10/03

29.95

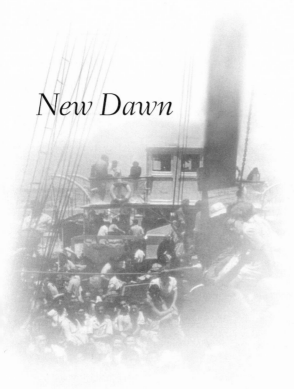

New Dawn

Religion, Theology, and the Holocaust
Alan L. Berger, *Series Editor*

OTHER TITLES IN RELIGION, THEOLOGY, AND THE HOLOCAUST

Exodus Affair: Holocaust Survivors and the Struggle for Palestine, 1947. Aviva Halamish; Ora Cummings, trans.

Himmler's Jewish Tailor: The Story of Holocaust Survivor Jacob Frank. Jacob Frank, with Mark Lewis

The Last Lullaby: Poetry from the Holocaust. Aaron Kramer, trans. & ed.

The Meeting: An Auschwitz Survivor Confronts an SS Physician. Bernhard Frankfurter, ed.; Susan E. Cernyak-Spatz, trans.

Second Generation Voices: Reflections by Children of Holocaust Survivors and Perpetrators. Alan L. Berger and Naomi Berger, eds.

Sun Turned to Darkness: Memory and Recovery in the Holocaust Memoir. David Patterson

Survival: The Story of a Sixteen-Year-Old Jewish Boy. Israel J. Rosengarten

War in the Shadow of Auschwitz: Memoirs of a Polish Resistance Fighter and Survivor of the Death Camps. John Wiernicki

Who Will Say Kaddish? A Search for Jewish Identity in Contemporary Poland. Larry N. Mayer and Gary Gelb

Will to Freedom: A Perilous Journey Through Fascism and Communism. Egon Balas

New Dawn

The Triumph of Life after the Holocaust

Helen Sendyk

With a Foreword by Yaffa Eliach

 Syracuse University Press

Library of Congress Cataloging-in-Publication Data

Sendyk, Helen.
    New dawn : the triumph of life after the Holocaust / Helen Sendyk ;
      With a foreword by Yaffa Eliach.— 1st ed.
    p. ; cm.—(Religion, theology, and the Holocaust)
    ISBN 0–8156–0735–0 (cl. : alk. paper)
    1. Sendyk, Helen. 2. Holocaust survivors—Israel—Biography. 3.
    Refugees, Jewish—Israel—Biography. 4. Jews,
    Polish—Israel—Biography. 5. Israel—Biography. 6. Holocaust, Jewish
    (1939–1945)—Poland—Personal narratives. I. Title. II. Series.
    CT1919.P38 S358 2002
    940.53'18'092—dc21   2002006027

For my precious grandchildren:

Rebecca Tamara, Ephriam Daniel, Shlomo Yonatan, Elchanan Shaul,
Zahava Adi, Elimelech Mordechai, and Mordechai Lev.

⟋⟍

These are the people and this is the land—both are the essence of your
existence. Pass this historic event on to those who will follow you.

Thus said the Lord:
A cry is heard in Ramah,
wailing, bitter weeping,
Rachel weeping for her children;
She refuses to be comforted for her children,
who are gone.
Thus said the Lord:
Restrain your voice from weeping,
your eyes from shedding tears;
for there is a reward for your labor,
declares the Lord;
They shall return from the enemy's land.
And there is hope for your future,
declares the Lord;
Your children shall return to their country.

—Jeremiah 31:15, 16, 17, 18

Helen Sendyk lives in Florida with her husband, Abraham. She is active in community affairs and is a member of the American Gathering of Holocaust Survivors of Hadassah, Amit, and Emunah, Jewish women's organizations. She is the author of *The End of Days: A Memoir of the Holocaust,* also published by Syracuse University Press.

Contents

Illustrations

Foreword

YAFFA ELIACH

N ow, in the first years of the twenty-first century, we, the living Holocaust survivors, are reaching the edge of the bridge of life. It is extremely important, therefore, to share with future generations how
survivors, despite great pain and suffering, managed to rebuild beautiful new
lives and were able to open new bridges for a safe future. Especially since
September 11, 2001, our experiences serve as a universal model.

In *New Dawn*, Helen Sendyk crosses the bridge from her previous book,
The End of Days, which documents the death and destruction of her family
from the Polish town of Chrzanow and her suffering in the death camps, to
the building of a new life in the land of Israel with her only surviving family,
her older sister, Nachcia, and her brother Vrumek.

For Holocaust survivors to rebuild their lives in Eretz Israel was much
more difficult than it was in the United States because of the British Mandate
and the Arab attacks. Despite the murder of millions of Jews and the suffering of survivors, there were great difficulties with the British government.
Immigration to Eretz Israel was considered illegal. Adults, teenagers, and
even babies who were born in DP camps were sent to camps in Cyprus. But
Helen, who became very friendly with members of the Jewish Brigade, managed to arrive legally with her sister in Haifa. They were welcomed by Golda
Meir and the mayor of Haifa. It was a magnificent and warm welcome to
their new homeland.

Although the British Mandate was difficult, eighteen-year-old Helen did
not yield to problems. She and her sister moved to Tel Aviv, where their
brother already lived, and began to rebuild their lives. July 1947 was a very
painful time, when the *Exodus* with its 4515 survivors was turned back;

three were murdered and thirty wounded. In spite of the pain, Helen managed to focus on life.

November 29, 1947, brought great hope. At the United Nations in New York, the partition of Palestine was decided. The Jews accepted, and the Arabs attacked.

Helen, a great dancer and singer, was delighted and danced with thousands of happy Jews on the beach of Tel Aviv. Her heart was full of joy and gladness for it was a major day in Jewish history. "We were a nation at last. After two thousand years of waiting, we were free to establish our own state."

Friday, May 14, 1948, was another important day in the two thousand years of Jewish history. In the museum of Tel Aviv, David Ben Gurion, with other future government members present, proclaimed the establishment of the State of Israel. None of the Holocaust survivors, as well as the other people in Israel, will ever forget that great proclaimation. (As a fourth-grade child who had survived the Holocaust, I was standing near the radio listening to Ben Gurion. Until today, every word of that speech is part of my mind and heart.)

During the War of Independence, attacks by the Arab troops from Jordan, Egypt, Lebanon, Syria, and Iraq and volunteer detachments from Saudi Arabia, Libya, and Yemen killed many Israeli soldiers. Among them were a large number of Holocaust survivors who were dreaming of building new lives in their homeland

Helen and her friends attended funeral after funeral including the one of the husband of her cousin Hania. Helen and Hania had survived the death camps together. Helen wept for "the lonely survivors of Hitler's Holocaust who gave their lives for the defense of their land, the land they did not have a chance to enjoy."

For Helen, even watching the emotional face of her brother, Vrumek, a soldier during the War of Independence, was very painful and meaningful; it expressed every element of the war, the pain of a Holocaust survivor, as well as his love for life!

Despite all the difficulties, Helen, her sister, and her brother built new lives. They got married and became parents of wonderful children, whom they named after family members who were murdered during the Holocaust, so that their names would always be among the living.

The members of the rebuilt family were very close. They restored many family customs during holiday celebrations, customs that had vanished during the Holocaust. Their apartments were open to friends who also were Holocaust survivors, for togetherness is central to Judaism. Although Helen's husband, Avremale, had to fight again in the 1956 war, their new life continued.

Eventually Helen, Avremale, their two children, and her brother and his family moved to America. Today, on the bridge of life, Helen is the last surviving member of her family. Her sister and brother have passed away. But they live on in her wonderful book, which is a special contribution to the public after September 11, 2001.

The terrorist attacks on the Twin Towers, the Pentagon, and a passenger plane in Pennsylvania, which caused the deaths of thousands of innocent people, is the most severe tragedy to take place on American soil. Holocaust survivors, in a unique way, share the terrible pain with the relatives and friends of the innocent victims.

Therefore, to read now the memories of Holocaust survivors will help people to understand the terrible human tragedy of the Holocaust and how people managed to build new lives and hope for a safe future, despite continued attacks of fighters and terrorists.

New Dawn is an excellent presentation how Helen, her sister, her brother, and other Holocaust survivors managed to rebuild their lives in Israel, despite wars and the terrorist attacks by Arabs in Israel that continue even now. Holocaust survivors are holding on to life and are documenting their tragedies and the rebuilding of their new lives for future generations.

God bless Israel and America, and bring peace to the world.

Preface

The world we live in, filled with strife, conflict, and contention, is a direct result of World War II. It is the residue of Adolf Hitler's quest for power, which encourages other maniacs seeking grandeur to promote and spread hate and crime. The technology we have acquired since then enables these individuals to carry out unthinkable crimes against society. Others, taking a cue from this atmosphere, settle for acceptance of violence, crime, use of force, and coercion. It is a sad state of affairs.

In my contact with people old and young at presentations of my first book, *The End of Days,* I am often asked, "How did survivors of the Holocaust cope with life and freedom upon their liberation?"

In this book, I tell the story of the people who came out from behind the barbed wire fences, the death and concentration camps, the partisans and fighting groups, and the hiding places. Homeless and penniless, alone and abandoned, they did not resort to revenge, violence, or vindictiveness. They did not turn to crime or sinful or evil behavior. Hard work, steadfastness, and a search for education were their goals. Pulling themselves up by their boot straps, using common sense and inventiveness, they found their way back to life. Fighting hard to overcome each hurdle, they became self-reliant and ambitious. They followed the traditions of their family upbringing.

New Dawn is a book of history, an account of individual miracles, a picture of a land so ancient but so new. It is the story of a people who suffered disaster after disaster throughout their history, who by all accounts should have become extinct, yet live flourish and grow in strength. It is a book about *Am Israel Chai* (The people of Israel live).

The survivors became decent, respectable, competent members of the human race. They are known to be tolerant, progressive, and freedom-loving.

This is the story of survival in the post–World War II world. Rehabilitated but not cured of the trauma they experienced, they nevertheless returned to what seems a normal life. The people in *New Dawn* are my surviving family members and my friends, people I knew well. Many are gone now. I became orphaned again when my dear sister Nachcia and my brother Vrumek passed away.

My struggle to tell the story of survival is not over. Read *New Dawn*, and may it be a catharsis and paradigm on the way to a better world.

Delray Beach, Florida   Helen Sendyk
March 2002

Acknowledgments

My thanks and gratitude go to the people who patiently stood beside me in my quest. They are: Dr. Alan L. Berger, Raddock Eminent Scholar Chair at Florida Atlantic University, for letting me benefit from the well of his scholarship and wisdom; Elayne P. Bernstein for her poetic soul, most generous heart, and friendship; Erica Jesselson for her warm Jewish heart and for keeping the promise; Isaac and Miriam Blech for their valuable attitude and gracious response; Professor Yaffa Eliach for being a model of courage and activism; Norma Hamburger for her prudent advice and perseverance; Sara Saaroni for preserving and contributing important photographs and for keeping the flame burning; my children, Howard and Lea Sendyk for their constructive practical technological help, and Alan and Sharon Shulman for being my pillars of strength; my husband, Abraham, for his deep love and kindness, his understanding and total devotion; Jean Weisser for her constant encouragement and concern; Dr. Robert Mandel for helping maintain my hope and for his gentle encouragement; John Fruehwirth, the acting director of the press, for his inherent instinct of cooperation and help; Ellen S. Goodman, assistant to the director, for her calm, soothing personality and kindness; Abe and Rose Rosenbluth for their trust and friendship; and Jay and Vivian Sendyk for not loosening that tight family knot.

New Dawn

Chapter One ✑

Clinging to each other, scared and lonely, we had only one desire, to board the train, to get on it. This train would take us back home. My older sister, Nachcia, who had always directed me, watched over me, cared for me, had become the passive one, seemingly dependent upon me.

"She is so young, so vibrant," she said to cousin Hania, our other companion, "how can I stop her?" Vigorously, I pulled them with me. Even Hania, also older than I, let me be the leader.

After having spent three years in a concentration camp, always so afraid, so tired, so cold, we were free. Free, able to walk out of the camp that had kept us captive. Can anyone imagine the feeling, the enthusiasm, the dream? Suddenly the barbed wire gates were flung open, and we were free to step outside. I could still feel the sensation, the mixture of fear, tension, and excitement upon seeing the Russian soldiers being brought into the camp, on the arms and shoulders of the girl inmates. One girl wore a red blouse, a symbol of recognition and respect for the Red Army. Where she managed to get a red blouse I will never know, but it was very impressive. She squeezed the soldier to her bountiful bosom with all her might.

Zdrastwicie! (welcome) we shouted to our liberators. They laughed, they hugged the girls, and we were sure they were as happy as we were, but they were happy for different reasons. They were happy to have young females converge on them, eagerly inviting them, even carrying them into the compound on their shoulders. As robust as the Russian soldiers were, they were still lighter than the barrels of water we used to haul as prisoners. Now they had come to liberate us.

True, they had fought to defeat their enemy, our murderers. They had saved our lives. How else were we to thank them? But they did not want

1

thanks, they wanted celebrations. We had nothing tangible to offer to celebrate the awesome occasion. They brought the vodka.

Na zdrowie (to health) they drank, to freedom they drank, to liberty they drank, to the end of Nazism they drank, to all that was dear to us they drank. We could not drink; we could not even eat. We tired so fast. The effort of bringing the soldiers in exhausted us. We wanted to rest, to lie down in our barracks on the wooden cots, being rid of whistles, screams, yelling, orders, and curfews, but that was not the soldier's idea of celebrating liberation. They were drenched in vodka and they were ready for *dziewuszki*—females. They lay down in our cots and wanted us there with them.

"How can you refuse us?" was their legitimate outcry. "You waited for us, you yearned, you brought us in on your shoulders."

"We are sick, we are emaciated, we are diseased, we are weak—can't you see? We are eternally grateful, we will never forget it, we will cherish you, we will honor you, but we cannot give you what you demand. Don't be so cruel. The Nazis are cruel; you are liberators, you are the angels of mercy, and freedom. Please leave us alone, please let us rest."

We begged, we pleaded for them to leave. They would not budge. All night we sat tense and tired, watching them sleep in our cots, making a racket when their heavy bodies crashed through the wooden planks of the flimsy three-tiered cots, plummeting down to the floor below.

It wasn't till dawn, when we finally managed to get hold of a high-ranking officer who identified himself as being Jewish, that we managed to get the Russians out of our barracks. We barricaded ourselves, pushing several cots to the door to block it. Some of us sat on guard duty, while the others rested.

The thrill of freedom was fading fast. Where were we going to hide the next night? What if they came back? What if they overpowered us? Liberation lost its glitter; the taste of freedom was becoming bitter. By the afternoon our determination was fueled by the familiar fear. We had to flee, to hide, not to get caught.

We were free to walk the streets yet afraid of the very people who gave us that freedom. With the help of several Jewish male prisoners from the neighboring concentration camp of Sportschule, we were able to leave the camp. A group of us settled in a house previously owned by Germans, from which the occupants fled. There we felt somewhat safer under the protection of the males. To the credit of the Russians, it must be said that they would not demand a married woman of a man. The irony was that there were only three males with twelve females. We had no peace. The Russian soldiers would show up day or night, banging on the front door, demanding to be admitted into our beds. Fending them off once did not guarantee we would not be caught the next time. It became dangerous for young girls to be without a male escort outdoors or indoors.

Right now we were still at the edge of the hell we were supposed to have left behind. We were holding on to the thread of life, with an ingenuity forged by an instinctive human reflex that makes one cling to life with one's last breath. Our oppressed, broken spirits were cleansed with the new breeze of liberty, fully absorbed by our desire to go home to our previous lives, our former house, our waiting family.

It was springtime, May of 1945. The sun shone delightfully, brilliantly. The time was ripe for celebrating, and the world did celebrate. The war has ended. Germany lay defeated. There was cheering and there was chaos. The people of Europe were going home. People were free, liberated from the bondage of the cruel Nazis. People were streaming east and west and north and south. All of Europe was in tumult. There was no orderly transportation, yet hundreds of thousands of people traveled.

We made our decision. We had to get out of there. Even as part of a group, we were each alone and afraid. Where could we go? Home was the only place we wanted to go. Mostly people whose home was in the same town stuck together. We had to separate from the others, but the three of us clung to each other, fearful of becoming separated.

With early dawn, we woke. Through the deserted streets of the city of Reichenbach, in lower Silesia, Germany, where we had been imprisoned, noiselessly we walked in the dark predawn. Like thieves, escapees, we were fleeing once more, watching, always looking back distrustfully, checking to see if we were being followed.

The railroad station was empty. Tensely we waited for the train to arrive, constantly glancing in all directions, alert to the most minute movement. A whistling wind, a falling branch, rustling leaves, alerted our sharp sense of danger. The whistle of the oncoming train brought mixed feelings of joy and fear. Careful not to fall into the trap of any Russian soldiers who might be on the train, we boarded and found a safe corner. Huddling together, suspiciously staring at passengers, perking up at every stop or station, we sat tense, tight, and edgy. My sister Nachcia had saved my life throughout our imprisonment, by watching over me, always hiding me behind her back in the lineup, sharing her meager portion of food with me, just like she used to do at home, watching over her baby sister. Our cousin Hania, the only one in her family, struggled throughout not to become separated from us. Glad to be together still, we watched each other, anxiously.

With the coming of daylight activity increased, and so did our unease and stress. Russian soldiers were visible at the stations, many boarding the train we were on. As long as they were not approaching the wagon we were in, we sat quietly, observing carefully, ready for any eventuality.

The train started moving, beginning its chugging, when we noticed a whole group of officers approaching our car. They were rowdy, laughing loudly and slapping each other on the back, having great fun. Immediately we anticipated trouble. We could not take a chance with this boisterous bunch. I grabbed my sister Nachcia's hand while she dragged Hania behind her. The three of us bolted out of our compartment, running toward the opposite door from which we saw the disorderly soldiers approaching. There was no need for words, for explanations, we knew what we had to do. The train was not yet driving fast, but it was moving. My thoughts raced through my head: we have to get out of here before they even notice us. Once they do, it might be too late to free ourselves. I could not take the time to hesitate, the situation demanded immediate action. Dragging Nachcia behind me, however, would have made her fall over me and make all three of us probably get injured badly. My brain worked fast for there was no time to lose. I heard the Russians calling out to us. I knew that if we did not escape we would be in trouble. Squeezing to the side of the door in front of me, I pushed my sister out the open door. My heart stood still for a second. I saw her tumble down into the ditch beside the tracks, and thought, "My God, what have I done, what if I killed her, how can I be so irresponsible, am I going crazy, to push my sister out of a moving train?" But the next second I saw Hania jump right behind her. There was no time for contemplation. I stretched my hands out in front of me toward my sister and cousin. I wanted to reach them, to touch them, to be with them. I jumped and fell into the ditch. The train had moved on. It was disappearing into the horizon.

I got up and ran back to where Nachcia was still lying on the ground. Reaching her, I could see her making an effort to get up. Her contorted face indicated that she was in pain.

"Are you hurt?" I asked, in spite of seeing so clearly that she was. "Can you get up?" I wanted to know, needing her reassurance. I did not know what I would do if she could not.

I was young and energetic, but in moments of distress immediately realized how dependant I was on my older sister. The peril hastened the fear that gripped me. Hania was at our side. Nachcia was making an effort to get up. She was not hurt badly, obviously just bruised and in pain. We helped her up. Limping, she began walking, supported on either side by the two of us. We stalked back to the station from which the train had brought us, some distance away. Nachcia was reticent. Hania wanted to know what we were going to do next.

"We have to get back on a train," I insisted. "Thank God we are not injured. We cannot stay here. We do not even know where we are."

"What will happen if the Russians come again?" Hania questioned.

"Don't be silly," I tried to make light of it. "These Russians are long gone, you know they remained on the train. We will be cautious, very cautious, we must get back home. It is the only place we can go, the only place we must go, and you know it as well as I do."

They did not object, they were just so scared and so was I. Waiting in the distance, hearts pounding, we heard another train approach. Carefully looking around, we checked to spot army personnel. Seeing none, we again boarded the train.

It was a long trip, the train sometimes stopping for hours, while we alertly poked our heads in and out of different compartments to check for signs of danger. Time was dragging on; we were getting tired but dared not relax.

Whom will we find when we reach home? The thought plagued me but I did not reveal my anxiety. There was no reason to worry them. They held on to hope, leaning on my enthusiasm. I needed them, my precious sister, my dear cousin. Without them I would die in freedom as I would have in camp. With pounding hearts and moist eyes we noted the sign KATOWICE coming closer as the train slowed to a crawl. Katowice, the big city our father always talked about. We knew we were nearing Chrzanow, our home town. Just a little more, I knew; if we endured, we would have reached our destination.

There was no welcome delegation waiting for us in our home town, Chrzanow. We were not disappointed for we had not expected one. Remembering the circumstances in which we left this town, we stepped slowly, carefully, cautiously.

In a daze we walked down the streets of the town we once called home. We passed Aleja Henryka, the nice avenue that we remembered as forbidden for Jews to traverse under the Nazi occupation, where we had spent summer evenings strolling when we lived in this town with our large families. There were no Nazis there, but there were no Jews either. It all looked so strange, these familiar places with not even one familiar face. We passed Mickiewicza Street, where we had lived before the war, where our father had owned two stores, without stopping to find out who was there now. Our legs carried us toward the last address, the house we were taken away from in the last raid by the Germans. It was the last home we remembered and was where everyone would come home to, we guessed, we hoped. We tiptoed up the familiar steps and I knocked on the door.

I looked up at the trap door on the ceiling of the hallway. The board still had the same scratches on it. There behind this board in this suffocating hole, in this cobwebbed cavity we had sat crouched with Blimcia, our oldest sister, her baby, Iiziu, and her husband, Jacob, when the Nazis came for us, when they dragged us out from our hiding place and shipped us to the concentration camp, Nachcia and me. Where were they, Blimcia, Jacob, and Iziu? Were we going to find them there again? A shiver went down my spine remembering how the German SS had dragged us all down on the shaky ladder, how Blimcia almost stumbled with the baby in her arms.

I looked at Nachcia. Did she remember the shove and slap she had received from the German when she tried to catch the falling child? Did she still feel the pain in her head from the impact of having slammed into the stone steps? Her contorted face mirrored her thoughts.

The door I had knocked on opened. Pipe smoke billowed from the hazy room through the open door. In the dingy room, a group of husky men sat around a table. Half-filled glasses littered the table. The men's dirty clothes and the sloppy hats worn in the house indicated they were farmers—strong, husky, rugged, evoking ferocity, automatically instilling in us that familiar fear of looming danger. The heavyset woman who opened the door, wiping her hands in her apron, asked in a hoarse voice, "What do you want?" Our ragged appearance must have warned her. The manner of her question was one applied to beggars, nuisances.

My tongue became stiff, my movements paralyzed, with one thought churning in my head. "What if I tell them the truth? What if I say I have lived here and I came back looking for my family who lived here with me? You have taken all away from us. I have come to claim my house."

I did not dare say anything like that. They were the masters of this house. They could easily kill all three of us, and no one would know about it. They were not accountable for anything. If there was one thing we knew, it was our predicament, our loneliness, the fact that no one would claim us or inquire about us.

"Excuse me" I said apologetically "I must have knocked on the wrong door."

"Let's get out of here before these men harm us, were I to tell them that this is our apartment," I said, running down the stairs.

Who were these people who now occupied our apartment? I thought. How were we to even begin explaining who we were and what we wanted? I did not think there would be any regard for us. Where were we going to wait for the other members of our family to come back? Nachcia and Hania were sending questionable glances in my direction. What was I to do?

This town where we were born, where we grew up, where we knew the joy of life with our parents, sisters and brothers, aunts and uncles, cousins, friends and neighbors, had become a hostile ghost town filled with strangers who had no regard for us, showed no kindness to our plight, and were upset to see the handful of us come back alive.

"Come, we have to go back to town."

"Let's try our house" said Hania. Totally distraught, troubled with worry about where we would sleep, we dragged ourselves down Koscielecka Street.

How relative is joy. The sight of a familiar face in Chrzanow was like a revelation at Sinai. Esther, a girl we knew, who had returned to Chrzanow some days before with her younger sister, Sala, stopped when she recognized us. She and her sister, with some other girls, were all crowded in their former apartment, which stood abandoned. The Poles had ripped out the heating stove, obviously searching for the gold, silver, and valuables the Jews were supposed to have hidden there. The windows were shattered, the floors and walls bare.

"Blessed art Thou, God of Abraham, Jacob, and Isaac, who has sent his emissaries into this wilderness to bring us into your tent."

We were taken in by the present occupants, the returned prisoners. We had no food or blankets. Huddling together on the floor, we rested through the night. Totally exhausted I lay next to my sister, contemplating our fate. Again the nagging thoughts kept coming back: we have been liberated from the concentration camp, what now? I felt my head spinning, my body weakening with hunger and exhaustion. I tried to get up to maybe find a drink of water or a splash of water on my face to restore my senses. But my legs refused to carry me across the room. With a great big bang I fell back to the floor, the noise waking everyone. It was the girls who splashed water onto my pale face, reviving me. They offered me a drink of water to strengthen my feeble body. They had nothing else to offer.

The next day, we found out that our cousin Sholek, Hania's brother, had returned from a concentration camp too, except that he was gravely sick in the local hospital. We immediately went to see him. The sight we beheld was gruesome. Sholek, the sixteen-year-old boy with round face and rosy cheeks we had last seen, was swollen and unconscious. Hania, choking on her tears, was trying to talk to him. She lamented, she cried she begged him to answer her. We were so helpless in the face of this tragedy.

Sholek, our cousin Hania's brother, was the only male survivor in our family to have come back. How could we make him hold on to life, what could we do to give him time to recuperate, to make him well? We all sat near his bed, Hania caressing his swollen face, kissing his puffy hands. Prayer was all we had to offer.

We visited again the next day watching, searching for signs of improvement. The doctors did not give any hope. The prayers and laments did not ease our distress. When we arrived on the third morning, Sholek's body and face were covered with a white sheet. They were waiting for us to claim him. With only the hospital sheet covering his body, his head bounced on the boards of a plain wagon, rolling down the cobblestone road, to the Jewish cemetery in the town of Chrzanow where he was born. We could not tear Hania away from his cold body. She had no strength to let him go. She collapsed onto the fresh soil of his grave, dug by several returned prisoners, who helped us bury Sholek. Her laments could rip one's heart out. Hania did not want to live, but she could not join him.

In the morning the sun shone brightly, and the people in the street were all smiles and happiness. The citizens of Poland were still celebrating liberation. We did not see the sun, we did not see the smiles. Our world was dark and depressing. We were utterly alone, totally destitute. We had come home carrying our hope with us, but found no one of our family. We had no home, no house to call our own, no place to put our tired bodies down for rest. Our former home was occupied by the Poles. We had no money, no clothes, no food, no means of getting anywhere. There was nobody interested in us; no one wanted us around. To come back to the place that was our home, where we were surrounded by loving family, so destitute, was so hard to bear.

Chained and choked in our loneliness, we went the next morning to the house on the Planty (the main street), where some of the returned refugees had already set up a soup kitchen. It was the plate of soup obtained there that brought life back into my emaciated, weak body.

We could not stay in Chrzanow, that was clear, but where could we go? In the soup kitchen, among our own, we found out about an agency in Katowice. We had to get there. It was the only hope. We had no money for the train ride. We could not hitchhike, it was too dangerous for three young girls alone. Russian soldiers were all over, plundering and raping women.

We rose early and marched to the train station anyway, indigence and fear our sole companion. At the office we came to, in Katowice, they registered our names and we were told to return the next day. We did not know exactly who these people were who registered us, but we did not care either. All that mattered was that they were Jews trying to help us. Not knowing a soul in the big city, we trekked back to Chrzanow, where we spent another night huddled together with the other returnees in the abandoned apartment. Eventually we made it to Katowice again. We just had to.

The people at the office were young Zionists attempting to organize groups of young people who had returned to Poland. Nothing was said to us regarding the aim, ideology, or destination of the group. Actually we were totally unconcerned when we put our names down. All we were looking for was someone to give us direction. We were alive but not able to continue living without some help. What a relief it was to find out that these other Jews would not let us fall. These young Zionists wanted to help us restart life, no less than in Palestine, in spite of the restrictions of the White Paper of 1939, a decree issued by the English Mandatory government that restricted Jews from entering Palestine.

These people, working for the Jewish Agency, whom we did not know, were really our saviors. Chrzanow, our former home town, did not offer anything to us. Not even shelter could we find in the town where we were born and where we lived with our families until the arrival of the Nazis. The only hope was these illegally established recruiting centers in the big cities, trying to gather the remnant of the Jewish survivors.

Together with other Jewish girls, we were transferred to the city of Zabrze, in upper Silesia, not far from Katowice. How good it was to become free of the burden of searching for a roof over our heads for the night and some food to put in our mouths. Here we were suddenly belonging to a family of Jews, Jewish girls and boys with an older man to supervise.

We were taken to a house obviously obtained by the organizers. Eagerly we embarked on the job of constructing sleeping quarters and setting up a kitchen. Slowly we began to mingle. It was like being in camp again, except that there were no cruel Germans to beat us, no long hours of forced labor to make our existence bitter. Here we were sheltered and fed. Here we revealed to each other our pain, our loneliness, the longing for our families. Here we found how the same we all were. Here we were able to open our hearts, to cry freely, for we all cried together, for our mothers and fathers, sisters and brothers. Here we were able to embrace a stranger and feel the closeness of family. Here we told time and time again the stories of our individual survival, until we knew each other's story by heart. Here we developed deep and emotional friendships, and we found healing for our loneliness, for we were never alone.

Zigmund, our *madrich* (leader), a big, broad-shouldered man, was a fatherly figure who led us with a strong but kind hand. A schedule was set up as to the different duties: cleaning, cooking and serving. All the free time was devoted to learning. We learned the Hebrew language, songs, and Zionist doctrine. There were among us some older people, experienced in organizational matters. There were ardent Zionists, zealous Hebraists, orthodox Jews, Jewish patriots, leaders and followers. We all had one goal, to get out of Poland and away from Europe.

The younger ones learned about our promised land in Palestine that lay wasted and uncultivated. It waited for us, for our spirit, our strength, to come and nurture it back to blooming fields and sweet-smelling orchards. We learned songs about our land, about the beautiful Lake Kineret, about the swamps of Hachula, about the arid Negev Desert. It became so close and yet so far. We became obsessed with the desire to go there. We were eager to do anything required of us just to reach that goal of setting foot on the soil of our promised land, our Holy Land.

We set up courses, learned Hebrew, and began conversing when we knew the first few words. We listened to lectures. Our lives began shaping up with new meaning.

The house we lived in was obviously acquired from the Polish government as an orphanage. We were not allowed to reveal our true purpose. When inspectors would visit, classes would be conducted in Polish history, Polish language, arithmetic, and the like. So we lived under false pretenses, conspiring to emigrate to Palestine.

Meantime our constant searches for loved ones were our greatest preoccupation. The boys who would be sent to Katowice to fetch supplies would bring back stories of people registering with different organizations. We all sent our names in, to be listed in Red Cross lists, municipality lists, and any other place they would take us.

Nachcia and I refused to believe that we were the only ones left in our family. After all, there were twelve of us in our family. People were still coming back. Every other trip to Katowice, by our envoys, enriched our ranks.

One late afternoon three new boys appeared. They wore Russian caps and *rubaszki* (Russian high-necked army shirts), and had on heavy, dirty, unpolished Russian boots. Moniek was a tall, heavyset fellow with dirty blond hair and a very Jewish hooked nose. Heniek walked swishing his arms back and forth at his sides. He was of slighter build with straight blond hair and blue eyes, a typical Gentile. He acted boisterous and protective of his bulkier, good-natured friend Moniek. And then there was Alex, a handsome, well-built boy with a round face and pinkish cheeks. He had dark, cheerful eyes and a lock of black hair that he always pushed away from his forehead. The three of them had survived in different places fighting with the partisans. It was Heniek, the most talkative, who would tell us the stories of his survival in the woods, of bloody fighting, of dark night watches, of nerve-wracking pursuits by the German enemy, and of actions of revenge. He spoke of the wild, uninhibited *Ruskies* (Russians), of daring expeditions and of freezing nights in the forest.

Alex was not the talkative type. No one knew where he was from, and where he had survived. He was friendly but did not become close with anyone in particular even after weeks. He was always pleasant, yet behaved strangely. No one ever saw Alex undress or wash and he slept in his boots even though it was already summer. It was assumed that Alex was scared, that he was used to running from place to place and could not afford to be caught undressed. We tolerated and accepted Alex's behavior and got to like him. He was extremely talented and very musical.

Each one of us in his or her own way acted strangely, trying to overcome our fears and our past and cope with the present. Our stay in Zabrze was not uneventful. The local populace was unfriendly at best. In openly hostile acts they would complain to the authorities about the Jews, bringing upon us all kinds of inspections. Commissars and directors would show up at our doorstep demanding more proof of our Polish patriotism. We had to have assemblies with salutes to the flag, political instructions, and exams.

An additional source of trouble were the Russian soldiers. Unexpectedly and uninvited, they would raid our premises demanding our girls. Ransoms were paid up in the form of vodka and food to lure them away from their animal desires. Petrified, we girls, would hide, leaving good-natured Moniek, impetuous Heniek, and quiet but determinedly steadfast Alex, to fend for themselves and to ward off the wolves. We girls would tremble with fear when late at night there would suddenly be rapping at the doors. Like scared mice we would search for places to hide, while Alex would grab a large kitchen knife and Heniek and Moniek would arm themselves with clubs.

One night, very late, the door was opened to a Russian officer, and we were surprised to see the boys at ease. From the overheard conversations between the Russian and our boys, we found out that he was Jewish and cooperating with us, helping our cause. When we told him how we are being pestered, he left a revolver for the boys to use for our protection. On his future visits he brought us news from the outside world. He told us of the plans that were being made for us to be smuggled out of Poland.

We were to pose as Greeks, displaced persons from the concentration camps in Poland (Auschwitz and the like) who were striving to return to Greece. We had to try as much as possible to resemble Greeks. The boys would receive berets they were to wear on their heads in the Greek style. The girls would organize some colorful clothes; brightly printed kerchiefs to be worn as head coverings were most desirable. The boys, too, should wear colorful scarfs as neckties, that being the popular way of dress in Greece. Dark hair was to be exposed, blond hair to be hidden. Cheeks were to be rouged and lips painted hot red. When we began to travel we should not converse among ourselves while in the presence of strangers. Jewish was forbidden and Polish was out of the question. The only language we could use would be Hebrew, assuming that the Polish population would accept it as Greek. We were taught some basic Greek words. *Kali mero* meant good morning, *kali spera* meant good afternoon, and *kali nihta* meant good night. The value of

Greek currency was explained to us so we would know the *drahmes* and the *lepta*. Preparing us for our eventual escape, the *madrich* told us that we would have to steal out of the house one by one and go to the railroad station. Once we reached the station successfully, we had to board the train but not congregate. We were to stay in different compartments and different wagons. We were to stay in touch inconspicuously.

We had been in Zabrze for close to three months. We were not familiar with the city, for we never went out on our own into town. The fear we had known for so long still gripped us, not releasing its claws. Only in the group did we feel safe, searching for new contacts and new friendships, yearning for the sense of belonging. There were girls who were absolutely alone. Nachcia, Hania, and I felt we were the lucky ones because we had each other.

There was Zosia, a somewhat plump, short, dark-haired fourteen year old. She had survived in a cloister. She never spoke about her parents or family. The only family she seemed to know was Mother Superior and the nuns. Zosia seemed still to be petrified. Every morning when she woke she would kneel down near her bed, cross herself, and say her prayers. It was most disturbing to Nachcia and me, having been brought up in an orthodox environment and having gone through the hell we just did, to see a Jewish girl pray to Jesus. Yet we were very tolerant of each other in every way.

The long, warm summer days of 1945 were fading slowly. We were gathered at the breakfast table, when Zigmund, our *madrich* announced that we were going to leave Zabrze, to escape Poland.

"You all know that we are here at the mercy and hospitality of the Polish government. They will not permit us to leave," Zigmund stressed, "but we are going to do it anyway. Remember what Theodore Herzl said: *Im tirtzu ein zu agada*" (If you will it, it is no dream), drilling into our heads the new theories so often discussed among us. "We are striving to reach our promised land in Palestine and we shall succeed."

With that he instructed us as to our behavior, conduct, and destination.

On Friday, September 7, 1945, *Erev Rosh Hashanah* (the eve of the Jewish New Year) quietly, in small groups of two or three, inconspicuously, we left the orphanage.

Nachcia, Hania, and I left together. We carried no luggage or bundles of any sort. We did not have any anyway. We had only a small bag containing some sandwiches for the road. At the railroad station we could see our people, scattered all over the platform. In the distance we could see a slowly approaching train. Emitting periodic puffs of smoke, it chugged into the station. People disembarked and boarded, amid a commotion of loud voices and the shoving of luggage, parcels, suitcases, and bundles. Our people boarded, two or three each to a different car so as not to congregate. Still possessed by our fear, which had become so ingrained in us in the past few years, Nachcia held on to me, cautious not to become separated, with Hania, too, sticking very close. That powerful fear, like an iron chain, kept us in its grip, strangling every move. We kept our eyes low, mostly staring at the ground. Feeling as if we were branded by the mark of Cain, we were terrified to be identified as Jews.

We peeked into the compartments, trying to find a suitable one. Eventually finding one, we sat down in a corner, close to each other. Soon the whistle was heard and the train moved with a jolt. Slowly at first, gradually gaining speed, it rolled through luscious scenery. Soon enough, the other occupants became engrossed in conversations, eating and drinking. We kept quiet, making only eye and hand contact with each other. We did not dare speak; we could not afford even to whisper. We did not want to eat. Our food supply was quite meager, and we did not know how long it must last us. Time seemed to stand still. Minutes dragged on, and hours stretched out to oblivion. It became burdensome when we began hearing people talk about us.

"Who are these strange creatures in the corner?" a young peasant woman was saying, it seemed to her mother, a plump woman with wide hips and a round face.

"Maybe they are deaf and dumb," answered the older one. Smacking her lips on a red apple she had retrieved from her basket, the mother said, "Maybe we should offer these poor devils something to eat."

Having understood, we anticipated the danger. Nachcia pressed her knee hard against mine to remind me to keep my mouth shut. Being the impulsive one, I needed Nachcia's presence not to automatically say something, like thank you. We kept on staring down. I pushed my foot against my sister's to let her know that it was okay, I remembered. Hoping that Hania's waves of black locks crowning her face would be the proper indication that we were Greek, I moved closer to her, saying *boker tov* (good morning) in Hebrew. Hania, a bashful type, so afraid to open her mouth, only smiled. Soon the woman picked up three apples from her basket. Holding them in both hands she offered them to us saying, "Here, take it, eat."

I made a surprised expression, took the apple and said, *"baruch haba"* (welcome). Nachcia caught on quickly and said the same. Puzzled, the women looked at each other.

"What did they say?" they uttered.

Not letting them end their sentence, I offered quickly, *"Greco, drahmes lepta."*

"Ah, Greczynki" (Oh, Greeks). They seemed happy to have understood that we were Greek. It spread fast in the compartment. I pressed Nachcia's hand and walked out of the compartment. Only outside in the hallway could we speak to each other quietly. Nachcia returned to the compartment while I went checking where the other of our girls were.

Sticking my head into the different compartments, I motioned with my eyes for some of them to come out. I found out that Mordechai, one of our older members, who was fluent in Hebrew, was sitting in the middle of the train. He could be summoned if anyone found himself in trouble. I was talking to Zosia, when two men passed by. They were talking about the Greeks on this train. They approached us asking questions, where we were going and where were we coming from. They had seen us conversing before their approach, so we had to keep talking. We could not answer their questions, supposedly not understanding them.

A Hebrew song we had just learned came to my mind, and it saved the situation. Totally ignoring them, I kept my face turned to Zosia and continued, "She kol hayom ani ovedet u-balaila ani rokedet. Mode ani lefanecha melech chai vekayam."

Zosia, sensing that I had run out of Hebrew phrases, answered me, "Hinei ma tov u-ma naim shevet achim gam yachad."

I heard one of the men saying to the other in Polish, "They speak Greek." He took his friend by his arm, and they left.

We did not dare giggle, even though we wanted to. Instead we tried to remember all the different songs we had learned, to store them quickly in our memory for immediate use.

I went back to our compartment, sat down, turned to Nachcia, and began repeating all the Hebrew songs and prayers in a litany with question marks and exclamations accentuating my speech. Nachcia kept nodding and answering, *"ken, ken"* (yes, yes).

After a while I became impatient again and went out to snoop around and to see how the others were faring. Stepping out from the compartment I could see Rachela and Jadzia in the distance. The two girls happened to be dark haired and dark eyed. They both wore red kerchiefs and looked to me more Greek than any real Greek. Their lips were hot red and I found out when I came closer that their cheeks were not rouged, but burning with the fire of embarrassment and fear.

There was one of the two men who had confronted Zosia and me before. I noticed that under his jacket he wore a priest's collar.

Jadzia was babbling, "Meal pisgat har hatzofim eshtachave lach apayim."

Rachela looked at me with panicky eyes. I understood what I must do. Turning my face away so the man could not see me, I strode by. I went to Mordechai's compartment, came straight at him, and vigorously shook his hand. He got up and followed me out. I quickly explained to him that it seems to me the two girls were in some trouble.

"*Ma kara?*" (what happened?) said Mordechai when we faced the girls.

It was the priest who answered in clear Hebrew, "I know that you speak Hebrew and not Greek. Who are you, and why are you running and hiding under false pretenses?"

Mordechai had quite a job convincing him that we were Greek Jews who speak both languages. We are trying to return to our homes, having been prisoners during the war in Nazi camps. The priest did not seem to be quite convinced but left us eventually. It was a close call.

Among our own, the apprehension was great. We did not know where to hide. We began changing compartments. The trip had been a long and tiresome one. We tried sleeping or pretending to be asleep. We knew we must keep in touch with one another, be aware of what was happening, not be laid open to any surprises. Yet surprises occurred.

At the other end of the train a group of authentic Greeks heard about us. Very excited, they sought us out. Enthusiastically talking they embraced Mordechai and Alex, who did not understand a word they were saying. Words flew back and forth, our boys speaking Hebrew and the others answering in Greek. Finally with hand motions and sign language our people convinced them that we are from a different part of the country where a different dialect is spoken. When they left us, they were not sure anymore who the real Greeks were, us or them.

In subdued excitement we noted that we had passed the Polish border when the conductor announced the town of Zabrzedowice. With rising anticipation we waited, knowing that we were nearing the Czechoslovakian border. When we passed the town of Bogumin, we knew we were out of the clutches of the Polish authorities. With lighter stomachs and hearts, we looked out at the rolling fields, conscious that we were distancing ourselves from the cradle of our birth, the cemetery of our families, and the source of our tormented souls. We knew not what awaited us but could not free our minds to think about it. All we were absorbed in was the trip.

And so eventually we disembarked at the railroad station in the big city of Bratislava in Czechoslovakia. From the railroad station we were led to a hotel named Dax. It must have been a quite elegant place, probably steeped in some splendor before the war. Presently it was a sordidly neglected building, with shattered windows, dirty walls and floors, and battered, nonfunctioning facilities. In the communal spirit of homeless people, we made ourselves comfortable in this ugly, repellent structure. We huddled together uncomplainingly, making the best of the circumstances.

With aching bones but refreshed spirits we rose the next morning, to find three other groups nestling in the same building. We met some girls from our home town of Chrzanow, who like us had joined these Zionist groups in the city of Krakow. There was a group of children from Warsaw and another one from Lodz. For fifteen uneventful days we stayed in the hotel Dax, wallowing in the dirty surroundings, distressed by inactivity, wracked by the waiting. It was the reality that we had no other choice and the bond we had developed with each other that kept up our spirits, the will to endure and proceed. Following the group leaders blindly, for it seemed no one knew exactly where we were going, we traveled to Austria.

We were trying to leave the Russian-occupied zone and to escape our liberating benefactors. We pushed on toward Vienna. Somewhere in the beautiful Alpine hills of Semering, we were finally stashed away in a small abandoned house.

We were a small group, only the Zabrze people. We were quite confined, not allowed out of the small cottage. Through the windows we observed the marvelous Alpine forests with their winding paths. Raindrops glistening on the yellowing leaves in the morning sun. Long, dark shadows slipped down the mountains at dusk, and the weather would get cool in the evening breeze. It was already fall of 1945. There was no room, however, for romantic appreciation of our surroundings. For us those hills represented a dangerous passage that would bring us closer to our destination. We looked at the hills and they seemed steep and foreboding. We waited each day for the setting sun and the evening shadow to bring us the heralds of advance. We sat to-gether talking about our hopes. Little was said about our past; it was the fu-ture we were eagerly looking forward to. And the future was so uncertain.

Finally one afternoon in late September, two men showed up at our cot-tage. One wore a Russian army suit and the other was an English military man. They both were of high army rank. In hushed voices the word was passed around that this is it, we were going to make a move. We waited until it was dark enough and in a small convoy followed the two officers. Tightly I held on to Nachcia's hand, with Hania in front of me to keep me between them, while we climbed the crooked paths among the tall trees. We did not talk, just watched each other attentively. Was our strength going to hold out? Our hope and our desire were the moving forces pushing us through this foreboding forest. It was our young minds that enabled the dream to over-take our bodies, giving us extraordinary strength. We came to a clearing and a guidepost. There were some soldiers stationed there. Our Russian officer approached the post while we lagged behind. Tensely we waited while there at the post some haggling and negotiating went on. Then we were motioned to proceed.

Carefully, the convoy of thirty-five people, mostly girls, wound on the path between the pine trees. Our ordeal was not finished yet. Next came the turn of the English officer to do his negotiating with his English compatriots. Hushed we squatted on the ground, impatiently waiting and watching. The officer motioned to us, and we began to move again. There were trucks wait-ing down below on the road, and we all piled into them.

Oh, how we wanted to burst out singing or talking loudly, expressing our exuberance on having made it. We had just smuggled out of the Russian-occupied zone into the English-occupied zone. We had crossed a border un-scathed. But we were instructed to be absolutely quiet. Mutely we sat in the military vehicle, closely squashed together. The truck was moving, rolling, bumping, jerking, making us topple over one another. Zosia was crossing herself with every bend in the road.

"Are you scared?" I asked her. She just grabbed hold of my hand and squeezed it. In the dark I could see her lips moving. I tried to see what she was saying to me, but then I realized she was really praying. I looked at my sister. Nachcia's lips were motionless but I knew she was praying, too. I saw it in her eyes. Hania was tensely pressing her hand against her mouth, afraid she might scream out with fear. Alex was nervously pushing away the lock of hair from his forehead, but his lips were smiling. What a peculiar group we were, I thought. Here is Nachcia praying to the God of Abraham and Isaac; Zosia saying her *pacierz* (prayer) to Jesus; Alex, a wild, untamed boy of war; and Mordechai, the intelligent scholar of Hebrew verse, wrinkling his forehead in thought. Here we were all huddled together, striving to leave our lives behind and make it to our new destiny, a destiny that was just a dream, a desire, for which we were ready to sacrifice ourselves. We were ready to give up all the nothing that we possessed and to go where ever we were taken.

In Kapfenberg on the Austrian side, we said good-bye to our guides. We found out that they were Jewish soldiers, Jews from Palestine serving in the king's army, known as the Palestine Brigade. We learned that the two officers that led us through the border were Jews as well. How good it felt to know that there were still Jews of authority around in the world. Our world until then had consisted of suffering, downtrodden, beaten, and dead Jews.

We boarded trains again to travel to Trofayach. Trofayach was a camp of barracks in Austria. It was an eerie feeling to be in a camp of displaced persons, where German was the state language. There were refugees from all over Europe stuck in this camp waiting for their turn to be taken out.

Many waited to be permitted to go to the United States. There was a kitchen where everyone registered in the camp could obtain a hot meal. There were families and groups. People who survived together usually stuck together. People who had survived in Russia were flocking to the Western occupied lands. We met again with the groups of our people from Lodz, Warsaw, and Krakow. Each was an entity unto itself, with its own supervisors.

In our own barracks we organized Hebrew lessons, talks, and communal singing, which was to become our constant pastime. It would be our entertainment and the essence of our lives in these temporary conditions. We waited.

One day we heard screaming from behind the barracks. It was Rachela calling for help. She was in pain and could not walk. Moniek and Heniek picked her up and carried her to the local hospital. It was a barracks room where people just stayed in bed. Rachela had had an attack of rheumatic fever. There were no medications except for a black salve they smeared on her legs to keep them warm. We visited her daily, bringing her all the gossip from the barracks.

It was October 1945, and the Austrian fall was wet and cold. Saturday morning I was on my way to the hospital with one of the other girls when we encountered a military truck full of soldiers.

As soon as we passed the truck I realized and said to Bala, the girl with me, "I think I heard Hebrew spoken. Or was it Yiddish? I am sure it was not English."

"You have such a vivid imagination," said Bala, who was a very calm, quiet, settled person.

"But I am sure," I insisted. "Let's go closer and listen," I pleaded.

Being the total opposite of Bala, I could not miss something that was happening, especially passing up an opportunity to be the first one to know. We turned back and came close to the truck. There were other people already flocking toward the truck.

"I must admit," said Bala, "your musical ear cannot be mislead."

There was a truckful of soldiers disembarking. They were wearing English uniforms but on their shoulder was an insignia, white and blue with Hebrew letters that said *Chayal Ivri* (Hebrew soldier). We were ecstatic. I would have wanted to hug and kiss every one of them, for my heart was filled with love. We shook hands when they greeted us with "shalom," and I became conscious that indeed they were speaking Hebrew, and we could not understand what they are saying. I wanted so badly for Nachcia to see them, right now, so she too could be one of the first to shake their hands and say "shalom."

"Bevakasha bou" (please come), I started saying and could not think of the word for "with us." With one or two of them understanding Yiddish, we managed to find out that they had come to this camp to entertain us refugees, to give a concert, to bring us greetings from our promised land, from the land of our longing. We left them to unpack, and I ran back to the barracks to be the herald of this fantastic news.

Promptly at eight we assembled in the dining hall. They were a mighty talented group of performers. There were skits and jokes in Yiddish in their repertoire, solo songs and choir performances. There were musicians playing the recorder, flute, harmonica, and accordion. There were dances, polkas, *krakowiaks,* horas, and other circle dances. The public was enchanted. Exuberantly they clapped and applauded each and every one of them. We were exalted when at the end of the performance they stepped down and began mingling, enticing us to join them in the dancing. Circles were forming, hands were joined, shoulder to shoulder we danced the horas. They were leading, teaching and instructing, grabbing us into the whirlwind. I danced and danced and felt alive again. There was no thought in my brain, only the exhausting jumping and kicking of feet. I felt I was flying through the air in the strong arms of Amos and Chaim and Yoske. They were so strong and so handsome, so proud and so free. *Chayal Ivri* it said on their shoulder insignia, and they came from that land of sunshine and orange groves. Slowly people began leaving, but I kept dancing. Elated, I did not hear Nachcia tell me to stop and rest and come back with her to the barracks. My body bathed in sweat, I danced. Emotionally involved, I danced until my legs buckled under me. There was a breaking dawn on the horizon when the fellows enveloped us exhausted girls in their warm army coats and walked us back to our barracks.

We did not sleep much the rest of that morning. In the early afternoon the boys showed up again in our room. We sat around and talked, using hand motions to help them understand. They spoke Hebrew, we spoke Yiddish, but we were not strangers. We were *Am Israel Chai* (the people of Israel live). They talked about their homes, the land of flowers, the aroma of the blooming orange groves and we were so happy.

There was a chill in the air when I walked arm in arm with Amos on the path winding through the barracks of the camp. He complimented me on my dancing, saying I was as light on my feet as an *ayala* (young doe), which made me blush but feel very good inside. He told me he lived in kibbutz Degania and invited me to come visit when I arrive in Palestine. It was a wonderful, positive, definite feeling. I certainly had to make it to Palestine, having been invited to Degania.

"How will I know where to find you, Amos, without an address?"

"Don't you worry your pretty little head," he smiled at me, "anyone you ask in Palestine will tell you where Degania is, we are the oldest kibbutz in the land and my father is one of the first pioneers. Our family name is well known."

Aware that I was not convinced yet, he took out a snapshot from his wallet, wrote something on the other side and handed it to me.

"Here, now you have no more excuses that you could not find me. Just show the picture."

It was raining by then. Amos bundled me up in his warm army coat, hat, and gloves. We saw the lights of the dining hall on, in the distance, and he lead me there. There was a crowd already there. We sat in a circle, where people were telling jokes. The soldiers suggested some games and again lead us in communal dancing.

"You are not tired at all?" Amos asked when he saw Yoske whisk me off in a whirling polka.

"You better save some strength for me," he yelled at me when I waltzed away in a jolly *krakowiak* with Chaim.

I felt so alive, so vigorous. I wanted this night to last and never end. I wanted to be compensated for the wretched suffering of the past years. A new life was starting for me, for us all. We were going to go to Palestine to build, to toil, and to dance, dance, dance.

The next day Monday, October 2, 1945, we were in our barracks. The room was drawn in the afternoon shadows, only the glow from the burning coal in the iron pot belly stove cast sporadic light. The flickering flames created dancing rays on the walls of the room. My back stiffened when I heard the knock on the door. The fellows had come to say good-bye. The dreams of last night and the night before were coming to an end. Like in the story of Cinderella, the clock was striking midnight. Soon they would be gone, and we might never see them again. We would be left with our struggle.

Amos sat next to me on my cot. "I know how you feel," he said. "I want to give you a gift." He took off the insignia that was pinned to his army shirt and handed it to me.

"But you cannot do that," I protested, "they will put you in jail."

"Don't worry your pretty little head. I will get another. I know what this means to you."

I took the insignia that was white and blue and had the inscription *Chayal Ivri Palestine,* on it and put it under my pillow, where it rested together with his picture. I smiled at Amos but he could see the tears welling up in my eyes.

"It is the best gift anyone ever gave me," I said, "I will cherish it, and I will come to Degania."

We walked them to the waiting trucks and stood there in the freezing wind in our light clothes, waving long and hard into the distance.

The days that followed the group's visit were drab and monotonous. We went about our daily activity without enthusiasm or vigor. Then one day Moshe, the *madrich* of the Warsaw group stationed in the nearby town of Judenburg, came to visit. By that time I had become popular in our group, with a reputation as a lively character. Moshe asked our *madrich,* Arye, to allow me to go for a visit to Judenburg. Accompanying Moshe and two other members, Wacek and Lola, we set out on our trip to Judenburg.

There was no direct train. In the waiting room of the train station in Leoben, our small group sat around talking when suddenly, Moshe came up with a brilliant idea. My possession of the insignia had elevated me to the status of a celebrity of sorts.

"Hela," Moshe said, "this trip is not going to be wasted. You have the insignia! We will pin it to the khaki shirt you are wearing, and you are going to be a *chayelet* (female soldier) that has come to visit the camps. I was lucky to procure you for our camp as well. You will bring us greetings from Palestine, and it will be exciting."

"But Moshe," I protested, "I hardly know any words in Hebrew, how can I make a decent speech?"

Quickly Moshe scribbled down a short speech and I embarked on learning it by heart. Lola found a safety pin to attach the insignia to my shirt.

On the next leg of our trip to Judenburg we were bubbling with excitement and anticipation for the spectacle. Every detail was carefully planned. Lola would go in first; she would warn the two girls from the Warsaw group, who knew me personally, not to reveal my identity. Moshe would lead me inside and make a proper speech of introduction.

Exuberantly we strode from the train station to the camp. There was a crisp frost yet I felt the insignia pleasantly warming my arm. Lola went in as planned and took Kazia and Krysia aside. Moshe gently took my arm, leading me in through the crowd. Eloquently he began talking while Wacek took off my coat. There was panic in his eyes when he could not see the insignia on my arm. I saw his frightened eyes and his mutely moving lips, asking me where is the insignia? Shocked I searched the floor to see if it had come off together with my coat. Then I realized that the insignia was on my shirt under the sweater I wore. Nervously I tried ripping off my sweater. The entangled pin revealed the insignia hanging on its end. Embarrassed I mumbled the learned words, mechanically, in a jumbled litany. Kazia and Krysia burst out laughing, and the audience applauded a good show, which sparked some fun and laughter from all. Everyone wanted to examine, admire, and touch the insignia, expressing their sense of envy at my precious possession.

The next day we traveled to Leibnitz, where we were invited to the official opening ceremonies of the establishment of Kibbutz Ichud, of which our group in Trofayach was also a member. *Ichud,* meaning unity, was to encompass all the factions of the Zionist movement.

Having survived the tragedy that befell the Jewish people of Europe, it was felt that we were all Jews striving to reach our promised land, Jews having the same interests and goals. There should be no more division among us. Our different political views were to be set aside. Ichud presented a broad coalition of members. There were some people who had belonged to Zionist organizations before the war and who became the organizers and leaders of the multitude. Mostly our population consisted of young girls and boys untutored in Zionist doctrine, happy with the ideology that was being fed to us, unity and togetherness, understanding and tolerance. Our *madrich,* Arye, was a dynamic individual. Dina, the second in command, was a warm, pleasant, responsible young woman. Their exuberance, enthusiasm and example were our driving force. We were ready for sacrifices, hardships, and suffering to attain our goal. That goal was clear and defined to us, with no alternative or deviation.

At the railroad station in Gratz, we met people from other camps also heading to Leibnitz for the big event. We all spent long, hungry hours waiting for the still sporadically scheduled trains.

The camp inmates in Leibnitz were all assembled in the barracks dining hall when we arrived. There were speeches by prominent Zionists, expressions of greetings and welcomes, and accounts of activities, followed by an original play based on our recent experiences. The performance was superb, the amateur actors extremely talented. Finally we, the invited guests, were served a festive meal. It was a big event in my life, being a participant among the invited guests. Stimulated we returned to Trofayach but not before we again waited a long time in Gratz.

Sitting on a bench at the railroad station we were approached by several English soldiers. They were young fellows with pink faces, trying to make conversation with us young girls. They offered us cigarettes and chocolates.

It had been years since I had that favorite sweet of mine. It reminded me of my home, of our store where I used to snatch chocolate candy and pop it in my mouth at will. It reminded me of my sister Blimcia, who was in charge of our store and who used to reprimand me for my frivolous behavior. I longed for my family, for Mama and Papa. Here I was helpless again in the face of these spoiled, wasteful, careless brats who had chocolate to give away. They lacked nothing in life. They were the authority that barred our entry into our promised land. I did not want the charity they offered us. I wanted freedom. They were smiling and talking to us and trying to be pleasant and enticing. I could not talk to them, not knowing any English. Suddenly I remembered a banner I had seen in the dining hall we had just left. It all came to me.

Clearly, I stated with a smile: "Palestine must be our National home." I took the offered chocolate, smiling broadly and enjoying myself. The English soldiers did not seem bothered by my expression of the political statement and demand but I was happy for the opportunity to express myself freely in the language they could understand.

Back in Trofayach, preparations were being made for our departure. All had to be done in strict confidence and secrecy. We were living in a camp for displaced persons with all kinds of people. There were quotas for staying and quotas for leaving. There were registrations and obligations. Our life of bondage had not ended. We managed to organize our own group life but were also subject to the rules and regulations of the camp authority and its strong men. There was a group of partisans, boisterous, rude men hardened by their immediate past, pursuing the girls in our group unsuccessfully. Aware of our conspiracy of illegal *aliyah* (emigration), they snooped around our barracks, curtailing our freedom of movement. When the order from Arye came that we were to move on, they stationed themselves conspicuously to bar our advance. We were to meet outside the camp gates to make our getaway to the railroad station. Under the cover of darkness in the early evening, we left in small groups. To our surprise, the partisans were waiting for us behind the gates. They commanded us to go back. They proceeded to threaten, shove, push, and even beat up our fellows. When we saw knives flashed, we retreated for our own good.

Tense days of planning followed. They threatened to assassinate our leaders. Arye, who would not abandon our plans, repeatedly proclaimed our ideology in the words of Theodore Herzl, *Im tirtzu ein zu agada*. After several days, a new attempt was made.

In twos or threes we left the camp, assembling outside the fence. Carefully listening to what seemed like whistles and voices, with beating hearts we proceeded slowly on the crisp, squeaking, packed snow. Every so often we hugged the frozen earth or icy snow in preparation for a new leap forward. Covered by a halo of thick falling snow we trekked, shivering in the chilled air, our aversion to the cursed soil growing with every fearful step. It was way past midnight when we met a few other people from our group trekking in the same unfamiliar path to Leoben.

All night we walked, losing our direction, shivering with cold, before we reached the railroad station in Leoben. From there we proceeded with the dawn to Willach. We still had to be inconspicuous until we recognized the familiar wink of a *chayal* (soldier), who came to direct us to the local camp. The barracks was packed by people lying on the floor. There was absolutely no room for us. We sat tired, cold, hungry, discouraged till morning. Then Dina and Arye arrived. We were happy to see them, for we felt like sheep without a shepherd. Vigorously Arye incited us to further efforts to continue on our trek.

We were led back to the railroad station, from where we were to embark on a journey into Italy. We were to cross the border illegally and somehow make it to Rome. There was again pushing and shoving and screaming and even rock throwing.

Everyone wanted to get on the train, and it was really an impossibility. It was half a year since the war had ended, but there still was absolute chaos, especially at railroad stations. Arye handed each one of us two rolls that were donated by the *chayalim* from the Jewish brigade and instructed us to get to Rome. Every individual had to fend for himself or herself. I held on to Nachcia's hand the way I used to do in the concentration camp, pulling Hania behind me, and we pushed our way by force onto the train. We were starving, and quickly the rolls disappeared into our mouths. We were tightly squeezed among husky Italians, plump peasant women, men, girls, and crying children.

We were crossing the border into Italy. We had no tickets, no money, and no food. We were as miserable as the day we were liberated from concentration camp, except that we were part of a group, and therein was our strength and the source of our vigor. We were a small group of girls who were separated from our leaders, but our spirits were sustained by the thought of Arye and Dina. They were our mentors, our leaders, and our moral support. We had a destiny, a goal to reach. We were to come to Rome, and there in our minds all our troubles would be over. There again we did not have to worry about a thing. They would take care of us, they would tell us what to do and how to do it.

Meantime, there we were, all young girls, vulnerable, and unprotected in this chaotic aftermath of a world war. We squeezed illegally into the train, escaping the conductor and by some miracle avoiding being thrown off the train. The world seemed very hostile to us, lacking signs or actions to the contrary. It was way past midnight when the train stopped at Bolonia. By three o'clock in the morning we disembarked, having been told that the train wasn't going any further and that it would be replaced by another train. The night was cold and dark. We were tired and hungry, not having eaten for more than a day. Using our bundles for headrests, we sprawled on the platform of the railroad station.

People were milling all around us. The Italians seemed to us a happy-go-lucky people, and they soon produced some harmonicas to entertain themselves. Circles began forming. In our group people began prodding me to start a song. I was hungry but there was nothing I could do about that. I felt worse for Nachcia's sake than for myself. She was the quiet, subdued type. My singing always attracted attention. I sang the songs taught to me by the *chayalim.* I sang "Laila afel" (Dark night) and "Mimromim bracha yoredet" (A blessing descends from above) and "Im ein ani li mi li?" (If I am not for myself, who is?). Some young Italians came to stand around our circle. Then more and more joined us. From their bags began to appear white breads and fruits, which they shared with us. Even Nachcia ate hungrily. The Italians drank wine and started dancing, and we girls, having gained back our resilience, recompensed the Italians by forming a circle and inviting them to dance with us. We taught them the hora.

The rewards were mutual, for a cattle train appeared into which we all piled, being pushed in instead of out and away by the Italians. It took the rest of the night to make it to Florence, where the scene was repeated.

We got off the train and found another group of our people. We hoped to be saved by them, for them to be the ones carrying the supplies of army rations that were provided to us by the *chayalim.* Our exuberant chatter quickly faded when they revealed that they were as hungry as we were.

In Florence the train stalled for hours on end, so the platform and railroad station became our shelter and sleeping quarters.

It was noontime when we arrived in Rome, the bustling city of Michelangelo, the Vatican, the Arch of Titus, and the Colosseum. But we did not know or see any of it. Our concern was how to get to Cine Cita (the city of movies), which had been converted into a refugee camp. In sign language and with a lot of prodding, pleading, and crying with exhaustion, we managed to get on a bus that finally took us there.

In the little barrackslike structures that used to serve as sets for movies, we found refugees of all sorts. Greeks, Czechs, Jews, and even Africans. We scavenged around for a place to stay. It was heartbreaking for me to see my sister, who was not a healthy girl, tired, pathetically silent, wearily shuffling along. But somehow even she bounced back when we eventually found Arye and Dina, our leaders.

Our sojourn in Cine Cita was intolerable. The long, demeaning lines at the kitchen window for our daily nourishment reminded us of our immediate past in the concentration camps. We did not have any living quarters as a group but were scattered in the enormous camp, which hampered our social activities. Our leadership persevered in pursuing the *aliyah* movement to grant us a place of our own. The vision we had in Willach, when Arye told us to reach Rome at all cost, vanished among the homeless refugees of Cine Cita, and the better tomorrow was still far on the invisible horizon.

Our dream came true after several weeks when a bus took us all to a suburb of Rome called Grotta Feratta.

On a small winding dirt road the bus clamored and rolled past the town of Grotta Feratta and finally stopped at Villa Cavaletti. The villa, obviously abandoned by its Fascist owners, was unbelievably beautiful. Set half a mile away from the main gate, it was constructed against a hill. The magnificent front entrance was surrounded by a small plaza adorned by small bushes, shrubs, and plants. The upper rooms in the back opened to a huge veranda on top of the hill. Miles of romantic walkways shaded by trees and shrubbery surrounded the villa. Even though it was meant to house a family, it now accommodated 130 of us.

With enthusiasm we embarked on setting up living quarters. The boys busied themselves building beds and long tables to seat all of us at the same time. The gigantic entrance hall with its imposing marble staircase was to become our dining hall, assembly room, and social activity meeting place. Groups of girls occupied the upstairs bedrooms. The fellows settled in the smaller rooms that must have served as servants' quarters. Even the elaborate bathrooms served us well to sleep two or even three people. The elegant tubs made comfortable beds when covered with some boards and the fancy bidets served as chairs. Besides the regular kitchen, a kosher kitchen was set up for the handful of people who demanded it. Nachcia, of course, became the cook for the kosher kitchen, preparing fine delicacies from the limited supplies. Enthusiastically we all worked together to make this place a happy home.

Kibbutz *Echud* group in front of Villa Cavaletti in Grotta Feratta, Italy.

In the back gardens there was a splendid gazebo where we would sit quietly enjoying the enthralling environment or talk dreamily with a friend about our wonderful future.

I had met Salek for the first time on my visit to Judenburg. He was not a member of our group but was an active member of our movement. In fact he was the brother of Moshe, the leader of the Judenburg group. His pale face and delicate features attracted my attention. He was very pleasant at our first meeting, and when he came to visit me in Trofayach, we walked for hours without noticing where the time disappeared. I saw Salek one more time in Italy. Admiring his tranquil but solid handling of organizational matters, I watched his medium build body move gracefully and felt a pang in my heart when he left.

Salek came to Villa Cavaletti specifically to see me. Being somewhat shy, he did not exhibit special interest in me when in a group, but asked me to go for a walk. I was quite worried about how proper it was to be found walking alone with him, especially because the walkways at the villa were very private and romantic. With my heart pounding a little faster, I did not dare look at his eyes while we walked side by side. He told me that arrangements had been made for him to go to Palestine. He would be joining the brigade, and that would facilitate his entry to the land.

We properly shook hands when he left. I mutely waited to hear him say something like, "I hope to see you again," but he just smiled bashfully, charming me with his blue eyes, which I noticed for the first time.

I tried busying myself working in the sewing shop that was set up on the premises but could not help running away alone into the gazebo in the garden, where surrounded by the singing birds I would dream about my prince. I would behold his sandy hair and blue eyes and imagine him holding my hand.

As time passed, our group was readying itself for the big event, the official opening of Kibbutz Ichud. Two of our most talented boys, Melech and Maurice, each in his individual style began decorating the walls of the downstairs hall with their paintings, except that for lack of material they painted directly on the walls. For weeks they worked, mainly at night when the hall was not occupied, creating scenes from our life. Melech composed a picture depicting the cattle trains taking our dear ones to the Auschwitz death camp. Maurice painted his own experiences. By the time the guests for the opening arrived, the magnificent masterpieces on our walls told our story vividly.

People shook their heads in reverence and admiration for their artistic talent. There was also a show put on for the opening. I had become known by that time for my love of singing and my pleasant voice. I was picked for a role in the performance, together with several other girls and boys. It was the busiest time we spent in Villa Cavaletti. Besides our regular obligations of room duty and work in the sewing shop, we spent hours upon hours rehearsing. I did not even have time to go to the gazebo to spend my quiet hours, but I was extremely happy to be with my friends, singing and performing, repeating and rehashing. It was a lively atmosphere and I loved it.

Then came the big day of the opening ceremonies. The cooks were busy preparing a special meal using all their culinary expertise. Melech and Maurice were nervously examining their works of art with a critical eye. The performers were in complete turmoil. Our director was sweating and screaming and throwing his hands in the air in total despair, bringing one or two of the girls to tears. Nervous stomachaches accompanied quick glances in the mirror, meticulous combing of the hair, and smoothing out the white blouses we wore for the special occasion. The performance was an absolute success. The audience applauded enthusiastically. The dignitaries seated in the front rows smiled with satisfaction and shook our hands when we the performers were introduced to them. Worn out with excitement and tension I fell asleep in the late evening dreaming about our future in Palestine.

But Palestine was still only a faraway dream to us. It was something unattainable. We longed for Palestine, the land that was the most frequent topic of our conversations, the goal of our fantasies and imagination. We spent the major portion of our day learning about it, discussing it, listening to lectures, learning to speak Hebrew in preparation of our life there. But it was not the only thought we were preoccupied with.

We thought about our families. I would sit with Nachcia or with friends and analyze all the possibilities. We knew our sister Goldzia could not have survived. She was crippled with polio. In our household the family had cared for Goldzia's every need and pleasure. It was Mama, however, who constantly handled Goldzia's well-being. Mama was the guardian angel of her lovely but unfortunate daughter. With sorrow we thought about her, bringing into our memory her pleasant, bright face. Deeply we mourned her death. From the stories we heard from our friends who had survived in situations different from ours, we learned about the atrocities, murders, and barbarism with which the sick and fragile, the old, and children were treated. We learned how our brethren perished, but we could not accommodate the thought that our loved ones, our Goldzia, was treated that way. The uncertainty and lack of knowledge about how she had perished tore our hearts to pieces. So many questions remained: Mama and Papa, were they alive? Were they tortured to death? Heshek, our brother who fled to Russia, he must be alive, for sure, but how would we find him and when? Vrumek, the most daring, and Sholek, the agile, witty one—our two brothers, younger than Heshek—they were alive too for sure, they must be somewhere in Europe like us, we felt. What about Blimcia our loveliest, oldest sister, with her cherubic baby, Iziu? Did she give him up? Was she able to save him? Did she go to her death with him? Was she able to hide to survive? We were troubled by these thoughts constantly and continually kept searching.

We listed our names with different agencies, with the Red Cross, but most of our hope was in survivors from our home town, people who had known us at home. Whenever we heard about people from our town who turned up in Italy, we would try to contact them. It was a difficult task, with more disappointments than accomplishments.

We were also not free to move around, and mail was absolutely sporadic. Once we heard that Blimcia had been able to be hidden by Gentiles. It was nothing concrete, someone thought that someone told them that someone had seen her. People did not remember when and how, but we clung to the idea trying to convince ourselves that it was true, that Blimcia was alive, that eventually we would find her.

The work of the Kibbutz went on, the work and the waiting. We knew that one day our striving would bear fruit and we would go to Palestine. We did not know how and when. Our whole life was one big question mark. How would we be reunited with our families and how would we attain our goal of getting to Palestine?

But we did not sit idle. Cultural and social activities absorbed much of our time besides daily chores and work. Our sustenance came in the form of food and lodging. We did not demand much and were happy with what we had. We had no money and felt no need for it. Our lives were contained in Villa Cavaletti, and we made the best of it. Our leaders would travel to Rome for organizational business and supplies. We never questioned any of their activities. They were our leaders, our patrons. We revered them and looked up to them. We respected them, and our hopes were with them. Like Moses, who lead the Jews out of Egypt into the promised land, we hoped our Arye and Dina would be able to lead us to safety in Palestine.

Sometimes on special occasions they would take someone along to Rome. These people would tell about the beautiful ancient city, and we would become awakened with desire to see the wonders of the city that was so close. Most of our travel took us on foot to the neighboring beautiful mountainous villages of Grotta Feratta, or Frascatti. We visited other villas where other groups of our people were staying. Even though we belonged to Kibbutz Ichud and thought that all Jews were already united, we found out that there were other groups. Not far from us was a group of *Betar* (revisionist Zionists) and another group of *Hashomer Hatzair* (socialist Zionists). Sport activities were organized, and our group competed with the *Betarim* or the *Hashomer Hatzair* group. Once after a match that our group won, we walked back to the villa dancing and singing all the way, expressing the thrill of victory.

One day Nachcia took sick. The headaches she suffered since the concentration camp became extremely severe. She vomited and could not get out of bed. Certainly she could not go to work, and having been cook for our kosher kitchen she was sorely missed. But most of all I became frightened. I could not conceive life without Nachcia. She had pulled me through all the camps. She had substituted for Mama in caring for me with love and endless devotion. Seeing her suffer devastated me. I appealed to Dina for help. After several days Nachcia was taken to a hospital in Rome, and I was allowed to travel to Rome to visit her. They did some tests on her and with no major improvement she returned to Villa Cavaletti.

As the weeks passed we all learned to know each other better. Many friendships developed and even some romances. There were two couples who were seriously in love and decided that they could not continue under the present conditions. They opted to get married. It was a wonderful feeling of excitement, as if a family member was getting married. The preparations had everyone working feverishly. In the sewing shop white dresses were made for the brides. The cooks labored and stocked special dishes for the occasion. The men built partitions from wood planks and blankets in one of the rooms to separate the bed from the rest of the room and give the newlyweds some privacy in their blanketed cubicles. The wedding was attended by all the members of our kibbutz and some invited guests. Everybody dressed as best they could for the occasion. The double *chuppa* (canopy) was put up outside in the beautiful setting of the villa, surrounded with trees and greenery and tweeting birds and nature. A festive meal followed at which we all lingered till way past midnight, to give the married couples this one evening of privacy in the room. We all felt a sense of fulfillment at the sign of our natural lives' continuation. We were so happy for the two couples who had found each other to love and share their lives.

There were happy times, like when one of our girls was found by an uncle from France and was promptly taken by him to France. There were tears of parting from her and smiles of happiness for her. There was sadness for not having found anyone from one's own family.

There were rivalries between the *kibbutzim* in the area. Each one tried to outdo the others at its opening ceremonies. Each one put up its own flag and the others tried to steal it. We had constant guards at the flag, as did the others, and yet we managed to steal them from each other.

My success as a performer brought me local fame and popularity. I loved to sing and learned songs in different languages quickly. One day Arye announced that we had been invited by the Jewish community in Rome to perform for the children in the Jewish school system and their parents. We prepared a poignant show under the able direction of Shlomo, our director, depicting our present life and our dream of reaching Palestine. We even built a ship for our stage decoration. Our resources were so inadequate that the ship slid down from the transporting vehicle en route to Rome. We scrambled around in the main street of the big city collecting the broken pieces. With our talented carpenter stage hands, however, the ship was ready and fit by the time the curtain went up. As predicted, the show was a success.

I had a solo song, which I learned from our partisans, called "Oisshtreken dem halz zum messer nein O keinmuhl nein" (Stretch our throat out under the knife, not ever again, no, not ever again). Emphatically I pointed my finger to my outstretched throat suggesting a knife, and in my strongest voice protested *"nein O keinmuhl nein."*

I felt like a real star when after the performance the chief rabbi of Rome and Dr. Nachon, a Jewish leader of the community, came over to greet me and warmly shake my hand. There were these moments of being in the limelight that I loved so well and quiet moments when I would sit with a close friend in the lovely gazebo and talk and dream.

It was in these quiet conversations that I heard how Clara escaped from Auschwitz, crawling underneath a truck and holding on to it, suspended between the fast-moving machine and the speedily disappearing road underneath. How Hershel, only fifteen years old, stuck a knife into a German's stomach in the woods of eastern Poland. Here in the gazebo one day Krysia talked about her survival.

Krysia had golden blond hair and hazel eyes. Her skin was milky white, and she was quite robust. "This hair is what saved me," she said, lovingly caressing the long strands of hair. "When the Germans came for us, my mother pushed me out of the house and said, 'Run, you must live.'

"I ran to the fields. I did not know where to turn, who would help me. It was all so strange and frightening. I walked for miles, getting tired and hungry. Totally exhausted, ready to just lay down in the field, oblivious to what might happen to me, I suddenly spotted a big house in the distance. I knocked on the door and asked the woman who answered if they had any work. Seeing the woman's surprised and suspicious look, I offered information immediately, claiming my parents died in a bombardment. To my total astonishment she took me in. It was a big estate. They had many hands working in their fields. When the fruit was ripe, the pickers came from the village to work in the orchard. With the sowing season came the farmers. After the harvest and in the winter it was quiet. But I was kept working around the house, and there was always work for me. I would prepare the feed for the pigs, help milk the cows, bring fresh hay for the horses, and help in the kitchen. The work was hard, from dawn to nightfall, but what troubled me was not the hard labor. It was the loneliness, the worry for my family, the fear, the pounding of the heart when the Germans would come around. The terror of the Germans never left me relaxed, always that thought present, what will happen when they discover that I am Jewish.

"One day something happened that eased my pain a little. The Chrabina (countess) came home in her coach on a late winter afternoon and promptly called me over to her carriage.

" 'Quick, Krysia' she said excited, 'take this child, wash her, and change her, and make her ready for bed.'

"I beheld the sight of a little girl of about five or six years of age, cringing in a corner of the carriage. Her clothes beneath the blanket that covered her were wet. Her light brown, shoulder-length hair was wet and tangled. Her sad brown eyes were filled with petrifying fear, and her teeth were chattering. She jerked and shrunk even more when I touched her. I spoke softly to her, *'chodz malenka'* (come little one). She did not budge or say anything, but she did not resist when I picked her up and carried her into the house. She just whimpered softly. I took her to the kitchen and sat her down in a chair. Her frightened eyes followed my every move. Stupefied, she watched me fill the wooden tub with water, her hands crossed on her chest as if protecting herself. When I came over to undress her, she began fighting me, trying pitifully to hold on to the clothes on her back, all the time crying, screaming 'no, no, no water.' I saw her misery and I understood. I figured she was a Jewish child, terribly frightened. I did not know what to do. Here I was having orders from the Chrabina to clean the child and put her to bed. I could not afford to disobey. On the other hand, my heart was breaking to see this traumatized child fighting, and I could not bring myself to force her. I sat down next to her and began talking to her, softly patiently.

" 'What are you afraid of? Tell me, you do not have to be afraid of me. I am not going to hurt you. I only want to clean you up and put you to bed. You can not go to bed dirty the way you are. Where did you get so dirty, anyway?'

"But all she kept saying was 'Please no water, no water.'

" 'Did you drown?' I asked her. 'Is that why you are scared?'

" 'Yes,' she said timidly.

" 'How did you drown?' I asked with surprise in my voice.

" 'I do not know,' she said, and a new wave of tears streamed down her face. She seemed exhausted, her eyes getting smaller and smaller. I took her to the cubicle behind the kitchen, where I had my straw sack, and put her down to sleep. I reported to the Chrabina that the child was too exhausted to be washed and cleaned but promised to do it as soon as she got up. The Chrabina informed me that the child was to sleep upstairs in the bedroom, since she was part of the family. I knew the Chrabina to be childless.

"The little girl was still sound asleep when I went to bed. I lay down next to her and felt her body shiver. She was talking in her sleep. 'Mama, *nein*, Mama come, Mama, no water, no, no, Mama don't leave me. I want to go with you.' I caressed her tangled dirty hair, and she seemed to relax somewhat in her sleep. When she woke she screamed, 'Mama, where are you, Mama?' But quickly she became fully awake and looked around suspiciously.

" 'Come, we go to the kitchen,' I said.

" 'No, no water,' was her instinctive reaction.

" 'No,' I said calmly. 'I will just give you breakfast.'

"Trailing distrustfully behind me, she came to the kitchen.

" 'What is your name?' I asked her, when she was eagerly stuffing a slice of bread into her mouth.

" 'Niusia,' she said very automatically, as if without thinking.

" 'Is it Hanusia, Hanale?' I asked playfully.

" 'Please don't tell this to anyone,' she now pleaded with me urgently. The Germans will take me away. 'Trust me, I will not tell anyone,' I said squeezing her small body hard to mine.

" 'Tell me what happened.'

" 'Please,' she pleaded again, 'I am scared, please don't tell on me.'

Sobbing softly she told me her story. Her mother left her with a Polish family, giving them a bag of money as well. She told her she must be a good girl and listen to the woman and call her Mama. Her mother told her that her name was now Niusia, and she was never to tell anyone what her real name was. She cried, but her mother told her she must not cry and must let her mother go. After her mother left, the woman began complaining and pestering her. She had to do hard work in the house, and all she heard was, 'I have to feed this lazy parasite.' It did not last long; she was kicked around even beaten, and finally thrown out. She wandered around for a long time—Niusia could not specify how long, did not have a very good concept of time anyway at her age—until she fell into the river. The next thing she knew, there were Germans pulling her out of the river. When she became conscious, she heard a woman screaming, 'Oh, my child, oh, my baby!' The woman retrieved her from the Germans and took her into her carriage. Niusia now felt comfortable enough with me to tell me her full name and the town she came from. I thanked her for telling me, but instructed her to follow her mother's advice, and never ever tell anyone her real name ever again. I told her she would have it good here because I would care for her, but she must remember that she is Niusia.

"My life now took on a totally different meaning," Krysia continued. "The Chrabina made it clear that she considered Niusia her child. She claimed the child was her brother's who died in bombardment, and she now adopted her. Niusia was treated very well and with time recovered fine. She would ride to church with the Chrabina in her carriage and take her meals at the dining room table. The Chrabina spent plenty of money to buy her expensive clothes. She did not, however, send Niusia to school, but hired a private tutor to teach her. The Chrabina herself taught her all the prayers. I would press her clothes, comb her hair, and eventually wash her. It took a long time for her to tolerate a bath. She became very close to me, but never mentioned her real name anymore.

Krysia sighed deeply, adding, "and when the war ended and I declared that I was leaving she clung to me and begged me, 'Please, Krysia, take me with you.'

"But I could not." Tears were rolling down Krysia's face. "I did not know myself where I was going, how could I take her with me? I knew that here she would be well taken care of, but my heart ached with the knowledge that we lost a Jewish child."

"Console yourself, Krysia," I said. "If it wasn't for the eagerness of the Polish Chrabina who was childless to have a child, Hanale would surely be dead like so many other Jewish children."

"But Hanale is not dead," Krysia sadly commented. "The burden of that truth is mine."

Our flag was our pride and joy, our most precious possession, and we treated it with extreme dignity. In front of the main entrance to the villa, in a small marbled entrance hall, the flag rested on a special pedestal. There were several names engraved on the pedestal, the names of boys and girls who had given their lives defending Jewish *yishuvim* (settlements) in Palestine. One of the girls was named *Ayala*.

We were all searching for Hebrew names to replace our European ones. Standing guard at the flag, I contemplated my name and decided then and there to be called Ayala. I had remembered how Amos, the Jewish Brigade soldier I met in Austria, called me Ayala, when he said, "You are as light on your legs as an *ayala*."

It was there at the *degel* (flag), standing at attention, that I heard the excited scream coming from an open window.

"Hela, Hela, come quick!"

I could not leave my post, yet I thought something, God forbid, had happened to Nachcia. Lucky for me, Dunia, who happened to be walking by at that moment, quickly saluted and took over my post. I raced up the steps, to find out what had happened. I saw Rachela holding a letter in her hand and screaming at me between hysterical tears and laughter.

"Vrumek, it's Vrumek!" I became frantic, not understanding what she was yelling.

"Vrumek, your brother, he is alive!"

She took hold of me and was shaking me by my shoulders, as if this would make me understand. Absolutely confused, I did not try to make sense of her words, instead running to get Nachcia, shouting to the wind, "Vrumek is alive, our brother Vrumek is alive!"

We both ran back to Rachela. She had just received a letter from a cousin in Palestine. In the letter he wrote that he had seen Vrumek Stapler from Chrzanow, who had arrived in Haifa recently. We were beside ourselves with frustration and anguish. Vrumek was alive. Someone has seen him in Haifa. So many questions suddenly popped into my head. I sat next to Nachcia on our cot, holding my head, trying to understand. How did Vrumek get to Haifa? If Vrumek is alive, so must be Sholek, the younger one of our brothers. The last information we possessed was that they were together. How were we going to find out? What must we do? We had to act, we had to find out, we had to get to Palestine, to see Vrumek, to see Sholek. I got up as if ready to run. I just could not sit there idle.

"Sit down," Nachcia commanded me.

My patient sister embraced my slender figure. I felt the usual motherly instinct that Nachcia so lavishly dispensed, which I always took for granted.

I, the impulsive brat, always leaning on this solid, supportive pilar of strength. Again we sat like so many times before, talking about our family. The nagging questions: Where were the rest of them? How did they perish? Mama, Papa, Blimcia. She should have lived, she was young and pretty and talented and so devoted to her family. Did she hold on to her baby, her Iziu? When did they tear him away? Or was she alive somewhere too? That hope somehow never left us.

We had heard about Vrumek, so it became possible that we could find Blimcia, too. The only thing we could do right then was to get in touch with the person who had seen Vrumek. I sat down immediately and wrote a letter to Rachela's cousin. We spent the whole evening and sleepless night pondering, dreaming aloud about our meeting Vrumek. The days that followed dragged, stretching our nerves to the limit.

It was Friday, March 29, 1946. Nachcia was busy in the kitchen, where she worked, preparing the Sabbath meal, while I sat at the gazebo with some girls just having a silly conversation.

"When I get to Palestine," Clara declared, "the first thing I am going to buy is a mirror and a comb."

Clara was obsessed with her beautiful copper-colored hair, which had grown back so marvelously after having been shaved off in Auschwitz.

"I will buy high-heeled shoes," Zosia said, "and will never let clogs be anyplace where I can see them."

Her feet were still aching from the freezing cold in the wooden clogs she wore in camp.

"I will buy a whole box of chocolate bars," I stated, "like we used to have in our store, and I will eat all of them at once."

Suddenly we saw Rachela running in the direction of the gazebo waiving a letter in her hand, and screaming at the top of her lungs, "It's from Vrumek, from your brother!"

I grabbed the letter from her hand, squeezed it to my heart as if it were alive. Shaking violently I sobbed, unable to control my emotions. My hands shook. All the pent-up anguish and sorrow poured out of my body, like a river spilling over her banks. Through the haze of tears I saw Rachela open the letter for me and push it into my shaking hands. Seeing and recognizing Vrumek's handwriting brought a new wave of tears. I could not see the words. I ran to Nachcia. We held the blotched and tear-stained letter between us and wept again. With hardly time enough to calm down, I wrote an

Villa Cavaletti, April 28, 1946.
This picture was the one we sent
to Vrumek to show that we were
alive. I am on the right, and
Nachcia is on the left.

answer to Vrumek, a four-page letter, letting him know how extremely happy and thrilled we were to have found him to be alive. How we longed to see him, touch him, hold him in our embrace, knowing that this was real, that we would always be together, that no force was ever going to part us.

That evening after dinner, Arye announced, "From now on, no one is to leave the premises, everyone is to go to his room, bundle up his possessions, and be ready." We had a visitor at the time, one of the members of the traveling theater troupe The Ensemble. I overheard him whisper, "I better get out of here. Otherwise I might end up in Palestine with you before my time."

We bundled up our things and brought it all down to the sewing room, where strict instructions were given. The packages were inspected and closed up. The final waiting had started.

Chapter Two ✑

We sat around quietly talking, speculating about our mode of travel. We knew we were at a crucial moment, finally embarking on the decisive voyage that would bring us to our yearned-for destination. However, we were absolutely not involved in planning or executing these plans. It was as well. We were young, inexperienced, and so glad there was someone else to worry about procedure. All we knew was we must listen to instructions and follow them, and we were happy to do that. We just were so anxious, nervous, scared of the unknown, wanting so badly to overcome, to succeed.

It was way past midnight when trucks showed up at the front gate. Hush, hush, we all walked down the main path, in the shade of the tall trees, carrying our bundles on our backs. The trucks were without light. In the stillness of the night the canvas tarpaulins of the military trucks were opened by the shadows of tall men, two to a truck. Moving quietly, the small bundles in our hands, we piled into the waiting trucks. Groping in the dark we could feel the benches against the wall of the truck. As soon as we were all in, even before we were all seated, the truck jerked and moved. We must have been speeding down and climbing up some winding, spiraling back roads, for we kept falling out of our seats and became sick with nausea and vomiting. Conscious, however, of the momentous situation, we sat reticent and subdued. Meekly we whispered in each other's ear, or caught catnaps, waking up queasy and disoriented.

In the morning the trucks stopped. Slowly we descended, suspiciously looking around the large camp. It was called Abiate and was located somewhere in southern Italy. We were directed toward some barracks where we accommodated ourself. Speculations and rumors circled around the camp. Some said we had been in a port and had to return to this camp, to sit and wait for the appropriate time to board a ship. Others claimed we were just traveling back and forth to lose our pursuers, the English soldiers who had spotted us.

All day long we stayed in the camp, a transit place for refugees, dirty, unorganized, repulsive. Exhausted we slept through the night and struggled through another day. After nightfall the trucks appeared again. Convoying on the twisted roads in the dark of night we proceeded. Suddenly we stopped. An eerie feeling possessed us. What was going to happen to us? We could hear some faint voices outside. We sat motionless, cooped up in the dark cavity of the truck, unable to comprehend what was happening. Absolute silence was observed by all. The minutes lingered, and the hours we spent suspended seemed to stretch to eternity. Finally a man came to the back of the truck opened the canvas tarpaulin a crack and in a hoarse whisper said in Hebrew, "Hakol beseder noseem halla" (all is okay, we are moving on). We understood that it was our driver. We wanted to explode but our exuberance was fettered. We would have liked to shout, laugh, express our joy at having succeeded, having outwitted the English, but knew very well how to keep all these feelings to ourselves for the time being. The convoy was moving swiftly again.

There was a gray dawn on the horizon when we beheld the sight of a ship anchored in the tiny port of La Spezia, in southern Italy. The trucks drove onto the concrete quay, where we exuberantly descended. There were hundreds of people already there, perturbed and agitated. Our group leaders tried to have the girls in our group board first, while the fellows waited down below. The tumult and commotion were great. Upon boarding we met a slim, muscular, curly-haired young man introduced only as Moshe. It was much later that we realized he was the Haganah (Jewish military underground) leader of the ship. Impatiently and eagerly we watched for the men of our group, who were detained on the pier. No sooner were they aboard than a jeep full of English soldiers showed up and boarded the ship. There was no panic, just undaunted resistance. We shouted back at them, "We will never leave this vessel, we will not go back to the Nazi death camps. We will go to Palestine, our national home."

People in makeshift tents on the pier in La Spezia with *Dov Hoz* at anchor. Courtesy of Sara Saaroni.

We threatened to throw them overboard if they did not leave us in peace and leave the boat. Indeed a boat it was, an old dilapidated cargo boat housing close to one thousand people, men, women and children, old, young, and in-between, rugged and austere, angry, frustrated, and tired.

Feeling outnumbered, the English left subdued, rushing toward their jeep. Triumphant and boisterous, we followed them down to the pier, where we quickly formed a circle around the jeep, dancing an exuberant hora, using the dance as our weapon, the encircling as a means of expressing our resistance, our fight with the might of the all-powerful British Empire. Then it was the turn of the English soldiers to be frustrated. Their rifles at their sides, they sat stiffly waiting for our steam to subside.

Finally drained of physical strength, we stepped aside, letting them extricate themselves from our midst. Hopefully, we settled into the narrow canvas bunks, sliding in like into drawers. We slept, absorbing each other's kicks through the flimsy canvas.

In the morning we found out that the ship was not going anywhere. Obviously we had been traced by the English since Abiate, and even though we raced them to the ship, their gunboats stationed around the *Fede* prevented it from sailing. It was not until we were safely living in Israel that we learned the details of our ordeal.

In the beginning of 1946 the Haganah, an arm of the Jewish Agency engaged in helping to bring survivors of the Holocaust into Palestine, chartered the first large vessel. The *Fede,* licensed in Italy to carry cargo, was clandestinely prepared to transport one thousand passengers to Palestine, to circumvent the British blockade. Anchored in the port of La Spezia, on the Italian Riviera, the *Fede* waited for its human cargo. The Italian authorities, although properly bribed, failed to inform the local police chief of the ruse. The enterprise backfired when the suspicious local police noticed a large convoy of trucks heading down the road. Suspecting contraband, they stopped the convoy. Apprehensive about falling into the hands of the British, the leader of our convoy risked confessing to the friendly Italians the real purpose of this human contraband. Aware of the hardships suffered by the refugees, the Italian Carabiniers were glad to cooperate.

So that was when we heard, "All is okay, we are moving on." But the inevitable delay had been long enough for the British to learn about the affair. Their gunboats arrived quickly at the pier, and although we were able to outrun the Brits to the quay, disembark, and dispose of the trucks in time, the British prevented the *Fede* from sailing. It was when they came on board and were confronted by our rage that they withdrew. The withdrawal of the single group of soldiers with their commanding officer, however, did not in any way, solve the problem or release us to travel. The British warship kept her vigil next to the *Fede.*

So there we were, a thousand refugees piled, squeezed, and crowded in this small cargo vessel. More and more we emerged onto the long, narrow quay. Idly we sat on the pier or lay in the canvas beds staring at the upper bunks, while the hours passed. So passed another day and then another and another. Slowly the people began settling on the quay, a concrete tongue jutting into the sea, several hundred feet long, just protruding above the water's edge with no fences or walls or barriers at its edge.

On one side stood our ship, where a constant flow of people, like an army of ants, scrambled up and down the metal planks. On the other side the murky waters of the Mediterranean slapped constantly against the pier. At the entrance to the pier was a chain-link gate, closed and locked, opened only to friends, who brought in supplies.

Crowded on deck of the *Fede*: Nachcia is facing the camera, second from left, and I am next to her, directly above the man with dark hair. Courtesy of Sara Saaroni.

The stagnant, rancid air inside the ship forced people out, and they began sleeping on the pier. Slowly, more and more blankets appeared on the pier, and like squatters, people were taking possession of small rectangles as living quarters, not bothering to go back into the ship's belly at all. Small group encampments were forming on the pier, totally blanketed to indicate occupance.

Our Ichud group had its camp, too, even though there was not enough space for everyone to sleep outside. We were a solid brotherhood commune by then, sharing and caring and spiritually supporting each other.

Kuba, one of our fellows who had been a medical student before the war, was addressed by all as Dr. Kuba. He had his hands full treating every possible ailment. No one was willing to leave the ship, even if seriously ill.

Alex, who had acquired an accordion back in Villa Cavaletti and was actively practicing, spent most of his time squatting on the ground playing popular songs. With some prodding he would stand up, putting on his embarrassed smile, and play the music requested, while we would whirl in a quick hora, putting all our pent-up energy into the dance.

As the days passed, necessity brought more and more organization into our lives. We would gather into a circle on the spread-out blankets and listen to Arye lecture on Zionism or lead a discussion. At the farthest end of the pier, the fellows constructed a toilet. Nothing fancy, just some blankets hanging on ropes to cover the people using the sea.

We did not know much of what was happening and were not informed of any intervention or negotiations about our being released to travel, but one morning we woke up to find another ship anchored next to ours. Our ship was called the *Fede;* the second ship was the *Fenice.*

In absolute awe we stared at the wonder before our very eyes. Another rusty, moldy old beautiful sister to our *Fede* stood anchored next to her. In a most orderly fashion the people were divided, and we luxuriated in more sleeping space. Half of the canvas bunks were dismantled and transferred to the *Fenice.* The space between the bunks doubled, making it possible even to sit up inside when the upper person was not in his bed. There was also additional deck room.

One day I was walking toward our encampment on the pier, when I saw a group of people congregating at the edge of the water. Curious, I went to see what had happened and was struck by the sight of my sister Nachcia being pulled out of the water. Hysterically I pushed my way through the throng of people to get to my sister.

Nachcia, who since our time in the concentration camp suffered from headaches and dizzy spells, had suddenly felt dizzy and tumbled straight into the sea when her legs gave out. The pier was not protected in any way at the edges. Luckily, there were always multitudes of people around and in very close proximity. Nachcia had gone under the surface for just a moment and was pulled out. She was frightened and disoriented, and I was happy, in the midst of my gravest distress, to be right there near her.

Nachcia recuperated from the shock, but our lives were beginning to deteriorate emotionally. Days were passing and nothing was happening. Morale was low and physical well-being was in a shambles. We had no sanitation facilities, and the overcrowding was slowly getting to us. Even with all our idealism, we could not control our emotions.

There were different groups each trying to keep up its own morale and sustenance, but there was friction between the groups. We were getting weaker. We could not undress, sleep relaxed, or wash. Eventually a contagious skin disease, *swiezba,* spread like wildfire.

In the midst of all this came the holiday of Passover, and even though we were still in bondage and not liberated, we celebrated. On the naked concrete of the pier some white paper was spread. We sat squatting in long rows on either side of the white paper representing the table, while a seder was conducted. Hastily and uncomfortably, like our forefathers when they fled the land of the Pharaohs, we ate our meal and chanted the traditional *Hagadah* (Passover story). As the children of Israel waited at the mouth of the Red Sea for it to part, so we the children of Israel in another generation waited for the gates of our promised land to open for us. At the edge of the Mediterranean we sat and sang "Bei dem breg fun dem yam" (On the shores of the sea), a song composed by one of our members, expressing our longing and waiting. Even though the name of the leader of our ship was Moshe (Moses), he had no staff and was not holy in the presence of God.

The holiday passed and our situation was still stagnant. A more drastic measure was needed to impress our enemy, the British Mandate government. It was decided by the leadership, with the unanimous consent of the people, that if they would not allow us to proceed to Palestine—and our lives had no value if we could not get there—we would resort to a drastic measure. Because there was no place we could go to, because there was no one that wanted us, and because we could not stay in Europe, the cemetery of our families and cause of our shattered lives, we declared a hunger strike. We refused all food, which was brought in daily from outside. We listened sadly to the sorrowful announcement coming from the bullhorn.

"It is our voluntary decision," it said. "Anyone weak, ill, or unable to withstand is free to leave the ship. Provisions will be made for such people."

No one budged, for there was really no place for us to go. We were all part of the group—the group was our family. Solemnly we talked among ourselves, approving the decision, conscious of its gloomy peril. Enveloped in melancholy, we retired for the night.

With the rising sun came some improvement in our moods. Even confined as we were, the brilliant sun twinkled with gold and color in the waters of the sea, encouraging our exuberance. God's world is so beautiful, we would endure, we would not perish, we would succeed. "Let's not despair, let's hold up our spirits, let's show the world our determination. In our unity is our strength, let us rejoice!"

Elated momentarily, we formed a circle and danced a hora, our favored expression of freedom and joy. We danced and people were joining, and the circle grew larger and larger, and the singing rose above the noisy flapping of the waves against the pier. Alex took out his beloved accordion and played "Im ein ani li mi li?" (If I am not for myself, who is for me?). The stomping and kicking and jumping increased, fueled by the ideology that it is only ourselves we can count on, and we must and will overcome. Exalted, we danced until there was no more strength, with people slowly leaving the circle, exhausted. Tired, we lay on the pier, trying to gather strength for more dancing. There was nothing else we could do in our frustration.

Meanwhile, meetings were constantly being conducted by the leadership. We danced some more in the afternoon, ignoring the warnings of the older folks to save our strength. There was no news from anywhere until we again went to sleep after twenty-four hours of the hunger strike.

The next day there were scores of people just sitting subdued on the ground. The girls and boys of our group were still in good shape. We encouraged and nagged Alex to play for us, and still managed to dance a lively hora. But the circle was growing smaller faster, with tired people flopping down. Arye, our *madrich*, came out of a meeting very agitated and headed toward the end of the pier, where the makeshift toilets were. Making a brief statement as to his disappointment and discouragement, he could not conceive of continuing; there was no alternative for him but to commit suicide. Then he headed for the water. The boys, of course, got hold of him, restraining him forcibly. He struggled fiercely but eventually succumbed. We tried to cheer him by dancing a hora around him, but we were devastated.

So the second day passed, forty-eight hours of fasting, and obviously no progress was made with the English authorities to release our ships and our people to travel to Palestine.

We drank only water, no food came to our mouths, and we waited.

The sun blinded my eyes when I came out onto the deck of the *Fede* on the third day of our hunger strike. There were not many people out. The throngs usually milling at the rails and on the steps were noticeably absent. Those that were around shuffled slowly, holding on to the railings, leaning against them for support when faint weakness washed over them. In the bowel of the ship, people lay in their bunks, motionless, staring just ahead, or quietly murmuring and contemplating what was going to become of us.

It had been seventy hours since we had begun fasting, and we were counting by the hour. There was a sign attached to the entry gate saying so.

I felt miserably faint in the rancid air of the moldy ship. With the remnant of strength left in me, I pulled myself out of the confines of the bunk and dragged my buckling legs up the ladder. The fresh air and sun felt good on my face but did not relieve the light-headed feeling and empty pit in my stomach. I saw an older man sitting on a chair on deck. Dr. Kuba was bent over him. I heard Moshe, the ship leader, and Arye, our own group leader, talking intensely to the man. In precise, clear words, they were explaining to him that being as sick as he was, it would certainly be advisable for him to leave the ship. Considering his age and his heart condition, he was really putting himself in danger keeping up the fast. They declared it would absolutely not be considered a desertion, only a preservation of life, which was our main concern. The man gasped for air and pressed his hands to his heart, yet he categorically refused to be removed from the ship.

His demonstration of such total dedication encouraged me, and I scurried down to the pier. There, too, the crowds were minimal. There were no hora circles, and most of the young girls and boys that were about just sat or lay on the blankets quietly talking. The mood was subdued and depressed. The placard at the gate read seventy-two hours of hunger strike. Passersby stopped, to stare and shake their heads in astonishment. There were even some reporters taking pictures of these strange human beings who barricaded themselves at the pier with the two fishing boats.

The sun was high in the sky when I went back into the confines of the *Fede* to rest. I must have dozed off, for suddenly I was awaken by faint cheering and hand clapping. In muted excitement, someone called down to us to come out, the strike was over. Overwhelmed, we pulled ourselves upstairs to witness the historical event.

On deck we saw a small circle of people attentively listening to a tall, distinguished man. Professor Laski, an envoy from England, had come to deliver to us, survivors of the Holocaust, the remnant of the Jewish people, who were ready to sacrifice their lives to break down the English blockade of Palestine, the good news that permission had been obtained for us to proceed. Through the efforts of the Jewish Agency and the Jewish world community, pressure had been brought on the British government to nullify the White Paper and issue certificates to more than the quota prescribed, in view of the disaster that befell the Jews. Professor Laski was explaining that certificates had been procured for us to emigrate.

We had won our battle. There were cheers and hand clapping, a feeble expression of our joy and excitement. The one thousand people in this contingent were permitted to enter Palestine legally. We were certainly happy, but the greater problem had not been solved, the problem of the many more refugees like ourselves waiting to be issued certificates permitting them to emigrate to Palestine.

The gates were opened immediately and supplies brought in. Each person received an orange and several biscuits, but even these were too little to build up the strength needed to express our emotions in the usual aggressive manner, by dancing a hora. Slowly people crept up from the hold of the ship to procure their ration of food and then returned for a rest.

By the next morning life began shimmering again. Food, that precious sustenance of life, restored our will, our mood, and our zest. Preparations began for our trip. In a small ceremony, the two vessels received their proper Hebrew names. The *Fede* was named *Dov Hos* and the *Fenice* was given the name *Eliyahu Golomb*. These two men, it was explained to us, were Jewish heroes who fought and sacrificed their lives defending the *Yishuv* (settlement) in Palestine.

The excitement of our approaching voyage was now felt. Again throngs of people were milling about, loading supplies onto the ships, talking excitedly, rushing about. Even the author of the song "Bei dem breg fun dem yam," which became our hymn, added a new verse stating, "and soon we will reach you, our promised land."

We stood on deck smiling and praying when the hoarse whistle announced farewell to the people of La Spezia. We saw their waving hands grow smaller, and then it was us and the sea.

Slowly the ship danced on the gentle waves, the brilliant sun accompanying her. A small breeze wafted on the surface of the water, and the salty smell of the sea filled our nostrils. Many people became sick even though the weather was superbly peaceful and the sea tranquil.

One girl became seriously ill, which caused the ship to seek the closest available port. We anchored on the island of Crete just long enough to take Helen to the hospital, where she was pronounced fit to continue the trip.

Saturday, May 5, 1946, was the tenth day at sea, and we strained our eyes for hours to spot land. The captain himself had promised that we would touch land that day. It wasn't until after the sun tumbled down into the sea that we saw twinkling lights in the distance, and they were not the stars. They were the scattered sparkling jewels on the dark outline of Mount Carmel. We were nearing the port city of Haifa. There was cheering and laughter and singing while the ship was anchored. We spent another impatient night on the ship.

On Sunday morning we had visitors, Abba Hushi, the mayor of Haifa, and Golda Meir, a representative of the Jewish agency.

It was Mrs. Meir who took a postcard I wrote to Vrumek to let him know that we had arrived. It all seemed like a dream come true except that the wish to see our brother still seemed remote, a dream unfulfilled.

Chapter Three ✌◦

I will probably never forget the taste of the two fresh white rolls with cheese I received upon our arrival in Palestine.

There we were, after having struggled a whole year to reach this destiny, having traveled, smuggled from country to country, prayed, dreamed. Finally we stepped foot on this longed-for land, a dream come true. We were filled with youthful energy, bubbling with happiness.

In spite of the still-unfulfilled goal of seeing ·Vrumek, my exuberance knew no restraint, and my legs would not stand still. People noticed me and came over to chat, and I was thrilled with the attention. I was eighteen years old. I had spent the last seven years—a third of my life—in the most dire conditions, the most horrible circumstances, in the ghetto, in camps, and only in the last year in hope for an end to this ordeal. We had achieved our goal, had reached freedom. Like all of us, I yearned for a life, a real life. It was the first time that courtesy was extended to me, attention was paid to me as a young female. The desire for that attention was surging forward.

I could not believe it when a uniform-clad English soldier came over to flirt with me and to my profound astonishment spoke Hebrew. Another young fellow in khaki shorts and shirt and a wide-brimmed hat folded on one side, stuck close to me. He said he was a *noter,* which I understood to mean some sort of local policeman. When we finally were transferred into buses, he showed up in my bus.

Rolling down the highway, we could see through the windows of the bus on either side of the road green fields basking in the warm sun. We inhaled the fragrance of the blooming orange trees. Nachcia and Hania were transfixed, looking at the scenery, calling out to each other, "Look at these fields all verdant and blooming! Smell the aroma of the sweet air; inhale deeply its freshness."

Symche, the *noter,* squeezing next to me on the bench, pointed to the fields, explaining the division of the land, astonishing me with his expertise. How could he know what he was showing us?

"This land is ours," he would say, meaning Jewish-owned, "and that is Arab-owned."

We were taken to the town of Hedera, and we disembarked in a large complex, explained by Symche to be an absorption center. The small white buildings looked neat and clean, and we made ourselves comfortable. A cool shower and fine dinner put us back into a celebrating mood, in spite of our fatigue.

Still in Symche's custody, we visited the *moshavah* (agricultural settlement), which Hedera was. It was on the outskirts of this settlement that the absorption center was located. Run by the Jewish Agency, the official governing body of the Jewish inhabitants of Palestine, the absorption center afforded a place to house us temporarily. At the *moshavah* we met some local residents, Jewish farmers, young people, obviously very interested in the contingent of young girls who just arrived in the country. Many of them later visited us at our camp.

For lack of a social hall, that evening a group of us sat on the cots in our room, in the company of the local fellows. With very little prodding, I sang and kept everybody entertained. I sang "Bei dem breg fun dem yam" in the original Yiddish, and soon in the Hebrew translation. It was Symche, the *noter,* who had heard me sing the song before, and had translated it into Hebrew. I sang my favorite song "Gei nit avek bleib du" (Don't go away, stay here) and Symche melted away. Years later he would remind me how fascinated and allured he felt when I sang this song.

My dear sister Nachcia, a much quieter type than I, did not get directly involved with the visiting boys, but I could see a smile broadening her sincere face when she watched me, singing, bubbling, enjoying. She was like a mother to me.

Hania, our cousin, looked around, a little confused by the Hebrew spoken by the local fellows, for she had not sufficiently mastered it yet. Her shiny jet black locks enhanced her exquisitely beautiful face.

At the port of Haifa, we had met an official who told us he was from Chrzanow, our home town, and that he knew that Vrumek was in Tel Aviv. I kept asking the man if he had seen Vrumek himself, unable to believe that this dream we had of seeing our brother again, alive and well, would really come true. He assured us that he had seen Vrumek himself.

In Hedera the waiting was becoming unbearable. Every now and then a commotion would start, when someone would come to seek out and find members of his family who had just arrived. I kept up a vigil at the entrance gate, anxiously awaiting our brother. We had notified him of our arrival. The postcard we handed to Mrs. Golda Meir in the port of Haifa, had he received it? Doubts were plaguing me, standing there at the gate for hours, watching.

Seeing others arriving, meeting with their loved ones, was a seesaw of happiness and distress—happiness hoping that soon I, too, would be in the embrace of our beloved brother, distress because he wasn't there yet.

Finally on the second day of our stay in Hedera, from the distance of the compound grounds I saw Renia, a girl in our group, run toward me.

"Your brother is here," she shouted, waving her hands, motioning for me to come, "I saw him at the gate!"

My head began spinning, my legs, always so easy to run, suddenly became weighted like lead and for a second rooted to the ground.

"How do you know that he is my brother?" I questioned her, "You never met my brother."

"Because he looks exactly like you," she declared.

Then I saw Nachcia standing nearby. I grabbed her hand and together we ran through the crowded yard toward the gate to meet him. All I could utter to the totally astonished Nachcia was, "Vrumek! Vrumek is here."

I had to stop, seeing Nachcia, my older, more serious sister breathe deeply to stabilize her heartbeat, the emotion evident in her gentle face.

Tall and slim, swaying in his gait, dressed in a good white shirt and gray pants with a summer straw hat, Vrumek looked a bit skinny, but well. We flew into his embrace and could not bear to dislodge ourselves from his arms. We clung to him on either side, walking through the whole compound, wanting to know that we would never have to part again. Fervently we searched for Hania, knowing how impatient she, too, was to see Vrumek.

Vrumek was emotional, kissing our faces, looking deeply into our eyes. The separation of years, the trauma of not knowing the fate of all the members of our family, was expressed in our cleaving to each other. The physical contact was the only tangible assurance that we had found each other and would not separate again. We looked at Vrumek's thin face, his cheekbones

First day in Tel Aviv. From left to right: me, Vrumek, and Nachcia.

somewhat protruding, his soft gray eyes that had so much pain in them. Choked up, we could not speak. We had so many questions to ask.

Vrumek, my older brother, who used to teach me ride a bicycle, when I was still a little girl, who invited me to visit him, in Bielsko, the industrial town in Poland, where he worked as an accountant, together with our brother Heshek. What a fabulous vacation he had given me that summer of 1938 in Bielsko. He was always so playful, fun to be with, a real pal.

Nachcia, too, must have been going over her own memories, but who knew which ones? From the mist in her blue eyes I guessed it must have been the sad memories of the war. There were no words to express all the pressing questions. We knew that it all had to wait. We just touched each other, embracing and clinging to confirm that we were together, that we were real.

Vrumek looked us over, his precious two sisters and his beautiful cousin Hania, for whom he felt a special affection even when we were still at home. We were still dressed in the skirts made in the concentration camp from the material I managed to steal from the weaving machine I worked on, and I was wearing a pair of men's shoes, received in one of the clothes distributions. He had a worried expression when he stated, "The first thing we have to do is buy you a pair of decent shoes."

The urgency of the present took priority over all else, Vrumek's sense of responsibility, so acute, immediately making decisions, worrying about our well being and appearance.

He spent the rest of the day with us. We walked the camp grounds, proudly introducing our brother to all our friends, who shook their heads and shed a tear. Some of the tears were in thanksgiving to the Almighty, in happiness shared with us, and some were maybe in pain for not having found anyone of their own. Mutely our eyes asked the questions: What happened to Mama to Papa, to Blimcia our most beloved oldest sister, with her baby, Iziu? "We will talk about everything," Vrumek assured us, "when we are finally together."

Toward evening Vrumek had to return to Tel Aviv to his job. In only two more days, he promised, he would come back to take us with him to Tel Aviv. Those two days of waiting were probably the longest in our lives. Impatiently we paced the dusty ground of the absorption camp, constantly glancing at the gate. In the crowded bunks we found no peace and could not concentrate on other people's conversations.

On the morning of the third day, we were right at the gate when he came. It was so good to feel his arms wrapped around our shoulders again, to know that he was real, and we were going to stay together.

He took us with him to Tel Aviv, where he lived. In awe we looked at the bright houses bleached by the intense sun, crowds drifting down wide boulevards lined with stores selling all kinds of goods. It all seemed so normal; it was so strange to see no traces of war.

We visited the place where he worked behind a counter in a coffee shop. Gladdened with the compliments and praise we heard from his employer, we walked proudly next to him. Next we met the people he lived with.

Vrumek had arrived in Palestine only a little more than a year ahead of us. Exhausted from his peregrination of Nazi-occupied Europe, he had finally reached his heaven in Palestine, while the war still raged on the European continent. His start in the freedom of Palestine was a new trial full of disappointments and loneliness. He was by then a boarder at a widow's apartment. Mrs. V had two sons and a mentally retarded daughter. She had taken Vrumek into her two-room apartment because she needed the extra income from his rent. Vrumek shared his room with her two sons, while Mrs. V slept with her daughter, Clara.

The family was not religious or traditional in any way but did not object to Vrumek's religious observance. Friday nights, when Vrumek would come home from synagogue, he would set out his meal on a corner of the table in his usual orderly manner and make *kiddush* (the blessing over the wine).

In the beginning, the fellows would ridicule him for his religious observance. Vrumek, however, was a man of strong character, and self-assurance, and their smirking, silly remarks and outright jokes did not bother him. Vrumek's adherence to tradition was unquestionable, nonnegotiable. Slowly Boris and Moishe abandoned their ludicrous behavior. Getting to know him better, noticing his decency, his tolerance, his pleasant manner, Vrumek gained respect in their eyes. Eagerly they began waiting for him to make *kiddush*, sing his *zemiros* (Sabbath songs), and even wanted to take their meals on Saturday with him.

Mrs. V, who was quite skeptical when she first met Vrumek and had hesitated to take a stranger into her house, eventually learned to love Vrumek and shed many a tear when he left her. By the time we arrived, Mrs. V was happy to let us sleep over whenever we visited our brother.

Vrumek had been struggling for over a year, totally alone, a subtenant in Mrs. V's house and a counter man in a coffee house with a meager salary. His joy at finding his two sisters, who had survived the war in Europe, was boundless. But with joy came worries. He had hardly saved enough money to buy himself some decent clothing, having come here himself totally penniless. Now he was confronted with two more people to care for. He wanted us again to be a family. We did not even have a chance to ask the burning question—how did you survive and get here? We had to satisfy ourselves with only the momentary happiness of having found each other.

After having visited Vrumek in Tel Aviv and spending a leisurely day walking down the shoreline enjoying the sun, the air, the freedom, the beauty of our land, we returned to Hedera. There with all our friends we awaited the settlement arrangements the Jewish Agency was working on.

On a Friday morning, May 10, 1946, buses showed up in Hedera. We were being divided into three groups. One group was going to a kibbutz of the *Zionim Klaliim* (general Zionists) called Tel Itzchak; another group was going to a *moshav* (agricultural settlement); Beth Yehoshua, and a third small group was going to Ayanot, an agricultural school.

Beth Yehoshua was one of the agricultural villages of the religious movement. Nachcia and Hania, being religious, were assigned to the bus destined to Beth Yehoshua. Distressed at being separated from Nachcia and Hania, I was in the small group of youngsters going to Ayanot.

Before we boarded the bus, a dispute arose among the leadership as to which of the youngsters were being sent to Ayanot, based on the need they had for education. I was told to step away. They claimed that there were those who were less educated or intelligent than I, and certainly more in need of some education. I was not convinced at all with this argument, especially in view of the fact that I was the youngest in the group, and no one else was assigned to the group going to Ayanot to replace me. The disputes among the people who were arranging our destiny only added to our misery. Another girl was asked to step away. More bargaining and bartering took place, and while all the people were already on the buses assigned to someplace I was still standing there my bundle in hand, unassigned.

Tears were choking me, I wanted to be with Nachcia and Hania, from whom I had never been parted in my whole life. My heart longed to be able to go to school, for I was very aware of my inadequacies. Yet there I was standing alone, unable to contribute at all to the turn my life was to take.

When the buses finally began moving and I still entrenched at the spot, despondent and crying, I was permitted to run to the Ayanot bus.

With the sweet fragrance of the blossoming fields penetrating our bus from the left, and the blue waters of the Mediterranean Sea seen from the windows on the right, we had a good glimpse of the country we had striven to reach for so long.

We arrived at the gate of Ayanot late in the afternoon. The gate had already been closed for the Sabbath, with no one in sight on the tree-lined walk leading from the gate to the main compound. The fellows who brought us there climbed up the fence, and I quickly followed suit. The rest of the girls were left waiting at the gate until someone was alerted to come and get them.

In front of the administration building we met Adda Fishman, the director of the school. A litany of rough remarks and angry screams came from the mouth of the stocky woman dressed in a plain dress, her long naturally curly graying hair pulled back in a bun on the nape of her neck. We were

At the Ayanot agricultural school (I am on the right).

shocked at the welcome we received and could not understand why this unfriendly director was so opposed to us.

"Who needs you here? Why did you come? Whom are you bringing
here?" she yelled acrimoniously at the man who brought us.

I was flabbergasted at being so unwanted. We had just come, after en-
during so much in the struggle to reach this promised land of ours, and again
we were faced with "who needs you here?"—bringing back the memory of
our neighbors in Poland, who had asked the same thing. It was simply unthinkable to hear the question repeated. It was burning our already scorched
souls. Why had we survived the awesome tragedy, struggled to get there, to
be rejected like that?

After some negotiations, Adda agreed to let us stay over Sabbath. We
were able to shower and change just in time for the Sabbath meal.

It was an overwhelming sight, when we were finally seated in the dining
room. After seven years of war, concentration camps, ghettos, hopelessness,
suffering, we were seated in a large, well-lit room, full of boys and girls our
own age, all dressed in their Sabbath best. The neatly combed hair of the
girls, the clean-shaven, bright faces of the boys, the pure white shirts worn by

all, made me think I was in heaven surrounded by angels. The tables were lined with white tablecloths, and the aroma of fresh baked challah was in the air. The *kipot* (head coverings) on the boys' heads reminded me of my own brothers. At the head of one of the tables Aharon, a teacher, was making *kiddush* over wine, while all stood and answered in unison, "amen."

We were eventually permitted to stay in Ayanot. A difficult period of adjustment began for us. We yearned to live like the local kids, but our emotions were severely scared. We suffered nightmares in our sleep. We were afflicted by diseases, some strange and some well-known.

One time when I was on duty in the kitchen, several of us stuffed ourself with some delicious sour cream. As a result we had to be hospitalized with stomach poisoning. Our intestines were obviously not ready yet for such rich food. Neither were our minds ready for the company of normal teenagers, with their frivolous sentiments and worries.

We mostly stuck together, the dozen of us, sharing our hopes, our feelings, our suffering. We felt close to our survivor friends, forming an artificial family. Yet deep in our hearts we longed for real family life.

I loved Ayanot, the symbol of my freedom—the green fields, the sturdy trees, the whitewashed houses, the bright dining room. I loved Zipora, the house mother, who stood at the entrance to the dining room scrutinizing every girl and boy. I loved her even when she would send a girl back to her room to change from her shorts or pants into a skirt, or asked a boy to go back to his room to put on a clean shirt before entering the dining room. Strict decor and behavior were always the rule. I loved Aharon's stern look at the head of the table, which made everybody behave. I learned to love Adda's strictness and her low, barking voice, for I knew what she stood for, although it was hard to forgive her the pain she caused us.

In time we found out why she was so hostile upon our arrival. Obviously things were very poorly coordinated in Palestine at that time. Supposedly Adda had no idea that a dozen newcomers were being shipped to her school, where it was her responsibility to house them and educate them. Not that the school was run so efficiently; her pride was hurt because she had not been consulted or informed.

I loved Shaul, the teacher who practiced defense with us. When he would hit the stick in my hand and yell, "defend yourself," the physical pain would dissipate against emotional pride. I loved the teacher who taught us fowl anatomy. We called her "The Chicken." Her speech was like the "tweet" of a chick. I loved running barefoot and in shorts, the warm sun on my arms and face. I loved the evening dances outdoor, when I would whirl in a hora, lifted off the ground by the strong arms of the boys.

It was there in Ayanot that a new chapter in our lives began. Out in the fields in the pure air, under the brilliant sun, in touch with our native soil, we were being reborn. It was there in the stall to which I was summoned to witness the birth of a calf that my body began budding with life and love. There was no more death, fear, and stench of dead corpses. There was, instead, the smell of animal manure, wholesome and natural and good.

I sat on the ground next to Aliza and Shimon, a pole looped through the ropes in our hands, the other end of the ropes attached to the calf's hoofs. In perfect rhythm with the cows pains came the order from our teacher Aharon, "pull." Using all my physical strength, I pulled and stopped and pulled again. When finally the calf plopped out my heart expanded in my chest with fondness and pleasure. A new calf—an addition to our family, our school, our land, our nation.

When I picked ripe red tomatoes, when I saw the little chicks hatch, I felt rich. It was all ours, and I was helping produce it. Eagerly we sat in the classrooms learning anatomy of birds, animals, and fish. We learned all the agricultural subjects, and most appreciatively we learned Hebrew. We were anxious to be able to communicate in Hebrew instead of our native Polish. We wanted to shed all memory of our past, of our tragic lives in Europe. We were eager to become the equals of the local kids. We participated in all the activities, enjoyed the socials, and harnessed ourselves with love to the work. We took part proudly in the military training even though we only used sticks as weapons. We adhered to the strict discipline of the school and seldom complained about anything.

I longed with great pain for Nachcia, from whom I was separated for the first time in my life. I ached to be together with Vrumek, whom I had seen for such a short time after finding him alive. But it was an emotional struggle, for Ayanot had so much to offer. After years of starvation, the food was so enticing and satisfying to us, even though it seemed boring to the local kids.

I will never forget a bright sunny day when I sat down to breakfast, and a girl next to me on the bench smelled her soft-boiled egg and complained, "it stinks." She dumped the egg into the disposal dish, picked up two slices of bread from the bread basket and covered it saying, "I cannot look at it." That was too much for me to bear. It was the straw that broke the camel's back.

Kitchen duty at Ayanot school.

"How can you do this?" I screamed. I was struggling against my spontaneous urge to slap her in that sour face and tell her what I would have done just a year ago to have what she was so sinfully throwing away. My whole body shaking with emotion, I stood up and yelled, "It's not enough that you are throwing away a perfect egg, you take two slices of good bread and ruin them."

I sat at the table crying. The poor girl was in shock. She did not understand what I wanted from her. Obviously, in her mother's house she would not even have been reprimanded. Her action was absolutely normal. Therein lay the immense gap between the refugees and the *sabras*. It was this gap that I would have to learn to overcome for the rest of my years. Never would I rid myself of the horror of wastefulness that I encountered throughout my life, the life of a survivor of the Holocaust. I sat and cried at the table, distraught, realizing that it was I who was at odds with the world.

Elsa, a petite girl with shoulder-length blond hair, came over to me after the girl left the table.

"I saw what happened" she said simply.

I was still shaking.

"You wouldn't understand," I said crossly.

"Why do you think I wouldn't?" she asked.

"Because," I said, "you do not know what hunger is. No one will ever understand what it is like to be so hungry that you would want to eat grass and even that is not available."

"What makes you so sure I don't know how it feels to be hungry?"

"Because you are talking about having an appetite for something, about a craving, not about hunger."

"Is that what I look like? And what gives you that impression?"

"Because you are a *sabra,* that's why."

"Well then, let me introduce myself. My name is Elsa, and I am not a *sabra.* I was born in Germany. Don't you detect my German accent?"

"Now that you mention it, I do, but it is very slight. You are not here with any group, though."

"No, I have come to Palestine with Youth Aliyah (young emigrees) and was the only one in my group placed here in Ayanot. I love farming and intend to go live on a kibbutz. This is my second year here."

"That's why your Hebrew is so good," I said a little more amicably. "So you are an immigrant, just like me. Unbelievable. Your healthy, tanned face does disguise your European origin."

"Soon you, too, will look like that, I promise you. And please don't get aggravated over these rude *sabras.* Try to ignore them," Elsa said pleasantly. "Let's go outside. I will show you where my room is."

I liked Elsa right from the start, and we became good friends. In the many evenings we spent together, I found out all about her. She was an only child. Her mother perished in Dachau concentration camp. She knew nothing about her father but was not concerned because her father had divorced her mother.

"Elsa, why don't you change your name to a Hebrew one?" I asked her once, when we were doing cleaning duty together. Barefoot in shorts with a colorful kerchief around her head covering her blond hair, only her high cheekbones and small nose were prominent. Her blue eyes smiling, she said, "When I came to Ayanot, Adda stood on these steps that we are washing now, at the entrance to the school building, and asked me what my name was. When she heard it was Elsa she stated, "From now on you are Esther." Do I look like an Esther? Tell me the truth. So I never took on Esther and remained Elsa, without Adda's knowledge."

"Yes I know Adda gave each one of us a Hebrew name. I was lucky, I had chosen my Hebrew name prior to coming here."

One day we were sitting on the lawn in front of our dormitory building. The sun was a fiery red ball quickly tumbling down on the horizon, and a bluish-gray dusk settled over the small buildings.

"Elsa, I am going to leave Ayanot," I said pensively, watching her face for reaction.

She sat quiet for a moment and then meekly, as if talking to herself, said, "I am very sorry, sorry indeed. I know you want to be with your brother and sister, and you have to do what is good for you, but I will miss you terribly. Throughout my stay in Palestine I have not made friends with anyone. Now that I have you as a friend, we are going to part. Probably forever. I was very fond of you, I opened my heart to you and you understood. I always feared being rejected, but you always made me feel comfortable."

She made me feel terribly sad. I put my arm around her shoulder trying to infect her with my enthusiasm and said encouragingly, "I am only going to Tel Aviv, and we will certainly stay in touch. You will have someone to visit whenever you come there. We will surely remain friends forever, you can trust me about that."

"I know I can trust you, Ayala, that is why I shared all my feelings with you, but there is a heavy burden in my heart that I did not share even with you, and now you are leaving and I will never have the chance to tell you."

"What is it, Elsa? Who are you in love with? You can tell me now. If you need my help I am still here, and if you do not want me to get involved, then I am leaving. Who is it, or should I guess?"

"If it were so simple you would have known already, but it is not. Even if I were to fall in love with someone, it would only mean hardship, and that is not what I want a relationship to be. That is why it was so good to have you as a friend. My friendship with you could not lead to any hardship. With a man it would."

"Now you have me puzzled. What in the world are you talking about?"

"You know I am all alone in this world, I have no one, absolutely no one."

"Oh Elsa, we all lost our families, we all must start from scratch. You will find someone to love who will love you, and you will build a home for yourselves, just like we all will do."

"But I have no tradition to build with," Elsa said desperately.

"You will learn, Elsa. You are intelligent, smart, and kind, you will make a good wife to someone. I have an idea: why don't we start right now? I have a beautiful name for you, not Esther, but Edna. Edna means delicate, and it fits your looks. You are of delicate build. It matches your pure skin and innocent blue eyes and your tactful, proper character. You will make a sensitive, wonderful Jewish mother."

"That is what scares me, Ayala. I will never be able to be a Jewish mother."

"Oh Edna," I exclaimed in shock and felt my eyes become moist with unshed tears. "You cannot be so sure. There are doctors who can probably help you. As soon as I settle, I will think about it and see what can be done. You will come to Tel Aviv."

"Why do you sit here in the dark?" Ziona called out to us in passing, "Don't you want to eat? The bell rang ten minutes ago. Come on."

We stood up and followed Ziona in silence to the brightly lit dining room, where the commotion of clanking forks and knifes mixed with exuberant voices of the boys and girls absorbed us into the mainstream.

I looked into Edna's eyes when I came to say good-bye the next morning, but she was calm and collected. She hugged me fiercely and wished me luck. It was a difficult period of adjustment. We yearned to live like the local kids, but our emotions were severely shattered.

Together with several of our girls I had plotted to leave Ayanot. With the first pound that Vrumek had managed to spare for me, I bought a bus ticket and went to Tel Aviv. Three other girls and I rented a laundry room in a fancy building. Located in the backyard of the building, the room consisted of four cement walls with a drain in the middle. We put up the metal cots provided to us in Ayanot by the Jewish Agency against the four walls. We had brought these cots with us, transporting them on the roof of the bus. The small washroom was filled. There was just enough room on each wall for a narrow cot, so three of them became stationary while the fourth had to be moved each time the door had to be opened.

We began scouring the big city looking for jobs. After several days clearing tables in a restaurant and some time in a factory, I got lucky. My next lead took me to the household of a fish store owner, as helpmate to his wife. The unpleasant part was the smell of fish on the owners' clothes and the disorder and filth in the house.

Vrumek was very happy when I came to live in Tel Aviv, in spite of the fact that it added to his responsibilities. We longed to live together, to practice again the tradition and lifestye of our family. Nachcia had left the *moshav,* and she completed our family circle.

Hania opted to stay at *moshav* Beth Yehoshua for the time being. What we learned much later was that there was a very handsome farmer living in the vicinity who visited Hania very often. Hania had very good reason to stay. Yaki, a strong muscular fellow with thick, dark blond hair, was absolutely enchanted with Hania. When he looked into Hania's smiling eyes he saw a happy future.

Hania was twenty-three years old. She had lost her parents, her brother Chamek, and her sister Gucia when the Germans took them away from her in the last raid in Chrzanow. Her brother Sholek, who had survived the horror of several camps in Germany and managed to drag himself home to Chrzanow when the war ended, had lived just long enough for Hania and us to see him when we returned home. Two years later, she still could not stop grieving for Sholek. Her loneliness was painful.

Yaki was big and strong, yet kind and understanding. He promised to make up for her pain. He promised to love her and cherish her for the rest of his life. He wanted to give her a good life. He took her home to his family to introduce her.

His father and mother, Jews who had fled the rise of Hitler in Germany, were established on a farm, with their three fine sons working side-by-side with their father. They were simple but kind, good-hearted people. They saw how enamored Yaki was with this charming girl and knew that he would not give her up.

In a small ceremony that we all attended, under the strain of living with the curfews of the British Mandate government, Yaki married Hania, and they settled close by in a small apartment. Yaki continued working his father's farm.

Living as we did under the regime of the British occupation, life on a farm afforded a much better life than that in the city. Hania learned to relax a bit. Yaki kept his promise: he loved her without bounds. Even as hard as he worked during the day, he would help her with the two little daughters that were born to them, eleven months apart. He would bathe them and feed them and play with them, never getting enough of the joy of his household.

Nachcia, Vrumek, and I could not see Hania much in those days of strife

Hania and Yaki's wedding,
July 1, 1947.

that the English created, but whenever we managed to meet we were happy
to see Hania bloom like a precious flower under the loving care of Yaki.

Our individual struggle was a mirror image of the struggle of all our
friends who had survived the Holocaust. In addition there was the struggle
of the *yishuv* (the Jewish population of Palestine), in which we actively
participated.

Chapter Four ✑

From the laundry room I moved to a tiny one-room apartment in the southernmost part of Tel Aviv called Schunat Shapiro, where I was sub-tenant and companion to an elderly lady. When the rains came, Salamy Street, the main artery leading from Schunat Shapiro, became a river to be cautiously negotiated. There were little ferries haphazardly constructed from some old planks of wood that would navigate us across Salamy Street.

Vrumek lived on the other bank of Salamy street at Mrs. V's, and so did Nachcia. Struggling to sustain ourselves in the dire situation in which the *yishuv* found itself at that time in Palestine, we slowly became aware of the difficult period ahead of us. Our dream of living together as a family was still just a wish.

Seeing young girls and boys slip out of the shadows in the evening hours, their faces covered with handkerchiefs, running from house to house on the main streets of Tel Aviv quickly pasting posters, alerted us to a new reality. We were not the only ones with problems. From these posters we learned about the struggle of our nation. With pain we realized how far away we still were from our longed-for freedom.

We learned about the disputes and ideological fights going on between different branches of our freedom fighters, the Haganah, the Palmach, the Lechi, and the Irgun. We heard about arrests the British soldiers of the Mandate Government were making. The underground fighters, whom they called terrorists, were just young boys and girls laying their lives on the line for the freedom of our people.

We had no sooner settled in Tel Aviv when we became painfully aware of searches the British soldiers were conducting, disrupting the peaceful lives of the populace. When the bullhorns sounded from the half-trucks of the English occupying army, announcing curfew, I was separated from my sister and brother, confined to house arrest. Scared and lonely, I would find solace in the company of my old landlady, the wise Mrs. Z, who, with her natural motherly instinct, wanted only to marry me off.

But it was Nachcia who found a mate in those early days of our lives in Palestine. We were so happy, Vrumek and I, to see Nachcia, who had lost the best years of her life in the inferno of the Holocaust, find a man she could love, a man to share her life. Nachcia was such a giving person, living only to care for someone. All her love she bestowed on me and on Vrumek. It was time for her to share her love with a mate.

Moshe was a short, dark-haired man, just the same height as Nachcia. He had a good job with the local electric company, Rutenberg, which was considered a great asset. Nachcia could quit her job as a household helper and enjoy her own household. That was very alluring to Nachcia, for she was very eager to establish a home not only for herself and her husband, but for her brother and sister as well. Moshe was a flatterer and knew how to draw Nachcia to him. He was also smart enough to recognize Nachcia's golden heart and her undivided attention.

So Nachcia was the first one of us to get married. Early on a Thursday afternoon, we went to the little restaurant on Alia Street, where we used to eat meals on the Sabbath. Vrumek helped the owner rearrange the tables, while I ran to several acquaintances to borrow extra chairs. Rachel, the wife of Yehudah, Vrumek's only friend from Poland, baked a nice cake and helped prepare some other dishes.

Toward evening the groom's family and some of our friends arrived. When Vrumek and I arrived with Nachcia, all our friends gathered around her, expressing their admiration at her modest, refined appearance. Nachcia, a quiet, shy girl, nearing her thirtieth birthday, was happy to have found a man to love and to be loved in return.

A solemn mood filled our hearts. If only Mama and Papa could have lived to see their daughter standing under the canopy, her eyes brilliant with love! My heart ached when Vrumek recited the blessings, his responsibility as head of the household visible in his taut face. Vrumek, who resembled our father in his habits and sense of humor, had become so serious.

Only after the shattering of the glass, in commemoration of the destruction of our Temple in Jerusalem, did the sadness lift, wafting away into heaven to rest among the stars. The mood finally became jubilant. Not only

Nachcia's wedding, May 8, 1947. Nachcia and Moshe are in the center, I am on the left, with Hania directly above.

was it Nachcia's wedding, it was also May 8, the anniversary of our liberation from the concentration camp in 1945, the day we gained our freedom, and a year later the day we arrived in Palestine, reaching final freedom. The festivity lasted well into the night.

A soft wind blew, caressing our faces when we walked home through the quiet street. A young boy and girl appeared from within the shadows. Their faces covered by plain handkerchiefs, the boy swiftly smeared some glue from a small pail onto the display window of a storefront. The girl pulled out from within her shirt a pile of posters. She peeled off one and pressed it onto the glue, smoothing it with swift strokes. Quickly they proceeded to the next window and as quickly vanished in the darkness. They were members of Etzel—Irgun Zvai Leumi (a national military organization). Vrumek whispered, "Let's see what the poster says." We stopped to read.

The Etzel accused the British Mandate government of reneging on their promises. The Jewish leaders demanded the abolition of the White Paper and the opening of the gates of Palestine to Jewish immigration. The Etzel demanded the British departure, termination of the mandate.

I was hardly familiar with the Etzel but felt a soothing warmth infusing my whole being. We were no longer cringing with fear but demanding our rights. How I wished I could be as brave as these youngsters, to help fight for our freedom, but I was still possessed by the ingrained fear inflicted upon us by the Nazis.

We learned about the constant actions carried out by the Irgun (one of the names of Etzel), sabotaging strategic installations, destroying bridges, penetrating military compounds, damaging civil administration buildings, even attacking and taking British soldiers hostage.

I did not reveal my feelings to Vrumek; he already had so much on his mind. It was in Mrs. Z that I confided when we talked about the trial of two underground fighters arrested by the British. The boys denied the legitimacy of the British justice, and they refused to plead guilty even though they were in possession of firearms when they were arrested.

"This is our land and you have no right even to be here," they said to the judges. I felt a bitter sadness when I learned that they had been sentenced to death. Sadly old Mrs. Z sighed, "Hinei lo yanum ve lo yishan shomer Israel" (The guardian of Israel neither sleeps nor slumbers).

Now that Nachcia was married and installed in an apartment of her own, we were able to have a family life again. Soon after she was married, she made Vrumek move in with her and her husband. In her kitchen there was room for Vrumek's cot. Her one-room apartment became the center of activity. We would meet our friends there, or have messages left with Nachcia. Every evening after work we would stop in. The apartment was centrally located, easily accessible, with an entrance straight from the street into the room and a small kitchen in the corridor in the back.

It was here at Nachcia's, in relaxed evening conversations, that we heard Vrumek talk about his survival.

"When Chrzanow became *Judenrein* (cleansed of Jews), Sholek and I went to Sosnowiec. We knew no one there. By chance I met Aharon, a man from Chrzanow.

"I wanted to live. I had come through so much, I was not going to give up now. I had managed to escape from Chrzanow during the last raid, when the Germans accomplished their goal of making Chrzanow *Judenrein*— when there was not one Jew left alive there.

"I was lucky in that tragic time even to have found Sholek, who also had managed to hide out during the raid. When the raid in Chrzanow was finished, we walked to Sosnowiec. I knew that there were still Jews in Sosnowiec. Sosnowiec was about thirty-five miles away, so it was reachable on foot, and maybe the only place where Jews still existed.

"There was nothing else besides giving ourselves up to the Germans. I was not ready to relinquish our lives just like that. I knew Sholek was not, either. It was still possible for us to survive, and we had to try. We agreed on it. Tired and hungry but full of hope, we dragged ourselves through the woods and the fields in the dark of night.

"When we reached the ghetto of Sosnowiec, and saw Jews in the streets, our hope was renewed. We were totally exhausted but ecstatic. If we managed to live through this trial, we would find a way to continue to live.

"Then I met Aharon. My hope awakened again—maybe this was an angel of mercy God had send to me.

"Aharon said he would ask his mother-in-law, in whose house he was staying, if he could bring me in, too. But two of us, Sholek also, was very doubtful. The mother-in-law agreed to one. My dilemma was heartbreaking. I did not want to leave Sholek alone. Especially not after having found him, when the Germans took all the rest of our family away.

"Again we were lucky. Sholek, too, met someone who was willing to take him in. Sholek's contact was in Bendzin, the sister city to Sosnowiec and very close by, which still had the Jews in its ghetto. There was no other alternative; we had to separate. We hoped to survive being sheltered separately rather than perishing together in the street. We went our separate way. Grateful, yet distressed, I went with Aharon.

"Then came the last raid in Sosnowiec. Sosnowiec was not spared and neither was Bendzin. I had dug a hole under the outhouse in Aharon's mother-in-law's house, intending to have a place to hide with Sholek in just such a raid. Protecting and saving Sholek never left my mind. I just did not figure that the raid would come in circumstances where Sholek would not be able to reach the bunker.

"So I grabbed hold of Aharon and dragged him along into the hole when the raid came. In that hole we were able to stand, tightly squeezed against each other. The Germans were upon us, and in spite of Aharon's complaints, I was glad to have him there in the bunker.

" 'I should have stayed with my mother-in-law,' Aharon said. 'We have no chance of surviving here. We are going to suffocate for sure. I cannot breathe.'

"Even with my own distress, I would not let Aharon lose his hope. Oh, how I yearned for the body touching mine to be that of Sholek. Our little smart brother would not have complained, never. He had courage. He was a fighter. He could understand me just by looking into my eyes. I would have hugged him and given him strength. Sholek would absorb and obey. He would wriggle his hands and toes, like I would tell him, so as not to become paralyzed. He would sniff the air coming through the cracks of the board covering us, even though the earth and grass camouflaged it. He would assimilate the words of encouragement and hope I would whisper in his ear and be a source of reliance for me. Sholek, our little brother, the only one left to me . . .

"But here I was with Aharon squeezed tightly against me and whimpering. I could not let Aharon lose his hope, either.

" 'Stop your crying, Aharon. Exercise your toes and hands,' I scolded him, 'for when we come out of here we will need our feet to keep running.'

"I did not expect the raid to last for seven days. In seven days God created the whole world! That same God, I believe, kept us alive for seven days in the grave I dug. Seven days without food, without water, with just a trickle of air, in standing position, next to each other, like twin children in their mother's womb.

"Stiff, faint, totally depleted of strength, we emerged into the ghetto of Sosnowiec. An eerie silence was everywhere. Aharon's mother-in-law and her family were gone. The ghetto was *Judenrein*.

"Now it was my task to keep on dragging the half-dead Aharon with me through the rest of our survival ordeal. Aharon, a stranger, not Sholek, our little brother. Still I nurtured a hope of finding Sholek, but I was happy to have someone with me, a person, a living soul, a Jew. Together we would make it, we would live, and we would not let ourselves succumb. 'Where are we going to run to?' Aharon wanted to know.

" 'I don't know,' I answered impatiently.

"I was well aware that thanks to my accidental meeting of Aharon in the ghetto of Sosnowiec, we were there together, and I was not alone. I was grateful to the Almighty for having bestowed upon me that chance meeting. Not that Aharon was a treasure; on the contrary, he was a burden, with his constant nagging and complaining. But in the present situation, to have someone, just another soul, was priceless. A human being, someone to whisper to, another pair of eyes and ears to listen, to watch, to guard.

"I had been dragging Aharon along since we came out of ghetto Sosnowiec. We trekked back to Chrzanow. I was trying to find shelter in the woods. At least it was a place I knew. There was no other place I could think of where we could hide from the pursuing Germans.

"In a large hollow tree we set up our quarters. There we spent the nights huddled together, covered by branches. From there we made our excursions into town to visit the barber. We could not afford to look like nomads. If that barber, *folksdeutsche* (naturalized German), had known who I was when he was shaving my face, he would have slit my throat.

"It was there in the barber's chair that I got my information about the war from the newscasts blasting from the radio.

"From the forest we made our expeditions to the cottage of an old woman who would give us some black coffee in a bottle, which I always kept in my pocket. That bottle, I believed, made me resemble a worker on his way to a factory. I preserved and safeguarded that bottle like an icon. There was nothing else to mask my Jewishness, to give me the confidence that I would not be discovered. Living under these dire conditions, posing as a Gentile, made me jittery all the time.

"It became harder and harder to obtain food. Even the resources of food in the fields, to which we resorted, scratching like animals for roots, nuts and grasses, became scarce when the weather got colder.

"I had the feeling that the old woman suspected I was Jewish, yet never said anything. I was grateful but could not risk finding out.

"My suspicions were confirmed when she said to me, 'the Germans are combing the forest. They are looking for hidden Jews. You had better not come here anymore.' It was a warning I could not acknowledge but appreciated and paid attention to. It was also a sign of the trap we were in, the absolute squeeze, the end of all refuge.

"Sure enough, that was the night.

"When we returned to the woods that night, I noticed that the little bundle containing my *tefilin* (phylacteries), which I did not give up in spite of it being the worst item of incrimination, which I kept buried inside the tree, was ransacked. I knew then that the woman had been a friend. I also knew the time had come to leave the shelter and move on. But where to?

"I could not think of another hiding place. I did not know what to do. I knew, though, that we had to leave if we were to survive. The Germans had found our traces.

"Again, we dragged ourselves through woods and fields, resting during the day if we were able to find a haystack, barn, or high wheat field, and traveling under the protection of the night.

"Like the ancient Hebrews who wandered in the desert under the protection of the *Shehina* (the presence of God), the divine cloud hovering above, so did we travel under the cover of darkness.

"The multiple incidents we encountered when we were so close to being caught, when the peril of death was just a step ahead or a step behind! The way we managed miraculously to cross borders under the noses of German patrols, swim through icy waters, traverse under watchful German guards, over stormy rivers, stretched our nerves and challenged our courage. We were constantly exhausted, edgy, terrified. Facing these enormous obstacles, having to invent more and more ways of survival, distracted by Aharon's constant complaints, I was getting weak, distressed, tormented. My strong determination to live did not leave room for despair. Each time, somehow, we were able to extricate ourselves from the most serious entrapments.

"When we finally reached Hungary in January of 1944, weary and drained, I was not able to relax. I wanted to go further, to escape the pursuing fires, the inferno of the Nazis. I would not acquiesce to the urging of the free Jews of Hungary to stay, to catch my breath, to recuperate from my ordeal. Like a possessed man I kept running, dragging Aharon along.

"We smuggled into Rumania, from where further escape was possible. I knew no peace until we were able to join other escapees boarding a dilapidated old vessel chartered by the Zionists. That boat got us to the Turkish port of Ankara. Even when we made it to the train, traveling for days from Turkey, through Lebanon, I was not calm yet. Only when our feet stood on the soil of the Holy Land, in the port city of Haifa, and I pronounced the prayer of *Birkat Hagomel* (praise for being saved) did I know that we were free.

"Once we were free, I felt no more obligation to drag Aharon along, and we parted ways."

A new struggle began for Vrumek—starting life again. Tired, emotionally drained, even physically weak, he could not give up. He harnessed himself to new challenges, searching for acquaintances, *landsleit* (people from his home town), seeking connections, staying alive. Pursuing all leads, he moved to Tel Aviv and found a job that afforded him the rent of a subtenant.

More and more people were coming from Europe now that the war was over. Maybe Sholek survived on his own, and would be able to reach the Promised Land, thought Vrumek. He could not lose hope now.

"And then one day at the end of March, as I was on my way out to work, I saw the mailman waving a letter, motioning to me to approach. 'Why isn't he putting it in the mailbox?' I thought. But the mailman made insistent motions, and I approached.

" 'This one is for you,' the mailman said, 'not for the Verchyks.'

"My heart thudded in my chest. A letter for me. Who could be sending me a letter? I looked at the envelope. Europe, Italy—my heart raced even faster now.

"With trembling hands I opened the letter. Unable to focus on the letters, I searched for the signature. Helcia! Nachcia! You were alive. 'Oh God' I cried out, 'Yehi Shem Hashem Mevorach' (Blessed be Your Name).

" 'Mrs. Verchyk,' I shouted, stepping back into the house, 'my two sisters are alive. I've got to go to work. I have my two sisters now, there is so much to live for again!' "

It was Chaimke, a boy of Yemenite ancestry, who enlightened me on the political scene of the *yishuv*. He would meet me at Nachcia's or wait for me in front of the Berlitz School of Languages, where I took English and French courses. We would go for a walk or sit on a bench in one of the lovely parks or avenues of the city. Enchanted, he would listen to my singing while making mental notes on my mistakes in the Hebrew language, which he would later correct and explain, becoming a wonderful resource for my self-education. He would teach me to pronounce the *chet* (h) and *ayin* (a) correctly. He would tell me about the Haganah, the Palmach, and the Etzel. He never told me which one he belonged to, but deep in my heart of hearts I knew. When he would part from me at the bus stop in the late evening all I could say was, "Please be careful, Chaimke." He would smile his mysterious smile, his moustache raised slightly, his dark eyes twinkling mischievously.

"See you Saturday night," he would say nonchalantly.

When he did not show up Saturday night, I would listen to the radio broadcasts very attentively and with pounding heart hear, "The King David Hotel in Jerusalem has been bombed. There were heavy casualties among the English officers."

Broadcasts of this kind would raise ambiguous feelings among the Jewish citizens. The English soldier had become the representative of the Mandate government, and thereby our enemy. The men in the street identified with the leadership of the land, the Jewish Agency, arguing for restraint on our part and belief in the decency of the international community, the entity that was promising the establishment of a National Jewish home in Palestine. There were those who believed in the Haganah, who advocated self-defense from the Arab marauders but no aggressiveness against the Mandate rulers. And there were others who supported the more radical organizations, the Lechi and the Etzel, in their struggle to get the English out of our land, so we could live as free people in our land, on our soil. When I learned of Haganah members denouncing their brethren from Etzel to the English authorities and having them arrested, there was pain in my heart. I could not help but feel that we were back to *Judenrats* (Jewish leadership in the ghetto) and *capos* (Jewish foremen in concentration camps), squealing to the Germans on their fellow Jews. That shouldn't be done in Palestine. I could not cope with the disunity of my people.

When we heard about the hanging of Jewish freedom fighters by the English in Acre prison, it broke my spirit. In retaliation the Etzel caught two English soldiers and managed to hang them, fulfilling our laws of an eye for an eye, a tooth for a tooth. It was a severe struggle fought by each of us in his own way, each having the same goal—to throw off the yoke of oppression of the English master.

Right after the hangings, I was on my way home riding on bus number 4 when I saw the English riding rampant in their jeeps speeding down Allenby Street, the main thoroughfare of Tel Aviv. There was tension in the street.

"They must have arrested someone again," the woman next to me said briefly, when suddenly we heard shooting. Everybody ducked, hitting the floor of the bus. The driver, who had immediately stopped the bus, jumped out to see what was happening. We heard screaming and saw the people running toward the bus just in front of us.

"The English bastards," someone proclaimed, were shooting through the windows of the preceding bus.

"We cannot even walk our streets or ride a bus anymore," said the woman bitterly. A young fellow attempted to run out of our bus, but his mother held him back, crying, "No Moti! don't! there is nothing you can do here all by yourself. I know how you feel, my son. Be patient; we will see the English leave our land, we will. It is the Arabs who worry me more."

The struggle against the British occupying power was a fierce and severe one. My understanding of that struggle came from Chaimke, when I would ask him to sing *Yesh chalil neelam* (There is a mysterious flute), and his voice would betray choking tears. His usually twinkling eyes would burn with fury, and I knew his longing and his desire.

"This land is ours," he would state heatedly. "I was born here and so was my father and grandfather and great grandfather. They have no right to dictate to us. We must get them to leave, we must."

"We will," I would answer, trying in vain to soothe his fiery heart.

"Those bloody British bastards hung Dov Groner," Chaimke spit out in a bitter rage. "They will have to pay for that."

My heart ached for Chaimke, for Dov Groner, whom I did not know, and for our Jewish people, who stood alone, unyielding against all odds. "I remember the hanged martyrs in my home town of Chrzanow," I said quietly. "No one pays for these crimes against us. The Nazis did not pay and neither will the British." My voice was bitter with the futility of our fate.

"Oh no, no," Chaimke almost screamed out. "Those times are over. The British must pay and they will! We here in the *yishuv* are not Europe's Jews of the *Galut* (diaspora). We are a free people. Our honor will be defended. If we shed blood, it is going to be for *Cheruth* Israel, freedom of our people from bondage."

I did not know how he proposed to accomplish that, or what part he played, but I knew that when I would say good night to Chaimke, my spirits would soar high with hope, and I would envision the day when we would be free.

On Sunday, May 4, 1947, Etzel attacked Acre prison, where Dov Groner had been hanged. In the skirmish, 251 prisoners escaped. I did not see Chaimke for three weeks. When we met on our bench in the *shdera* (avenue), he seemed to be calm and relaxed. He sang beautiful songs. He rolled the *ayin* with feeling in his throat, looking at me with his dark, burning eyes but did not as usual put his hand on my shoulder to keep me close. His hand remained in his pocket throughout the evening. I did not need to ask questions, I was so happy to see him.

I would always wait with trepidation for Chaimke to come. There was no place I could contact him, so when I beheld his slender figure standing at the corner, leaning against the light post, when I would leave school, my whole being would reveal joy. He would embrace me, and with our hands intertwined we would stride down Allenby Street toward the seashore, the popular promenade. We would talk about the most mundane things, only my eyes expressing the question. His reassuring smile would tell me that everything was fine. We would sit on the shore playing with the golden, soft sand, searching the dark horizon. When we would spot some dim lights in the distance, our hearts would pound with hope, for we knew that far in the distance a small boat was unloading illegal immigrants, evading the searchlights of the English ships. Under the disguise of darkness, they would swim ashore and be hidden in the most outlying communities. We knew also that on the day after the arrival of a boat with immigrants, the English would declare curfew and conduct searches, but the night before was ours to celebrate.

When the lights stopped flickering we would buy ice cream at Witmans and walk back to the lights of the city.

Not all the boats managed to land in the dark. It was a star-studded night in July 1947 when the *Exodus,* on her way from Marseille, France, with hundreds of men, women, and children, survivors of the concentration camps and inmates in post-war DP (displaced persons) camps, tried to reach the shores of the promised land. The British barred their way with war ships, and demanded that they return to Marseille, the port of origin. The pitiful, exhausted crowd rebelled with all their might. Determined to choose death rather than be forced to return to the graveyards of their original lands, they resisted the British brutes. Undaunted, they fought back bare-handed against the unleashed terror of the soldiers, who opened fire, brutally killing several innocent victims and wounding many. Vicious power prevailed and the passengers were transferred to a British war ship and escorted to the island of Cyprus, where they were placed in a camp.

When Chaimke picked me up on Saturday night and wanted to go to the movies, I knew he was scheduled for action and wanted to have a good time. I did not ask any questions, only helped him laugh and enjoy. He caressed my face and squeezed my hand when we walked home, arm-in-arm. I searched his eyes when we parted but found only the usual twinkle. He was so brave. Or was he scared but could not tell me?

Next day we heard about the ammunition depot that was raided by the members of Etzel. The British were outraged again.

I quit my job at the fish lady's household and got a job in a vegetable store. I became such an expert that all the housewives would wait for me to pick the watermelon for them.

"Is this good?" they would ask, "Will it be sweet? Will it be red inside?"

I would pick the large round ball-like fruit up, pat it, squeeze it, tap it, and pronounce, "this is just right for today's use. It will revive your guests with its sweetness and juiciness." Sometimes I would just give it a pat and say no, take the other one. That made me trustworthy and an expert. Lucky for me, the melons were at the peak of the season and at their most delicious state.

Unfortunately, the three hours I worked in the morning did not afford me the pair of shoes I so badly wanted and needed. I had enough to eat, but buying clothes was out of question on my budget. I would not accept any money from my brother; that was below my dignity. After all, I was grown up, healthy, and able to work. It was just a question of finding a job.

The opportunity arose when the rabbi, whose wife had expired at the birth of her fifth child, married the nanny who took care of his children. A new nanny was needed, and I was it. From my morning job in the vegetable store, I would rush to pick up the rabbi's children from school. It was my afternoon job to take them home to have lunch, and then take them to the park for afternoon play. When we got home, toward evening, the bigger ones would do their homework, while I fed the smaller ones their dinner and got them ready for bed.

Aliza, the cook, would have their meals ready. She was a lovely lady in her thirties. Her blond, frizzy hair pulled back in a bun, a clean white apron around her waist, she would scour around the kitchen, fast and industrious, like an ant. She would always put up an extra plate for me. A little embarrassed, I would succumb after the second invitation, and devour the delicious *pyrogen* and blintzes. I would lick my plate clean when she made eggplant in tomato sauce, or stuffed cabbage and stuffed peppers. Sometimes she would slip me a piece of cake that was left over from the *rebbin's tish* (the rabbi's dinner table) as she would comment, "You look so young and so hungry, and there is plenty here, it will go to waste."

I certainly did not waste it, smacking my lips with every bite.

"How old are you?" she questioned me. "Where did you survive the war?" I told her about the concentration camps, and she confided in me that she was a widow with a young son. She bemoaned her fate, being all alone in this world, just her and her son. She had lost all her family in Europe. She mourned the loss of her parents and her sister and her husband, but most of all she bewailed the loss of her little niece, Chanale.

"Every night", she would say, "when I fall exhausted onto my bed the nightmares start. I will never see my parents and sister anymore, I know that in my heart. Nor my brother-in-law. I do not know how they perished but they are among the dead. My little Chanale is the one who is in my dreams. I am only a poor widow supporting myself and my son on this cooking job but I would have a place for Chanale. She could grow up together with my boy, like a sister. They could share the room, go to school together. Whatever we eat, she would eat. If only I could have her."

I soon found out that Aliza knew that her sister, who had lived in Poland under the Nazis, had given the child away to a Gentile before she herself was deported. Aliza did not know how to find her but nurtured her hopes. Who better than I could understand this yearning Aliza had, to save the child, her sister's baby? The child was the only link Aliza had to her family in Europe, who had been so cruelly slaughtered by the Nazis. That child might be living somewhere, unaware of who she was, at a time when her own people were fighting to recapture their own country. She could have a chance to live as a Jewess and a free person, without being ashamed or afraid, in Palestine, where she had blood relatives, Aliza and her son.

Who better than I could know the pain Aliza felt? I who would give anything to know where my own little nephew, Iziu, my sister Blimcia's son, was. Iziu, that pride and joy of my father and mother, their first grandson, born into the cruel world of Nazi occupation in our home town of Chrzanow on March 17, 1940.

As we talked, I suddenly realized that I held the key to Aliza's mystery. Her Chanale was in fact Niusia, the girl left in Poland on the estate of the Chrabina (countess), where my friend Krysia from Kibbutz Ichud had survived the war years, serving as a maid. Aliza almost fainted with excitement when I revealed to her my thoughts.

Promptly thereafter I contacted Krysia and arranged an appointment with Aliza. We met at Nachcia's. In a lengthy conversation that lasted way past midnight, the story crystallized. Krysia identified Niusia by a birthmark she had on her left shoulder blade. Aliza brought a picture she treasured of her sister's baby girl. That night it was determined beyond a doubt that Chanale was indeed Hanusia-Niusia.

Action had to be taken. A plan was drawn up. Aliza was to contact the Chrabina, introducing herself first. Then she was to hint delicately that since she was the only living relative of Niusia, she would like her niece to come live with her.

After the first letter, Aliza was panicky. The Chrabina was indignant, Aliza said. She asked Aliza to leave her and her only daughter in peace. She called Aliza an opportunist; she accused her of taking advantage of her good heart.

After another consultation with Krysia, Aliza followed up with a gift, a case of oranges, a most generous investment for poor Aliza. The oranges were accepted but not acknowledged. Another plea from Aliza was rejected with contempt. Aliza's requests to inform the girl of her aunt's existence were answered with: "Over my dead body."

"What am I to do now?" Aliza lamented when I arrived at the rabbi's house for work. She showed me the last letter.

"Maybe we should contact the Red Cross and ask for their intervention. A lot of people are still searching for relatives through the Red Cross," I stated. Aliza was not too familiar with official channels.

"I'd rather contact the Jewish Agency," she said decisively. "Maybe they will be able to help."

The following Friday I went to the main bus station and boarded the bus to Kibbutz Tel Itzchak, where Krysia lived. Krysia was rather surprised when I told her I came to spend the Sabbath so that we would have plenty of time to talk and work out a strategy for how to help poor Aliza get custody of her longed-for niece. Saturday afternoon, when the meal was over, we walked down to the fields, where we could be alone.

Krysia reminisced about the time she spent on the Chrabina's estate. She spoke about her loneliness and longing to be free, her fears and anxiety about not being found out to be Jewish. She spoke of evenings spent serving dinner and perking her ears up to the conversations at the table. She described the Chrabina as quite primitive, very religious, and extremely superstitious. She told me that she consistently took Niusia to church, regularly supervised her daily prayers, and in general imbued the child with religious beliefs, and how earnest she was about silly superstitious stories and calling on spirits for major decision making.

"If nothing else works, tell Aliza to tell the Chrabina in her letter that her dead sister, the mother of Niusia, came to her in her dream and said, "My spirit cannot find peace until I return my child to her flock. I will hover over the house where my child is imprisoned and curse it until my child is set free."

"She will let her go," Krysia said. "She is petrified of curses."

Enthusiastically, I conveyed the message to Aliza, assuring her that this would work. Aliza was not convinced at first. "What if she mistreats Niusia as a result?"

She still wanted to try with pleasantries. So she sent another gift of oranges, and a note saying she hoped they would enjoy the fruit but asking her to let Niusia know where it came from.

"As long as I live, my Niusia will not know anyone but me as her mother," the Chrabina wrote. "She knows that I adopted her when my brother, her father, perished with his wife in a bombardment.

Aliza had no choice anymore. She had to take Krysia's advice.

The next time I saw Aliza, she showed me the last letter she received from Poland. The Chrabina was outraged.

"For all I did for the Jews during the war," she said, "is this how you Jews are paying me back? Don't you dare write to me anymore."

"All is lost" Aliza stated. "I must learn to bear my pain and adapt to the fact that I will never see my sister again, nor her child."

I was extremely sad but did not know how to console the grieving woman.

I had left the rabbi's employ and moved on to another job. I found work in a factory but was not happy there. I felt I must do something with my life, not stagnate as a factory girl, so I kept looking. Eventually I was engaged as a waitress in Bikowski's restaurant on Allenby Street. Allenby Street at the corner of Balfour Street was the center of town. All day long and even into the night people milled around. Wherever one had to go, one had to pass Allenby Street. On any given afternoon, anyone who was someone would stroll down Allenby Street, to see and to be seen. At Bikowski's, traffic started by eleven in the morning. Customers were served while the restaurant also served as a forum for discussions. Politics were debated. People would come in for their meals and bring with them loads of communication, politics, and news. The issue of partition was debated in the restaurant as intensely as in the United Nations. On their portion of mashed potatoes the customers would draw the map of Palestine and partition it to their own satisfaction. Many a time I would stop heated discussions with a cool cup of fruit soup, the house special.

At the United Nations, the Jewish people were having their fate determined. Partition of Palestine was being debated, fought over, manipulated, discussed.

Toward evening, the discussions would become heated. Young girls and boys, their faces covered by handkerchiefs, would float down Allenby Street, quickly running from one showcase to the other, pasting bulletins. The Etzel was announcing in these bulletins the punishments they would dole out to the British Mandate authorities.

From Manshiye (a neighborhood in Jaffa), the Arabs were shooting. Someone was wounded passing by on Allenby Street near the beach. The tension was rising like the tide of the nearby ocean. Arguments were taking place among friends and families, some siding with the Haganah, others defending the actions of the more nationalist-oriented Etzel and Lehi.

Gradually all the boys were being mobilized. Nachcia's husband, Moshe, was called, and Vrumek became a soldier, too. The cot he used to sleep on in Nachcia's kitchen was free for me to use. In that tiny L-shaped nook a cot was put against one wall with a couple of nails above it serving as cloths hangers. Against the other wall on a shelf stood a *primus* and a *ptiliya* (a gasoline-burning cooking contraptions, one fast and one slow), the main furnishing of the kitchen. In the other corner, Moshe, my brother-in-law, had hung a small water drum, which could be heated with the *primus* to afford us a nice warm shower. A plastic curtain divided it from the kitchen and my bedroom part.

On November 29, 1947, a Saturday night, I went to the restaurant to listen to the radio (we did not have a radio yet in our possession). Mr. B let the radio blast loud. People were congregated outside the store.

The United Nations was voting on partition. Like an electric current, the waves of emotion swept through the people assembled. Every "yes" vote would be greeted with explosions of joy, every "no" vote would travel through the bloodstream of the people, eliciting a sorrowful outcry. With trepidation we counted, waited, anticipated. When finally all the votes were counted—thirty-three for, thirteen against, and ten abstentions—the crowd exploded. Strangers hugged and kissed each other, boys lifted girls into the air, dancing wildly around. The mood was so elated all the worries of yesterday were momentarily forgotten. Only one thought was absorbing everyone: We were a nation at last. After two thousand years of waiting, we were free to establish our own state.

Multitudes of people streamed down Allenby Street toward the beach. At the end of Allenby Street, on Herbert Samuel Square, the crowds formed circles. The soft wind saturated by the salty smell of the nearby sea cooled the overheated bodies that swirled in an enthusiastic hora.

I was swept along into the hora dancing. With all my exuberance I danced, stomping, jumping, the way I had danced with Amos in the D.P. camp in Germany after our liberation. Amos was not there, but my heart was full of joy. In total ecstasy I kicked my feet, threw my head back, my hands linked with my fellow Jews, feeling like a *chasid* (very religious Jew), absorbed to the core of my being. All night long people kept coming, streaming, filling the circles, expanding them, until we thought we would push out the guard rails of the promenade and tumble down into the sea. We were drunk with happiness, with the awe of the moment. We knew we were making history, we, the remnants of the Jewish people, the shreds that had come back from the death camps, were witnessing the rebirth of our nation. We also knew we would have to fight for our freedom and existence, but we could not think about that right then. It was the time to celebrate, to swirl in that insatiable dance till we were totally drained of strength. The sky was the soft gray hue it always is just before the sun rises when we walked slowly up Allenby Street, dragging our feet, exhausted, but oh, so happy!

We did not manage to sleep much before we learned that the Arabs were attacking Jews everywhere. In Manshiye, the snipers from Jaffa played havoc with the Jews living in close proximity. Shuk Hacarmel (the Carmel marketplace), the source of food supplies, located at the perimeter between the towns of Tel Aviv and Jaffa, turned into a battlefield. People were being wounded by sniper fire coming from the city of Jaffa while purchasing their vegetables. Arab sharp shooters and snipers hiding on rooftops picked their victims from among innocent strollers in the streets of Tel Aviv. Unaware of their exposure and vulnerability to these hidden bandits, the citizens of Tel Aviv continued conducting their daily lives. The Jewish *yishuv* was bleeding in the process of giving birth to its nation, while we, the citizens, were struggling for our meager existence.

Chapter Five ✐

It was two weeks before Pesach, the most elaborately celebrated Jewish holiday. At that time, however, the preparations at Nachcia's were meager. Shortages of food were common, and even when food was available it was not safe to stroll around the *shuk* (marketplace) for fear of sniper fire coming from Jaffa.

The Passover holiday that started April 22, 1948, was a mixed bag of deep sorrow and profound hope. In Jaffa, the city adjacent to Tel Aviv, fighting was fierce. The boys from Etzel were fighting against the well-equipped English soldiers, who stopped hiding their anti-Semitism, their hostility, their ugly hatred. They had removed the political white gloves, revealing their abomination and their prejudice, fighting openly against the Jews, defending the Arabs. Blood stained our streets, dripping from the wounded fighters being brought back to Tel Aviv from Jaffa. While the severe fighting went on we attended funerals of the fallen.

One plain sunny day I saw Mania, a friend from our kibbutz group, walking toward me on Balfour Street. My heart suddenly thudded in my chest. Her appearance heralded bad news. Her head bent, her gait resembled a shuffle rather than her usual stride. When she came closer I noticed her red, swollen eyes and pale face. She wore a dark dress and had the traditional rip on her chest done at the time of burial, as a symbol of renting one's clothes. Her head was covered by a dark kerchief.

Mania was a friend whose wedding I have attended just six weeks earlier. I did not need ask any questions. I knew Mania to be the only survivor of her family. She and Shmilek, who was an only survivor as well, had found each other when we were still in Italy. They were very much in love but had not wanted to get married there in Italy. With great yearning they waited to reach the shores of our promised land, so they could marry properly in the ancient Jewish tradition in the homeland. They kept dreaming and talking about their obligation to *lehakim bait be'Israel* (build a home in Israel), build a family again. They spoke about the need to replenish, to rebuild the lost family they both so miserably missed.

They were planning to have a large family of their own. With no help from anyone else, they worked hard and saved every penny to have a proper wedding. It was indeed as large and as cheerful a wedding as they could afford at the time. By word of mouth the news spread, and many friends participated. I remembered Mania's flushed face when she whirled in a hora at her wedding, elevated by excitement and happiness. I saw in my mind's eye Smilek's loving eyes cast upon his bride with such admiration and anticipation.

Now I beheld her face dark with pain. We had no words for each other. I embraced her slender figure. She buried her head in my shoulder, and we stood in the middle of Balfour Street, weeping, bewailing her loss, the loss of our people, of a Jewish soldier, husband, lover, companion, future father, builder of Am Israel, the people of Israel.

People passing by just stopped for a minute, shaking their heads in sympathy, wiping away their tears. They were so used to these scenes.

This was the first time since we lived in the land that the four of us sat down to celebrate the Seder as a family. After all the years of war, destruction, and dispersement, we were in our land, in Nachcia's apartment, celebrating a holiday. Reading the *Hagadah* (The exodus from Egypt), recounting the exodus of our forefathers from the enslavement in Egypt, added significance to our own participation in the historic events. The present inadequacies of the environment were not our major preoccupation.

It was the first time we had the opportunity to reminisce about our lives as a family in our old home in Chrzanow, Poland. We talked about Mama and Papa, remembering the Passover seders we used to observe, and the songs Papa used to sing. How proud he was of his four sons seated around him, helping with the singing! How pleased Papa had been that his sons all continued in his footsteps, observing the tradition, following the religious observance. How Mama's pink cheeks had exhibited her excitement when she saw her four daughters, all in their holiday best, so pretty, so modest, exactly the way she wanted them to be.

We talked about the foods Mama used to prepare, the delicacies we liked and the ones I, being the baby of the family, did not want to eat.

And then we heard Vrumek tell us how he and our brother Sholek, younger than Vrumek, met in the house from which the Germans took all the rest of us for the last time. Vrumek's gray eyes would cloud and we could hear the pain in his voice when he spoke about Sholek. Vrumek felt such responsibility for his younger brother. With bitterness he blamed himself for not being able to save Sholek. We had to console him. With all the dangers he had lived through, hanging on to life by a thread, it had been impossible for him to do more than he had done in his attempt to save Sholek. We all cried bitterly for our dear family.

In the end, however, we did not let our hope vanish totally; we held onto the fading possibility that we might still find someone else in our family alive. Vrumek remembered how our oldest sister, Blimcia had taken care of him when he was so deathly sick in the ghetto, and pronounced the fervent hope that maybe Blimcia had had a chance. Maybe she had been helped by someone, maybe she was alive somewhere, maybe we would still one day hear from her.

With great fervor we read the Hagadah, following the liturgy, discussing the different passages, trying to emulate our father, conforming to the tradition we loved so well, the way we knew it from home.

The English were destined to leave the country soon, their mandate having been exhausted, while our boys were registering for military service. They were going to defend that precious piece of land from the Arab hordes who were voraciously waiting to swallow up whatever they could.

Vrumek went to register for the army the day after Pesach. Three days later, he was gone.

The settlement of Ramat Rachel, near Jerusalem, had been invaded by the Jordanian Legion. When I met Chaimke several days after Pesach, he was worn and tired. We fought hard at Ramat Rachel, he told me. I felt his sadness and knew he was aching at the loss of his friends. He did not sing his favored *chalil* song for me. We sat at the *shdera* (avenue), the fragrance of the trees wafting through the air. We were young and desirous of each other's company, but we were also as old as our land. We carried in us the responsibility to make that land free. We mourned Chaimke's friends, but in that torment there was the affirmative feeling of their having fallen for the just cause of our independence.

"We fought hard at Ramat Rachel," Chaimke stated simply, but in those simple words was a well of unexhausted yearning for our freedom, for the justified urge to snatch back our home, which the ferocious enemy is trying to seize, invade, and destroy.

The battles had intensified all over the land. Arab marauders, supported by the legitimate armies of Egypt, Syria, and the Jordanian Legion, had attacked settlers and settlements. The road to Jerusalem was the most dangerous thoroughfare.

On the night of April 13, 1948, the Arabs attacked a convoy of Hadassah workers on their way to the hospital in Jerusalem. There were seventy-six people, all doctors and nurses, in a convoy of home-made armored cars that were supposed to protect them from bullets. But the Arab attacked in full force. With the English standing by, making themselves invisible, the Arabs slaughtered all the passengers of the convoy.

When the news reached us, we were devastated. Our boys and girls, the fighters of Haganah and Etzel, with their almost-empty caches of ammunition, who traveled all over to stall, hold back, and defeat the murderers, failed to prevent the massacre. The population grieved the loss deeply, and the only response we could find was to mobilize and strengthen the ranks of our fighters.

I had just finished putting the chairs onto the tables at the restaurant where I worked, for the afternoon cleanup, when the announcement came through on the radio. On Friday, May 14, 1948 (Hey Iyar, 5708) at the Tel Aviv Museum, David Ben Gurion read the proclamation of the establishment of the State of Israel.

From among the three brothers in the Bikowski family at the restaurant, only the youngest, Moti, was still home working next to me. His other two brothers were mobilized. I jumped up and down and so did Moti. Mr. B, his large frame shaking, stammered slightly unable to control his emotions. Short, plump Mrs. B wiped her tears into her apron. We opened the doors and saw passersby excitedly laughing, crying, shaking hand or hugging. A crowd immediately gathered in front of the store, loudly debating, talking, screaming, shedding tears of happiness and frustration. The joy was overwhelming. We had a country of our own! It was unbelievable; it was historic.

Our prayers of millennia had been answered. After two thousand years of yearning and hoping, the moment was here, and we did not know how to perpetuate it, how to react. Should we drink *lechaim* (to life)? Should we celebrate? Our hearts were overflowing with emotion unparalleled at any time of our lives. Uncontainable jubilation exploded from our midst, mixed and overshadowed by trepidation.

With dread we acknowledged the great shadow hovering over us, the Arab armies poised ready for battle. I ran down the short block of Balfour Street to Yochanan Hasandlar Street, where I lived with Nachcia.

With Moshe and Vrumek mobilized, there were only the two of us, survivors of our family, worrying about our family members who were in danger. The next morning, Saturday, the news spread quickly. The Arabs were attacking everywhere. Five Arab armies—the Egyptians, the Syrians, the Jordanians, the Lebanese, and the Iraqis—augmented by other Arab irregulars, all surged forward in a wild cry of "Kill the Jews, push them into the sea!" Fierce battles were raging everywhere, and we were ill and morbid with worry about our men. The news on the radio was sad and bitter.

Jerusalem, our precious city, was fighting a decisive battle. The city was being strangled, and there was no access to it by Jewish fighters. Convoys attempting approach were mercilessly cut down. The old city was under siege as she had been so many times in her history, devoid of food and water. The Jewish defenders, fighting house by house, were outnumbered and overwhelmed. The fiercest fighting took place at *Abu Gosh,* an Arab village, where the Arabs entrenched in the fortress controlled the only road, the lifeline to Jerusalem. The only topic of conversation among friends was who was fighting where or who had fallen.

We attended funerals, crying our hearts out for the lonely survivors of Hitler's Holocaust who gave their lives for the defense of their land, the land they did not have a chance to enjoy. Neither would their successors, for they had been the last of their families.

I must have slept just a short while when the piercing sound of an air-raid siren woke me. The Egyptians had penetrated the depth of our land and had come as close as the city of Tel Aviv, to bombard it. I jumped out of bed and saw Nachcia throwing on a house dress while struggling with the back door.

Like a rocket I shot out of the room through the front door into the street. Stumbling over the two steps in front, I ran along the brick wall that divided our house from the tall three-story building. Nachcia had obviously grabbed Raizia, a friend of mine, who slept in the kitchen on my cot whenever she was in need of a place to stay, and dragged her along through the back door. I saw them jump down the couple of steps into the yard, and shoot through the gaping hole in the brick wall (opened exactly for that purpose). Together we pushed and plunged into the dark hallway under the staircase in the adjoining building. This small hallway, now crowded with people, tenants and some outsiders, did not afford much protection in an air raid, but was still better than our room covered only with a flimsy shingle roof.

On Friday, May 14, 1948, at Tel Aviv Museum, Ben Gurion had read the proclamation establishing the state of Israel, but it wasn't until the next month, after the signing of the first truce on June 11, 1948, that we found out how bad things were.

Vrumek came home in June for a short leave. He had been at an outpost where the Arabs sat atop the mountain, in the fortress, shooting down at our convoys. He was among these fighters using the last of their might to try to break down the siege on Jerusalem. I saw Vrumek's emotion when he spoke about the fighting that was so severe. His burning gaze, his parched lips, told me more than any words he could use. He had just come down from a post on the hill. "There were three of us left," he recounted. "We had no ammunition left, so I took a branch of a tree and banged it into an empty can to make a lot of noise. They ran away scared, the Arabs. We were lucky that they are such cowards." The stories became fantastic when we would gather at Nachcia's when Vrumek and his buddies would come for a short visit.

Nachcia's room became headquarters, with everybody stopping there, some for a minute and some for an hour, Vrumek's soldier friends and my girlfriends. We strolled down Allenby Street when they had a short leave, walking them back to their waiting trucks at Mugrabi Square.

It was June 1948. The sun peeked through the window spreading its rays over my face. I lay in bed and turned over, realizing that it was Saturday and I need not get up for work. Lazily I basked in the sunshine while Nachcia went into the kitchen to get her hot drink from the overnight tea kettle. Moshe and Vrumek were at the base, so we were alone.

After lunch, friends came calling and together we strolled down toward the beach front. From afar we already could hear a commotion. Suddenly shots rang out and the crowds surged toward the beach, where we beheld a ship several hundred feet away from the shore. The shoreline at this section had no harbor. It was only used as a bathing beach and was always crowded with people—bathers, sunbathers, ball players, strollers, splashers. People were running in all directions as the beach was being cleared and a battle started. On the upper boardwalk soldiers were hastily setting up machine guns and barricades. At the ship's side thick black smoke was bellowing out in curly ribbons. Shots were heard again, and people ran in panic. No one knew what was happening. Curious myself, I scrambled up closer to the soldiers. I saw a broad-shouldered, husky man run over to a group of soldiers and scream something into their ears. Then he picked up his binoculars and looked out into the sea. He was absorbed, his face turned away, only his profile visible to me, but I recognized the brown curls protruding from underneath the helmet, and that prominent chin. Coming closer I could see not the soft smiling eyes I had known, but fierce, haggard eyes tracking an enemy.

"Amos," I yelled out. He turned abruptly. Stunned he looked at me, and in quick succession at the soldiers, at the sea, and at me again. I could see his confusion, his predicament. I saw his lips move but no sound came out. He motioned to me to wait but stay away. I stood at the sidelines among the crowd, excited and confused. Soon it became clear that the ship was not the enemy. Another group of soldiers appeared, pushing their way through; they were members of Etzel trying to get to their friends on the ship. The confusion was enormous. I did not budge even when the police got involved trying to disperse the crowds.

Then I witnessed the most horrible sight, when they began to bring down the stretchers into the boats. Twelve bodies were brought back to shore. There were also scores of wounded lying on stretchers on the shore. I craned my neck to see what was going on. In total disbelief I recognized a face resting on a stretcher, pale as if all the blood had been drawn from it. The contrast of the black curls made the face even whiter.

"Chaimke," I screamed but no one heard me. I thought he was dead and felt as if my heart was going to stop too. But suddenly I saw him move and knew he was alive. He had blood all over his body but not on his face. His hand was resting on top of his stomach, which was all bloody. I became frantic wanting to get closer to him and found Amos barring my way. Furiously I tried to free myself from his embrace. I felt his strong hands take my face. He looked at me and said, "I wanted to meet you again, I wanted it to be in Degania. Why do we have to meet here?"

"Amos," I cried, "he is my friend," pointing at the stretcher. "Take me to him."

"Ayala," he said in his clear Hebrew accent. "I want to see you and talk to you, but please go home now, this is not the place for you. Tonight, when it is over, I want to meet you right here. Please don't worry about your friend. It is only a slight wound. They are getting him to the hospital right now."

"Where are they taking him? I have to know," I cried.

"Come tonight, and I will let you know," he answered.

The crowd was breaking up, people walking slowly, sadly. Upset, they whispered, "Civil war, is that what we need now? Brother killing brother? I went home and lay on my cot for hours just crying, even though I did not really know what had happened.

In the evening, I washed my face and went back to the beach front. Leaning against the balustrade, Amos stood facing Allenby Street. His eyes were searching the street. As soon as he noticed me, he started walking toward me. I felt his strong arms lift me up.

"Let me look at you," he said after he set me down. "Its been three years, Ayala, but you have not changed even one iota. Let me see you smile," he said, looking into my eyes. "Do you go dancing? You must dance with me again. I have not found anyone else who can dance like you."

"I am so happy to see you, Amos. You have to tell me all about yourself, but right now I want to know what you are doing here, what happened here today, and most important where is my friend?"

"Come, let's sit down, and we will talk." We walked over to one of the sidewalk cafés on the seashore, which were open again now.

"You know I am a soldier. After all, you met me in Austria as a soldier. I have been an officer of the Haganah for a long time now, but the time has come, as you surely know yourself, that we have a country, and we cannot continue having bands of marauders. We have a regular army now. I am no longer an officer of the Haganah; I am an officer of I.D.F., Israel Defense Forces, Zva Haganah Le-Israel. Your friend is obviously a member of one of the bands who do not understand the situation. We have our freedom now, and we must become legitimate soldiers obeying a central command. He is a member of Etzel, and they have not conformed. Ben Gurion gave orders, and we must carry them out. Begin is not cooperating. We cannot have two heads of state and two armies; it just will not work."

"Is that what it is? So you are ready to shoot your brother. No wonder I heard them saying 'civil war.' I cannot believe my ears. We are in such dire need of fighting men and weapons, and you, instead of shooting at the enemy, are shooting at your brothers? Is that what we are fighting for? Is that what I had to struggle so hard to come here for? Oh, Amos, I cannot believe what is happening to us. I have just attended the funeral of one of our boys who came with me from Europe. He died defending our freedom, our pride. Where does he fit in? He was neither Haganah nor Etzel, but he would not fight his brethren; he fought his enemy. He gave his young life so that we could live here and enjoy our freedom, our country, but not this way. You claim that Begin is a nonconformist, that Ben Gurion gave orders. I haven't been in the land as long as you have, but I have heard how Begin fought the British. I have heard how people from Haganah have cooperated with the British, handing over members of Etzel to them. Now, when we finally have our country, is that going to continue? Jews fighting Jews! When I met you, Amos, after having come out of the concentration camp, you were the symbol of our pride. You wore the insignia of Chayal Ivri. How can you shoot at your brothers? Even if you have to disobey Ben Gurion's orders, that must not be done."

"Please let's not fight, you and I," Amos said calmly, taking my hand into his. "Things will get straightened out, you will see. Right now let's talk about you. Tell me all about yourself. It has been such a long time."

"Oh, Amos, I cannot believe all that is happening. When I first met you I had such dreams, and now look at us, three years later. This is the only place on earth for us to live in peace, at least with each other. Why can't we agree on issues? Why do we always need an enemy to persecute us in order to be united? We do not even have our country yet, there is still so much fighting to be done."

"Precisely because of that we must have a strong hand to lead us at this crucial moment, and if unity has to come by force, so be it."

"Who decided that you are right? When I speak to my friend from Etzel, he seems to be as right as you."

"That's why we will have elections soon, and the people will decide who will lead us."

We sat for a while yet looking out at the sea where the ship *Altalena* stood. All was quiet now, the barricades dismantled, the soldiers gone, people again strolling by at leisure. But deep in the hearts of the people, there was a chasm, a division, a deep cleft of mistrust. Ben Gurion would rule, we knew, but the iron fist he was using was what many people questioned.

"Please come to Degania after all of this is over. I want to show you the good life," he said before leaving.

Absorbed in demure thoughts I walked back. I had liked Amos so much when I first met him. He represented the heros of the Bible to me, the heros of our Jewish people. Now this hero was fighting and killing my other heros.

Chaimke's dark curly head rested in sharp contrast on the white pillow of a hospital bed. Even his olive-colored skin seemed pale. He opened his eyes when he heard me enter the room but did not smile at me. I came close and touched his hand.

"Shalom," I said, a little chokingly.

"I did not want you to see me like this," he said bitterly. His eyes were melancholy, the usual twinkle gone.

"How did you find me here?" he asked.

I told him about Amos. He went into a rage. He tried to sit up, and I could see how painful his struggle was.

"That bastard Ben Gurion," he spit out, "sets himself up as king of the Jews and like Herod of old turns against his brethren. Do you know how much Jewish blood and money it took to bring the *Altalena* here? Do you know that we were ready to share with them that precious cargo, even though it all came from our supporters? We were ready to give them so much. All we wanted was that our boys get equipped, too. We are fighting side by side with them. We bring in the weapons, we buy them, we transport them, we take the risks, we endanger our people, and he wants it all. Why? Why? This land is mine as much as his. We brought freedom to Am Israel, we chased the British out, now Ben Gurion wants to be master over us. He wants to have all the power, all the say; he will not let us share in the victory for which we shed so much blood. I can tell you one thing, I will not live under his dictatorship. If they will not let us share this land, I cannot stay here. I will not fight my brethren. My commander will not be David Ben Gurion. My commander would not order us to shoot at our brethren, at Jews. I'd rather leave."

Chaimke was echoing the words of Menachem Begin, who proclaimed, "There will be no brother fighting brother, there will be no Jewish blood shed by Jews."

I sat next to his bed, speechless, subdued, perturbed. I had no words of consolation to offer. My heart was aching for him, this hero of Israel, but I was helpless in the face of history. I cried a long time into my pillow that night, unable to make peace with the fact that although we finally had our country, we had no unity.

Several weeks later Chaimke came by to say good-bye. He was leaving for South Africa, he told me.

"Will I ever see you again?" I asked poignantly.

"I don't know," he answered, gesturing with his eyes toward the sky as if to indicate, only God knows.

I saw the melancholy in his eyes again and felt the sorrow in his voice. I knew he felt that he was being exiled from his homeland now that he had finally won freedom for his people. He held my hand in his for a long while, and I knew I would never see him again.

Yigael was not a Holocaust survivor. He had come to Israel with his family. He was mobilized, with his family's delivery van, serving together with Vrumek. That gave him tremendous advantage, being mobile at all times. He would come to Nachcia's even if Vrumek could not. After a while I learned that he was really not looking for Vrumek but for me. I was flattered by Yigael's attention. He was very handsome, with blue eyes and a crop of ash-blond curly hair adorning his smiling face.

I had not heard from Chaimke and was lonely for companionship and attention. Yigael paid a lot of attention to me. He would take me along whenever the opportunity arose and would stop in to see me even when it was for the shortest of moments. He was lively, talkative, and fun to be with.

The fragile truce that had been so laboriously negotiated ended, and new fighting resumed. Vrumek and his buddies stopped coming home, and the commotion at Nachcia's apartment died down. I had gotten used to Yigael, having seen him so often in the past weeks, so I missed him. I missed his honking the horn upon his arrival, his spontaneous decisions to take me along to wherever he had to go, his show-off character when he was introducing me to his friends. I knew he admired me, and I loved when he fought hard for us to go out alone, without the company of other friends. He would claim that he had absolutely no room in the van, or that he was on an important errand, only to avoid having one of his friends accompany us. He even totally ignored the girls who tried to flirt with him. I liked his gentleness and gentlemanly behavior. Yigael was a *Yeke* (person of German descent). Now I worried and wept into my pillow, unable to communicate with him or to find out his whereabouts.

When on a Sunday afternoon I suddenly heard the familiar honk, I jumped out of my skin with excitement. I ran outside straight into his open arms. He told me that another cease-fire had been accomplished. He also assured me that Vrumek was fine. He knew very well how important it was for me to know about Vrumek, how I worried for his safety and well-being. He assured me that he had opportunity to see him. He did not know how soon Vrumek would be able to come home. Then he said that he himself must run, for he had not even been home yet to see his parents, but he promised to see me the next day.

Jerusalem had been under siege, with no convoys able to negotiate the dangerous road dominated by the police station fortress at Abu Gush, which was occupied by the Arab Legion. A new temporary road had been built to bypass the main blocked road. They called it Burma Road. Yigael was going to Jerusalem and insisted on my coming along. "I want you to be among the first people to reach Jerusalem via Burma Road."

Early in the morning he honked his horn once. I was ready and jumped into the cabin beside him. The sun was strong by the time we reached Burma Road. There were several vehicles bouncing in front of us on the dusty stretch: a military truck, a jeep, and a half-truck. Yigael was shifting gears energetically, trying in vain to keep up with the other vehicles. The road was a winding clearing, just wide enough for a car to pass. Big rocks and little stones were bouncing off the freshly created road with every wheel revolution, and many small stones hit the windshield. The dust clouds were so thick we could hardly see ahead of us. Sweat running down my back, my heart pounding, I sat stiffly holding on to the seat with cramped hands.

"Are you scared?" Yigael asked, glancing at me from the corner of his eye. Sweat poured down in streaks on his face, but his hands maneuvering the wheel and his disposition were calm. I looked at the surrounding cliffs in awe, and even though my stomach was turning inside out with every bounce and jump of the vehicle, I could not help but admire the beauty of the surrounding hills.

"These are the mountains of Judea," Yigael said, noticing my interest. "This is where our forefathers walked, where our biblical heroes fought. This is where the Assyrians, Babylonians, Greeks, and Romans all laid siege to our holy city of Jerusalem. This is where we have shed our blood since time immemorial, swearing, 'If I forget thee, O Jerusalem, may my right hand forget her cunning. May my tongue cleave to the roof of my mouth, if I remember thee not; if I set not Jerusalem above my chiefest joy.' * Again we stood in these hills witnessing the siege of our holy city, but we did not give up. We fought like lions, we died like martyrs, but we managed just in time to open this road to save our city from starvation and thirst. A day before the first truce went into effect, on June 11, 1948, this road was opened, and the first convoy passed through with supplies. You have no idea what welcome we received in Jerusalem! There was no water, no food no electricity. There was fighting all the time. The soldiers who were in the city were exhausted. Everybody fought—old folks, children. You cannot imagine the courage and determination the people of Jerusalem showed, the sacrifices they made, the losses they suffered. Then the convoy came. It was far too little, but thank God not too late. Don't be scared," he said faintly, "we will make it to Jerusalem. I want you to see and to remember."

I looked at the terraced mountains, at the protruding cliffs and rocks, and tried to imagine the battles these hills had seen. I saw the valley of Ayalon where, according to the *Tanach,* the sun stood still. In my mind's eye I saw Yehudah Ha Macabee in his high-laced sandals, jumping from rock to rock shooting his arrows at the Greek soldiers. I saw Bar Kochbah motioning to his men to follow him in his fight with the armor-clad Roman soldiers, and I tried to see our boys running up the mountain, their Sten guns extended, exposed and vulnerable in the brilliant sun.

Another jolt of the vehicle brought me back to the dusty road. We were

* Psalm 137:5, 6.

reaching Abu Gosh. Several scattered stone houses in this Arab village were now occupied by our soldiers. They were jubilant to see us and invited us to share their field lunch. Yigael went to take care of his responsibilities and left me with the fellows. When he returned it became clear that we would not go to Jerusalem after all because we had to return to Tel Aviv. We were disappointed but these were army orders, not a pleasure trip. Back we trekked on the unstable, rough Burma Road, his van now filled with soldiers loudly exclaiming their discomfort with every bounce of the van.

I looked at the sparsely growing trees, bent in the hot wind on the uneven slopes. They were not really beautiful but in my eyes they were precious. This was our ancient land, to be our new homeland. My heart filled with joy and sadness and fear. These boys sitting next to me seemed so calm, yet I knew that they were the heros of which our future generations would learn. I looked lovingly at Yigael—he, too, was my hero.

As usual trying to please me, Yigael surprised me with a stop at Hulda, the camp where Vrumek was stationed. Vrumek was so happy he gave Yigael a hefty smack on the back and embraced him, thanking him for the gesture. We spent some time with Vrumek's friends, whom I knew well. Being that it was a period of cease-fire, the mood was calm and relaxed. The boys took pictures with me, all crowding around, dressing me up in uniform with a helmet. The sun was just tumbling into the sea when we arrived back in Tel Aviv. Nachcia was happy to hear that I saw Vrumek and glad to see me back home.

Shraga, a casual friend, brought Branka and Lola, two of our girls that were serving in his unit, in his jeep with him to Nachcia's apartment.

"Look at her," Shraga said, pointing at me. "Who else has it as good as she does? She does not have to trek back to camp tonight with us. She is *datit* [religious]."

"Get off my friend's back," Lola interrupted excitedly. "Not every person is an *apikores* [atheist] like you, living like a *goy*. You do not know what the interior of a synagogue looks like. Your forefathers must have been communists or Bundists."

"My grandfather was a rabbi, if you must know. So what did that do for him? He was angry with my father for being a Zionist and leaving Poland as a *chalutz* [pioneer]. My grandfather died, what he called for *Kiddush*

Hashem [sanctification of God's name]. God must be very holy with six million holy martyrs. Is his being so holy going to help us to establish our country? Not in my book. When I sit on an outpost and make in my pants, I will be dead. I am there because I am going to show these bullies that I am strong, and I am not going to take any crap from them. I am going to protect my land because it is mine. My grandfather and all of them went like sheep to the slaughter. Not me, not here, not my father, and not our kind. My father drained the swamps of Hachula, and I must fight at Abu Gosh. We are building a country, every generation in its own way, with its own obligation. To be a draft dodger is not something to be proud of."

I was incensed. "If you are implying that a religious person is a draft dodger, it just comes to show how brainwashed you are, with your indoctrination of socialist ideology. I bet you are a member of the socialist workers party. My brother is a religious fellow, so is my brother-in-law, and they are serving in the army. Vrumek's unit—all religious fellows—were sitting on the farthest outpost and took most of the fire, yet they managed to pray every day before every battle.

"Moshe, my brother-in-law, was wounded and is right now lying in a hospital bed. Is that not idealistic enough for you? Just because you do not pray, you think you are better equipped to bring freedom to this land?

"As far as your grandfather having gone like a sheep to the slaughter, have you heard about the Warsaw Ghetto uprising? Do you know how they fought the German tanks? Don't be such a big shot, sitting in Sarafend base! I would like to see you up at a *mishlat* like my brother's religious regiment. Don't you think we know by now what a membership booklet in the party does for you?"

"Look at your friend Pepa," Shraga said, getting excited, running his fingers through his thick brown hair. "She has a religious deferment, yet every night her room is full of boys hanging out till wee hours. What do you have to say to that?"

I was getting furious now. I knew Pepa; she came from my home town and she had been in camp with me. Pepa had been a mere child when she managed to be taken to a concentration camp instead of being sent to Auschwitz. She was in my barracks. We all protected Pepa—she was so vulnerable, so young, so fragile. She was also neither the prettiest nor the smartest girl, yet she was lucky; she did survive and came to Palestine with us. But here there was no more camp and no one to watch over Pepa. All her family had perished. She found no one when she came back from the camp and had no one here in Palestine, either. Now Pepa lived alone in a tiny room, struggling to make it on her own. Pepa was not very smart, but she adhered to her family tradition. She knew enough to get a religious deferment and not go into the army. She wanted to get married and make a home for herself, and someone who would share his life with her. She had friends who would visit, boys and girls. I felt my heart going out to poor Pepa, my aching heart, which was also searching for that decent someone who would help me make that new life. I, too, had gotten a religious deferment. I did not think my father and mother would have appreciated their youngest daughter going to the army, which did not have a reputation of keeping its young girl soldiers protected. Soldiers are just guys, whoever they might be. I had a reputation to protect. Nachcia and Vrumek thought so, too. Unfortunate Pepa, she did not even have a brother or sister. Now I vented all my anger at Shraga.

"Yes, all you guys have on your mind is to have girls in the army to use when you get the urge. The girls do not do any fighting anyway. We know very well what is going on in the army. So if you cannot have it, you go around making accusations of ill repute about a decent girl. I know Pepa better than you, and I can guarantee her behavior is proper and respectable. The fact that she has a lot of friends just shows what a well-liked girl she is. I have a feeling that the truth is that you are jealous of Pepa because she would not go out with you, because you behave like a *goy*. We suffered too much from the *goyim* for being Jewish. Now that we are in our own land we should live like Jews, a life based on morality, decency, a life conforming to the teachings of our sages, a life of righteousness, a life of brotherly love, with no political parties and political strife. When we came out of concentration camp we formed one party. We called it *Ichud*. I do not understand how again we are being split up into groups, factions, rivals, even now when we are just fighting to establish ourself as a country."

"If you think Shraga is interested in Pepa," Lola interjected, "why don't we invite Pepa to come here so they can meet? Maybe Shraga will change his ways."

"Do you really want competition, Lola sweetheart?" Shraga was smiling now. "I am not about to change. I will settle for a type like you, darling. But you, Ayala, I will tell you what kind of Jew I am. My father was a Zionist. He left his home and his family and as a young boy pursued his goal. His ideal was to regain this arid land for our people, to make this land bloom, to restore it to its ancient splendor, to make a home for us, the Jewish people, who have lived scattered all over the globe, being chased and thrown out of land after land. I wish my grandfather had the foresight my father had, but I am sure glad at least my father did. If my grandfather had been as wise as my father was, we would not have had a Holocaust. I was born here on this land. I do not know any other country, and I do not want to know any other. I live as a free Jew without prejudices, free of ancient customs that do not apply to life here. What we need is people to devote themselves to the land and not to the book. I am fighting for our freedom so that my children will not have to."

And so, as always, we discussed politics until it got late and Shraga took the girls back to camp. The fighting had stopped.

Rosh Hashanah 5710, equivalent to September 24, 1949, and the Jewish New Year was over. It was Yom Kippur, the holiest day in the Jewish calendar. Nachcia was in the ninth month of her pregnancy, and her legs were swollen and her stomach protruded. Nevertheless, she prepared for the holiday as usual.

We were already seated at the table for the traditional pre-fast meal, when Nachcia grabbed the arm of the chair. We could see her squeezing the wooden frame so tightly that the veins in her hand were turning purplish blue. I looked at my sister and recognized the symptoms. The time had come, I thought.

"What is it, Nachale?" Moshe asked.

Her lips were squeezed tight, her sky-blue eyes were filled with panic. She did not answer until the pain had passed. With a small, faint smile on her lips she said, "I think I have to go to the hospital," and than more forcefully. "Oh, my God, just on *Erev Yom Kippur,* what a time! We must hurry up and finish eating," she prodded, "it is time also to go to shul. I have to clean up still before I go."

She was meticulous about her household, this tiny apartment where she lived with her husband and made a clean, pleasant, warm home for all of us. Even now, at this critical time, her concern was for us, rather than for her own pain and discomfort.

"Now stop making us nervous," I interjected. "Let Moshe take you to the hospital, and I will clean up here and take care of all the rest."

What I could not tell her was how worried I was for her, her well-being, her health. After all, she was all I had. She was my sister but also my substitute mother, my friend, my support, my guide.Now Nachcia was about to deliver a baby, who would be the link between our past and our future. A baby who would continue our family. Who would be reborn in this baby? Would it be a girl to be named after Mama? Would it be a boy to perpetuate Papa's name? Certainly Nachcia would name the baby after one of them. What about the others, Blimcia, Jacob, Iziu, Shlamek, Heshek, Goldzia, Sholek? Their names must live, too.

On the way home from shul, after the *Kol Nidrei* (evening service on Yom Kippur) was finished, Vrumek and I stopped at the Hadassah hospital on Balfour Street, just around the corner from Nachcia's house. In the corridor we saw Moshe all excited.

"I was waiting for you, you may wish me *mazal tov!* It's a girl! Nachcia is doing fine, thank God."

When Nachcia was well enough to go to shul the baby was named. Mama was finally put to rest in our minds. Until now we lived with denial, never thinking about Mama as dead. Somewhere in a corner of our minds a fantasy was hidden, a feeling that we would one day see her again. As we named a grandchild after her, we put up a *matzevah* (monument) for her. Sar-ale, we called the baby, for Sara Miriam Laufer-Stapler, the matriarch of our family, and for Sara, the matriarch of the Jewish people.

I had been dating Yigael for almost a year. We would spend our free time together, mostly at Nachcia's with my brother Vrumek and their army buddies. Yigael was always at my side, tenaciously watching out for my safety and comfort and jealously guarding against rivals.

I loved Yigael for all his qualities. I appreciated his being so handsome, was proud walking down the street holding hands with him. His advantage of serving in the army with the family van enabled him to come home very often and spend many nights at home, thereby having much time to spend with me. We would sit on a bench in one of the lovely boulevards of the city, his gentle embrace so sweet and pleasant, talking and planning our future. We knew we came from the same background, a religious orthodox up-bringing that was important to both of us. I was very eager to meet his family, to know that I would be accepted. My deep longing for family life, my yearning to establish myself as a family member in the broader sense, was weighing heavily upon me.

Our country was struggling, fighting, losing lives in the process of its birth. Soldiers were fighting on fronts, coming home for short intervals. Amid all of that, individuals were eager to establish their own identity, start a household, end the life of refugees and stragglers. So was I anxious to have my own place, my own home, my own person to love and dedicate my life to.

On Saturday evening October 9, 1948, soon after the high holidays, Yigael presented himself at my doorstep, theater tickets in his pocket, and declared that his mother would be joining us. When he saw my surprised expression, he said. "You wanted to be introduced to my family, right?"

I dressed carefully and walked solemnly next to him after we picked up his mother. I had the distinct feeling that it was done intentionally so she could look me over, for she would not want to invite me to her house for fear of misinterpretation. After the show, Yigael's mother insisted that they take me home first. It must have been the look in my eye that convinced Yigael to act maturely. With some protest on her side, we took his mother home first.

We were all seated around the table in Nachcia's living room/bedroom. The doors at both ends were open to let some of the steamy summer air circulate. Nachcia scurried in and out between the room and kitchen, fetching cold drinks for the girls and boys who had just come in straight from the army base for a short break.

Moshe was home from the hospital. He had injured his back while on duty but was okay now. Vrumek came home, thank God unscathed. So did the men from his unit.

Yigael, too, was back, so we had more of a chance to be together undisturbed by the call of duty. He would come by every evening honking his horn to announce his presence. We would go out, walk toward the boulevard, and our empty bench would summon us. With the soft fragrance of the trees wafting by, the warm summer evening breeze would embrace us, while the strollers floated by locked in embrace. For hours we would talk, discuss subjects of concern, sometimes heatedly debating, other times just sweetly whispering words of endearment.

I loved Yigael by then and knew that he loved me. He was such a gentleman, a quality I appreciated. I wanted to spend the rest of my life with him but was getting impatient waiting for an overture on his part. We talked about our future in very distant terms, but I needed some concrete commitment. My situation was quite desperate, living at Nachcia's in her tiny kitchen. All my friends were marrying in brisk succession.

I was twenty-one years old and just like all the girls my age wanted to settle down in my own household. The main reason for my hurry was the fact that I had known Yigael for over a year and was painfully aware that it was absolutely improper for me to keep dating him without a basic commitment. The fact that I did not have parents emboldened my awareness of people's scrutiny. My two guardians, Nachcia and Vrumek, watched over me with gentle persistence, safeguarding my good name. In my own conscience my behavior was spotless and decent, but I did not want to jeopardize my chances of a proper engagement.

In an evening discussion at Nachcia's, it was decided that Vrumek would go see Yigael's parents to inquire about Yigael's intentions, and ask for the parents' consent. The appointment was set up. With a pounding heart I waited for Vrumek's return from the fateful meeting.

Intently I watched his taut face when he walked in. The last rays of the setting sun cast long shadows on the table that stood crowded between the sofa and buffet commode. Vrumek's futile attempt could not disguise his exasperation. A gloomy grimace replaced his usual familiar smile when he said, "I am sure you are anxious to hear what happened."

"So tell me," I asked awkwardly.

"They were extremely cool, even unfriendly," he said with annoyance.

"Who was there?" I wanted to know. "Where was Yigael? Was he present?"

"He was there but did not make his presence known. We sat in the living room. He never came in, but I saw him in the adjacent room. The mother was the main spokesperson. She said, 'He is so young.' She sees no point in his getting tied down yet. He has older brothers and they are not even married yet. Obviously you have no money to fix up a household, and he doesn't either."

"I tried to argue," Vrumek stated. "I told her, 'they love each other, they are both young and will work together to establish themselves. I am ready to help my sister with whatever I can.' The mother was adamant. 'This is not the way I want my son to start his life, he has plenty of time.'

"The father smiled lamely, shaking his head approvingly. I tried my best," Vrumek said bitterly, "but I don't see any chance. I would not humiliate myself and you by giving the impression that I was begging for some-thing. You are a beautiful girl, you are smart and pretty and kind, and you will find someone who will be worthy of you, who will want you with all his heart. I could not act otherwise," Vrumek said now apologetically. "They are greedy and insensitive. I see no point in your continuing seeing Yigael."

I felt the blood rushing to my face in a hot wave and a sting in the eyes, which were filling rapidly with tears. An unpleasant silence filled the room that usually pulsated with lively conversation and laughter. Nachcia got up and spread a tablecloth on the table.

"Let's have dinner," she said. Grateful to my sister, I went into the kitchen to help her prepare the salad and carry the food to the table. I stuffed a bite of bread into my mouth, forcing myself to eat, but the lump in my throat was getting bigger.

Luckily, Frydzia, one of the girls, came in and joined us at the table, which was the habit at Nachcia's house. Anyone was welcome; anyone who came in joined us at the meal. Nachcia, as always, produced another plate and soon Frydzia was enjoying the meal, talking and laughing, unaware of the disturbing tension that had pervaded the room just minutes ago.

From the time of that momentous meeting, our relationship began to de-teriorate. Yigael did not show up that evening. The next day when we went out, he was demure. I was silent, trying to think what words to use to describe my distress. We sat down on our bench, the atmosphere thick with unspoken words. Yigael tried to take my hand and only brought tears to my eyes.

"You know that Vrumek went to see your parents," I started.

"I know," he answered curtly.

"You know what they said," I persisted.

"No."

"Why not?" I said annoyed this time, "You were there."

"I was not in the room," was the excuse.

"You should have been," I was getting angry. "You could have said something. Aren't you interested in our fate? Why do you make me waste my time?" I pleaded, "when you know that your family does not approve of me and you know that your parents will not let you marry me?"

"Don't talk like that, that is not so. It is just the circumstances right now."

Yet Yigael had nothing concrete to offer to counterbalance our predica-ment. He himself had never made any commitment or given any hint of con-crete plans for our future. I was in a rotten mood, getting depressed. I realized that I loved Yigael and was not ready to give him up, yet I could not afford to keep seeing him. It was improper. I was shocked to know that the only objection they had to our friendship was financial. They knew I was from a fine home and proper upbringing, which they valued, but the fact that I had no money, no apartment, no means, made all the difference. It brought closer into my consciousness the sensitivity of being a poor orphan. They were a quite well-to-do family, sons all gainfully employed, father in his own business.

"I should have known it when your mother wanted to get rid of me, suggesting that you take me home first, that time when you invited her to come to the theater with us."

"Well I did not, as you remember. I took her home first, didn't I?" he said unrelentingly.

"You say it with such fervor, as if you were doing me a favor."

"Do you want to quarrel? Is that what we came here for?"

"No, I do not want to quarrel," I said in an imploring tone. "I just want you to understand how I hurt, for I do love you, Yigael, I love you very much, but it seems to me that we have to part."

I told him how I was always dreaming, wanting to be a daughter to his mother, the daughter she never had. I thought she could fill my empty heart with a mother's love and care, which I missed so much. Obviously, however, she does not want a daughter, she wants a girl for her son with a sack of gold and a heart of stone. All I have to offer is a sack of stone and a heart of gold." I now cried bitterly when I told him, "I will miss you, Yigael, I will miss you terribly, but it is all finished between us. I hope you too will remember me and think about me sometimes."

He in turn tried to assure me that he loved me and would not let anyone stand between us. "Please, Helush, do not talk like that. I love you, you know I do. Why do you want to break up?"

Ignoring the point, twisting it all up, trying to put the blame on me for breaking up seemed like a good tactic, but I could not let it finish in anger.

"You are trying to ignore the problem knowing perfectly well that it cannot work anymore. I do not have money, but I do have my pride and my decency. I know when I am not wanted."

"If you are so determined to break up and finish our relationship, I will respect your wish." Always the gentleman.

"You know the tradition we follow as well as I do. I cannot besmirch my good name and keep on seeing you just because I love you. It will pain me to live without you, but I have been used to suffering. Suffering does not kill, it only breaks one's heart. My parents deserve to be proud of me, of my behavior. I will not obliterate their honor, I know they are watching over me and will help me persevere."

We clung to each other in a sweet kiss and then I left abruptly. I did not look back, but I think Yigael remained sitting on our bench.

For many a night I poured tears of bitter longing onto my pillow, bewailing my fate, but mostly wanting him. Every caress, every touch, every word of kindness kept coming back, sounding sweeter than ever. I blamed myself for harsh words I had used, and I planned to go find him and make it all good again. During the day, however, having sobered up from sweet dreams I would become conscious of the realities and know I could not have done otherwise.

My sister and brother supported me and praised me for my bravery, while from the corner of the eye they would watch to see if my pain was diminishing. Friends and neighbors tried to set me up on dates, enumerating the virtues of the fellows, but I was not interested. I wanted Yigael or no one. Slowly my pain dissipated, leaving me numb and empty. I felt life brewing within me and was curious to know if I would be able to love again. I wanted to find someone to love and to be loved in return, someone to understand my pain and to share his feelings, his life, with me, on a pure basis without preconditions. I felt my heart overflowing with love and pain and had no one to share it with.

With fervor I immersed myself in work and study. I spent the evenings reading, and the days taking courses that would enable me to find a better, more prestigious job than the one I had as a waitress.

The shimmering water of the Mediterranean was picking up the bathers on its soft waves, buoyantly floating to the shore and back. Heads were bobbing out of the water and then disappearing in the white foam. We were playing volleyball, the ball flying above the heads of passersby. The beach was crowded with the usual crowd, sunbathers, ball players, gymnasts, and muscular body builders.

I let the approaching ball fall when I suddenly saw Salek coming toward me. His lean body was pale and reddish from too much sun, his sandy hair wet and tangled. He extended his hand in a handshake, appearing to be very pleased to see me. I smiled broadly in happy welcome.

"Where have you been all this time, that I never bumped into you?" I asked in surprise.

"Oh, here and there," he said evasively. "And what have you been up to? Where do you live?"

"I live here in Tel Aviv at my sister's. She is married. How is your brother Moshe?" I asked.

"He is fine, thank you. I'd better let you continue your game," Salek said politely, "but maybe I could meet you Saturday night so we can talk about old times?"

"That will be fine. I will see you then, Saturday at eight, on the corner of Allenby and Balfour, not far from where I live."

"Stop dreaming," my partner shouted at me, noticing that I was staring at the disappearing figure. "Come on, throw the ball."

With renewed vigor I threw the ball, pouncing it rhythmically, repeating to myself, Salek is back, Salek is back. That night I lay in my bed physically fatigued, emotionally awake. Aroused by my original enchantment with Salek, my thoughts were churning. Why did I meet him now? Was this invitation just a friendly courtesy call of reminiscence, or was there more to it? My sanguine nature kept me on my toes throughout the week.

Saturday at eight I walked to Balfour Street. I was prompt because I never liked to keep my dates waiting, but Salek was already there.

"Where would you like to go?" he asked, looking at me with smiling eyes.

"Doesn't matter. Your wish is as good as mine."

We walked down Allenby Street to the shore. The well-lit street was full of strollers. Very soon we were caught in the crowd proceeding to the promenade. The sidewalk cafés were packed with couples romantically looking into each other's eyes and sipping cool drinks, groups of youngsters loudly conversing, fellows smoking and turning their heads to follow pretty girls with their gaze. We sat down at a small inside table and ordered soft drinks. He wanted to know all about my time here in Israel.

"You do realize we have not seen each other for a very long time," he said with interest. Ostensibly he was not in touch with other people from our group and was curious to know about everybody. He told me about his being trained in the air force. At length he described his first visit to the United States. Enchanted again with his presence, I listened and laughed at the funny stories and vivid descriptions of his travels and encounters. We sipped our drinks while he described a very fancy dinner he was invited to, in America.

Waiters dressed in uniforms brought out shiny bowls of water and placed them before each guest.

"I was about to begin drinking," he said laughingly, "when I peered at my host and saw him dip his fingers in the bowl. Just then I understood why the waiter stood at my side at attention, a white towel hanging over his arm. Quickly I, too, dipped my fingers in the silver bowl and submitted my hands to the anxious waiter."

We sat at the café till very late, the soft wind just wafting by, its salty taste on our lips. The ink-black sea reflected a crescent moon. From time to time, twinkling lights appeared in the distance, and we were calm, knowing these were friendly lights.

"I remember the boats of immigrants that disembarked on nights like this," he said with melancholy, and I understood that he was involved with *aliyah bet* (illegal emigration) before our independence.

"How was it when you first came?" I asked.

"We will talk about that next time," he said, taking my hand and helping me get up. Unusual behavior for an Israeli boy, but Salek was not an Israeli boy, and that was exactly what I liked about him. We walked home at a leisurely pace, and I promised to see him again.

I did see Salek one or two times more, but with each meeting my conviction grew—Salek was not for me. We were worlds apart in background, outlook on life, goals, and ambitions. My enchantment slowly dissipated, leaving me free again.

Hania, our only surviving cousin, who had been with us throughout the war and had come to Israel with us, was a source of envy when she met Yaki.

Hania was a beautiful girl, with jet black hair crowning a pretty face, passionate black eyes, and a small, perfectly shaped red mouth with lips like rose petals. Hania looked distinguished even in the hand-me-down clothes we received in packages from our relatives in America.

It was considered that Hania had a good catch in Yaki. He was a handsome hulk of a man who carried his big frame with poise. What made us so envious was his background: second son of a fine family of farmers, prewar refugees who emigrated from Germany, well established on their farm, with three sons in the family, all young, healthy, big, strong and handsome.

Yaki fell deeply in love with Hania, and they were married on July 1, 1947, not long after Nachcia's wedding. Hania was twenty-three years old, and at the peak of her beauty. With overflowing love in our hearts, Nachcia, Vrumek, and I watched Hania's beautiful face shine with love when she raised her dark eyes to look at her beloved at her wedding. We felt hopeful that Yaki would help Hania overcome the pain of losing her brother Sholek, the trauma she felt of having being the sole survivor in her family. Yaki's stare, so full of admiration and love, reenforced our confidence that Hania was happy.

They had immediately registered for a *shikun* (government-built subsidized housing). Hania, of course, had not a penny to her name, and it was Yaki who put up the money for a down payment.

Yaki was madly in love with his bride and exhibited tremendous concern, understanding, and caring. After their first year of marriage, Hania gave birth to a cute baby girl, and even though war raged all the time, Hania was soon blessed with another baby. The two girls were one year apart. Yaki was ecstatic with his two babies. He helped feed, diaper, and bathe them. Their smile was his sunshine. Their small but fine apartment was in walking distance of his parents' farm, where he worked with his father and brothers.

With fighting continuing and food scarce, there was never a dire need for food on the farm, although the city people suffered. Yaki would bring home eggs, milk, vegetables, and an occasional chicken, so Hania was better off than most of us. Hania lived right near the triangle, however. With Jenin in the north, Nablus in the south, and Tulkarem in the west, it was the most dangerous nest of Arab hatred toward Jews. With Kalkilye just a stone's throw away from her house, Hania lived in constant danger. Arab marauders would attack Jews at random, and it was never safe to be out alone.

In spite of this danger, the girls grew and developed nicely. Their parents went about their business like the other inhabitants of the new country that was under attack everywhere.

A cold wind blew, permeating my light clothing. I said good night to my friends without the usual procrastination and nimbly turned into the darkened yard. My body shivered somewhat while I fidgeted with the key in the narrow cubicle in front of my door. There was a calm silence in Nachcia's room, indicating she had not waited up for me. Adroitly I opened the door. The tiny kitchen that served as my bedroom was cozily warm, and the cot with its blanket was inviting. I lay there on the cot hugging my cold body, remembering other cold nights on the wooden planks of a three-tier bunk, in an enormous hall with so many prisoners, all shivering, their teeth chattering. These thoughts were often my companion at night.

"I must not think about it now." I reprimanded myself gravely. "After all, here I am in our homeland, where the sun will shine tomorrow and warm me through and through, even in the winter. Here, in the next room, my beloved sister Nachcia is sleeping next to her husband, cradling a baby in her arms. A beautiful bouncy baby, with corpulent thighs and pink cheeks, making Nachcia the happiest woman in the world. And so should I be happy, too, for my sister and for myself."

I must have dozed off and was awakened by Nachcia's clamoring in the kitchen.

"What happened?" I demanded sharply. I was always angry when awakened suddenly. I immediately regretted my outburst. "What happened?" I said now in a softer tone, when Nachcia did not answer me at first. I knew something had happened. It was not Nachcia's habit to wake me that way. She would always apologize when she woke me, and tell me to go back to sleep. Now she did not. She looked at me sadly, and I saw her choking on the words she was saying. She seemed to force the words out of her throat.

"Not good news, bad news."

I sprang out of bed and stood barefoot next to my sister.

"What happened?" I pleaded, dark thoughts fast crowding my mind.

"It is Yaki," she said softly. "He is no longer here."

Suddenly I was fully awake.

"Yaki? Yaki? What do you mean no longer here?" I questioned, my head feeling light as if I were going to faint in a moment.

"His brother Zvi was just here," Nachcia stated, crying openly. "I don't know what exactly happened, but he said the funeral is tomorrow at twelve."

The next day was blustery and cold. In fact, snow had fallen during the night. Snow in Tel Aviv was a most unusual occurrence, even though it was only a dusting.

We assembled in Hania's house. We sat around talking and waiting. I looked at the two babies in the cribs, so innocently oblivious to what was happening. The older one, Esther, eagerly sucked at the bottle someone had handed her. The tiny second one, Leah, only six months old, was squirming, twisting, bouncing her little fists in the air. Kicking her small legs, a grimace on her face announced that she was going to cry soon.

Hania was in total shock, absolutely unable to control her weeping and lamenting. Someone picked up the smaller baby and stuck a bottle into her mouth, too, to prevent her from burdening the already very upset crowd with her crying.

They arrived bearing Yaki's body on a stretcher. Hania leaped toward it and was held back by the strong hands of Yaki's brother. She was screaming at the top of her lungs, begging Yaki not to leave her alone. It was so pathetic. I could not digest this terrible tragedy, the repetition of it. Just a few years earlier, Hania had buried her only brother, who had survived the camps and died several days after his return home. That same plea I witnessed then and now. It was tragic.

People crowded around her, talking, promising her faithfulness. "You are not alone, you have us. We are your family, we will not let you down," Yaki's brothers were saying. There was Yaki's father, his face dark, his wrinkles deep furrows, holding his face in his arthritic, twisted hands, lamenting, exposing his deep sorrow. Yaki's mother was shriveled, bent, wringing her old bony hands in a nervous, agonizing fashion.

We formed a line behind the fellows who carried the stretcher. Staring at the body covered by a black blanket, I saw Yaki sitting in Nachcia's apartment just a few weeks ago, when he, as usual, stopped in for a short visit when in town. Crunching sunflower seeds, we sat at the table debating politics. We were just over one war, strongly aware of the danger of more fighting that loomed on the distant horizon.

"When my girls grow up," Yaki had said, "I will not let them serve in the army."

"When they grow up, we will have peace," I'd said optimistically, and we all chuckled.

"I will marry them off before they reach the age of eighteen, so they do not have to serve. They are not going to fight, not my girls."

We knew we had a long way to go fighting for our newly established freedom, but he was so sure he would be able to control the destiny of his girls.

Now he was being carried out to the cemetery. Who would decide his girl's destiny, I wondered. Who will raise them, feed them, clothe them? At the open grave, the father broke down.

"As long as I am alive," he wept, "I swear to you my son, that I will provide for your girls."

It sounded so earnest, so true.

When Hania got up from her low chair at *shivah,* she immediately began searching for a job. Carrying her two girls, one in each arm, she took them to a nursery every morning. From there she proceeded to her job as dishwasher in a local restaurant. The pay was meager, the work backbreaking, but still Hania considered herself lucky to be earning some money. The visits of the family were slackening as time passed. The country had won her independence, but the widows and orphans faced a bleak existence.

Nachcia, burdened with a family—a baby to care for and her husband an invalid, wounded in the very beginning of the fighting for independence—had very little time to offer to Hania. Vrumek, too, was absorbed with establishing himself. It was me, young, single, and free, who visited at every opportunity. Communication was very poor at the time; buses ran at specific hours and stopped in the early evening. Telephones were nonexistent in private homes. So whenever a fellow I dated had wheels, I would use him to drive me to Hania's for a visit. At the oddest hours I would pop up at her doorstep, always warmly welcomed.

On my days off I would make it my business to spend time with the children. They loved to sit next to me on the stoop of their house and listen to stories I told them or read them from books I brought. Many a time I would also help Nachcia with that same trip, bringing back some valuable hard-to-obtain farm products, eggs, vegetables, chicken. These were at a premium in the city.

Chapter Six 〜∕∂

Y ou are just the person I was looking for," David, a boy from our group,
exclaimed when he bumped into me on Allenby Street on the shady side
of the pavement. Dressed in khaki shorts and cotton shirt, his feet clad in
sandals, he slipped his arm through mine and brusquely accompanied me.

"What for?" I was curious to know.

"We are looking for people with good singing voices for the choir I have
just joined. You will love it," he said pulling me along.

We went to Achad Haam Street, where in a second-floor apartment he
introduced me to a short, somewhat pudgy man with gold-rimmed spectacles
on his round nose. After an informal test of the musical scale, he warmly
shook my hand, congratulating me on having become a member of the first
musical theater to be founded in the State of Israel. I was flabbergasted with
the firm and speedy induction, thinking to myself, "What will happen when
he hears me sing and most probably changes his mind?" My suspicions, however, were unfounded. Next evening at five forty-five David stood at my door.

"I have come to pick you up. Aren't you ready? We are going to rehearsal."

On the way, David assured me that I would not be asked to leave. On the
contrary, he said, Conrad, the conductor, would be very pleased to see me.

Slowly my trepidation dissipated. There were several boys and girls
seated already in the living room. Conrad handed out mimeographed sheets
with some verses on them, no notes. With delight I realized that no one read
music. Conrad clapped his hands, and everyone stood up. He pointed to
where he wanted me to stand, in the alto voices section. He played the music
on his piano once, and we began to sing. Like an acrobat, Conrad would gesture and gesticulate to bring out the proper tone in his charges. His hand
cupped on his ear indicated: do not whisper, sing. His hand stretching from

his forehead to the front as if pulling on some invisible string meant: from up here, from the head. Or he would squeeze both his hands upward from his stomach to bring up our voices louder and clearer.

Three times a week David would pick me up to attend the rehearsals. It was a wonderful time of learning, enjoyment, and being motivated to perform to the best of our ability. It was a time of broadening of cultural horizons, of striving to be ready for the performance, the final goal. We all learned to adore Conrad and marveled at our own progress. Our group grew by word of mouth and we had to rehearse in a public place because Conrad's apartment was too small. My sister and brother were thrilled to see me happy again, involved with young people, and I was perfectly satisfied to be involved in an activity I loved so much.

Time passed quickly, and in a few months, a real performance became a possibility. Unlike the beginning, when we did rehearsals only with the choir, we now rehearsed together with the main characters of the show. A larger hall was necessary to accommodate us all, and one was acquired far down on Ben Yehuda Street in Tel Aviv.

My dilemma started when the date of the premiere drew close. The rehearsals became a daily affair and required us to be present even on Saturday. Most of the participants were not Orthodox. My problem was getting to the rehearsal hall—singing was permitted on Saturday. Immediately after the traditional Saturday meal at Nachcia's, I would start my trek to the hall. Two hours later my friends would pop out of a taxi, fresh and relaxed after an afternoon nap. Many would look at me in amazement, others would try to convince me that they would be happy to take me along in their taxi.

"You won't have to pay," they would state innocently, intending to spare me from performing a transgression.

They amazed me, these youngsters, many of whom were sabras, with how little they knew about their own religion. How carelessly they desecrated the holy day of the Sabbath. I wanted to give them a lesson in religious behavior but felt it was useless. Me, the new immigrant, telling the sabras! They were the proud, the know-it-alls, looking down at the newcomers with their ancient, outdated habits. *Yehudi Galuti,* the diaspora Jew, they called us, the Jew with the bent back. They were the new Jew, the proud, the strong, the fearless.

Calmly, without arguments, I would let them all disperse after the rehearsal before starting my own two-hour walk back home, absolutely happy, convinced that mine was the right way of behavior.

Having been ridiculed at first, I slowly earned the respect of all. Even Conrad who was a devoted, active, convinced communist, expressed his admiration.

And so, after final rehearsals with the whole cast and in costume, came the big moment, the premiere. Absolutely enthralled, we watched Conrad the communist, dressed in a tuxedo, tails flipping, standing on his little stool to make his short husky figure visible to us, give the first strike of his baton. With pomp and fanfare the music began, and all at once the hall, which was filled to capacity, exploded with melodious voices performing *Baron Hacoanim* (*The Gypsy Baron*) an operetta by Johann Strauss. Conrad's wild lock of hair danced on his forehead while he gesticulated, his round face expressing every move, his short body almost dancing on the tiny stool. Every voice rang out loud and clear on the large stage. Smiling broadly, we acted out our parts with conviction.

I remembered my performance in Villa Cavaletti in Rome Italy, and felt satisfaction for having attained this stardom. With zest I sang the Hebrew translation of Strauss's operetta in the prestigious Beth Haam Hall on Balfour Street. It was the first Jewish operetta performance in our new homeland, and I was taking part in it. Thrilled, I accepted a beautiful bouquet of roses from a friend who honored me by attending the premiere. After the show, there was the traditional celebration of our victory at an elegant restaurant. We all exploded in a dance of joy the next day when the reviews came out and they were very favorable. A milestone had been attained: an operetta performed in the Hebrew language, by Jewish performers, with a Jewish conductor, a Jewish director, in the Jewish country. And I was a rising star.

The musical theater group went on to perform other plays but I did not participate. With time I found it too taxing. As much as I enjoyed and strove to be involved in the entertainment field, I felt that as a young religious girl, it was not the place for me. The bohemian world was not exactly appropriate milieu for a young lady who observed the Sabbath. I eventually found suitable companions in a club of young Mizrachi members, a modern religious movement. To satisfy my desire to sing and perform, I would entertain the group at every occasion. Their outpouring of praise and their enthusiastic applause was gratifying, fulfilling, meeting my needs.

Performing in *Gypsy Baron*. I am fifth from right.

Edna, the girl I had befriended in the school in Ayanot when we first arrived, had left Ayanot, but instead of joining a kibbutz as she had planned, she joined the army. After basic training she took a course in nursing and was stationed in the military hospital at Tel Litvinski.

Our friendship was as fresh as if we had never parted. When she had time off from her job, she would come to Tel Aviv and stay with me in Nachcia's kitchen. We would sleep together on the narrow cot talking long into the night.

She had met Yigael when I was dating him, and she became my open well, into which I poured all the pain of our separation. I confided in her the most intimate of thoughts. Only with Edna did I analyze my relationship with Yigael and the stand that his parents took against me. " 'He is so young and good looking,' his mother probably said," I stated, " 'Why does he have to tie himself down with a refugee girl, who has absolutely nothing to her name? No schooling, no trade, no money, no family of substance. He can surely get a rich girl from a fine family maybe even from a German back-ground, someone we would be proud of.' "

In costume for *Gypsy Baron*
performance.

"But he loves me," was my argument. Doesn't that count for anything?"

"Oh, silly children," I would imagine his mother saying. "Love! What do you know about love? Today it is here, tomorrow it is gone. He will get over it."

"But I cannot get over it, I know I can't. Doesn't she have a heart at all?" Sometimes in my anger I would say, "God will punish her for her sin against me."

"Do you want me to talk to her?" Edna would ask. But my answer was silence. Instead I immersed myself in study and work. I would also spend more of my free time at the Hapoel Hamizrachi, a religious youth organization.

There were lectures, trips, study circles, and entertainment, enough to fill one's desire for the companionship of young people, and enough food for the brain.

One day when we lay in bed, Edna and me, she said, "Remember in Ayanot, before you left, I told you about my worry?"

"Yes, I remember," I said, suddenly feeling terribly guilty, for I had never pursued my promise to Edna to inquire about a doctor for her plight. I was sure that what was on her mind was the fact that she probably could not have children, probably as a result of what the Germans had done to her.

"I never told you why I worry," Edna said sadly.

"I can figure it out," I intoned subdued.

"I am dating someone and am afraid I might reveal my secret," she said. "I feel an urgent need to tell someone."

"You know you can trust me, Edna," I said with conviction. "I would never reveal something you do not want anybody else to know. You know I have told you things I did not want even my sister to know."

"I told you my mother perished in a concentration camp, but I know nothing about my father. Well, that is not the truth. My father did not divorce my mother. My father sent us both to the concentration camp because my father was a Nazi," she blurted out through agonizing sobs.

I was stunned into total immobility. Right next to me, so close that our bodies touched, lay a girl sobbing hysterically. She was my friend. I loved her, but at that moment I felt petrified. She had just shed an enormous burden, which suddenly possessed me. I felt as if she had thrown a rock that had landed in my lap, and I was sinking under its weight. I did not know what to do or say. I wanted to embrace her and tell her not to worry, I would not reveal her secret. I wanted to tell her that it did not matter to me, that it would not change my relationship with her, that to me she was the same Edna I had known before. I wanted to tell her I would help her with whatever I could, but I felt paralyzed with an eerie fear. I wanted to ask questions, to understand what she meant by "my father was a Nazi." I wanted to understand how a girl who was in a concentration camp, whose mother perished there, could have a father who was a Nazi. Edna sobbed for a long time and I just lay there listening to her crying, speechless and subdued. Finally she turned around to face me and quietly recounted the whole story.

Her mother was young and beautiful and Jewish, when she married a fellow student attending the same chemistry class at the university of Berlin, where they both studied, in Germany. They were happy at first; their life together was a beautiful one. Edna remembered how, when she was a young child, her father would take her to the park to ride bikes. He was always a strict parent, but she loved him anyway. He took great interest in her schooling, and she knew she must do well. She remembered time spent with her parents on hikes in the woods. Such happy times they were! Her mother was always smiling, caressing her long blond hair. Her father would be playful, chasing her around in the forest, rolling on the fragrant grass in the meadow, where they would picnic on sandwiches brought by her mother in her basket. Her father showed lots of affection and love to her mother in those times.

But then things began to change. Her father became very patriotic and spent a lot of free time with his buddies in the *beer halle*. He became very enthusiastic when Hitler came to power, and he joined the Nazi party early on. It was his buddies who challenged him to get rid of the shame he had in his own house, he claimed.

"Hans and Gretchen, the loving couple, were no more when they came to take us to concentration camp. He even stood there motionless as my mother pleaded with him to save me."

How horrible it must have been for Edna, I thought, to live with the memory of a father who was the enemy, a father, who does not prevent the destruction of his own child. Would she ever be able to forget his image standing there when they took her away, not lifting a finger to save her?

A Nazi uniform inspired in me the ultimate fear, the reminder of the murderers of my family, the torturers of our people. What did a Nazi uniform mean for poor Edna? I felt her pain, but the knowledge that there was nothing I could do about it was churning in my brain. I compared it to my own frustration, the loss of my dear ones. I realized that at least I had my wonderful memories of my father, the cheerful, loving, always joking, devoted, hard-working man he was. I felt my father was a king I revered but did not fear. I could not think of him any other way.

After the war, Edna continued, when she found herself the sole survivor, she refused to stay even for a day in Germany. She did not want to know anything about her father, but her past kept her a prisoner. She felt she could not take that torture any longer and had to tell someone. She was grateful to me for listening. On my part I just hoped I helped ease her pain by being there for her when she needed someone to confide in.

Edna went on to marry Zvi, a Jew born in Germany. They loved each other deeply. We stayed in touch after her marriage for a long time, but eventually we lost contact.

While the delegates at the United Nations in New York debated and Jewish representatives negotiated an armistice agreement with the Egyptians, Jordanians, and Syrians, Jewish soldiers in their trenches in forward positions were being replaced by new recruits. Thousands of new immigrants were streaming to the embattled land in the first year of its independence. The formerly barred gates had been opened wide to the tide that flowed legally. The Jews from the Eastern European countries had been released from the iron fist of the Communist regimes, and they flocked to the newborn homeland. Those immigrants who had been in Israel for three or four years or more became the big brothers to the newcomers. Released from the tension of fighting and war, the citizens concentrated on their personal lives.

Among our boys and girls, activities normalized. People were returning to their jobs, boys pursued girls again. Vrumek was back, too, as the fighting had ended. He felt a surge of new enthusiasm and new strength. It was time to think about his own life.

He was thirty years old; he was ready. His older sister was married, and so was Hania, his cousin. It was his turn to seek happiness. He was going to find a girl to love, to share his life. We were absolutely thrilled when Vrumek brought Esther to Nachcia's house to introduce her to us.

Esther had fiery copper-colored, thick hair, and soft brown eyes. When we saw the sparkle in Vrumek's eyes when he looked into Esther's, it warmed our hearts. Vrumek deserved to be happy. Finding his happiness with Esther pleased us very much, for Esther was one of us. She was the first person we had met in our home town of Chrzanow when we returned from the camps. It was in Esther's apartment, in which she let us sleep when we had no other place to go to, that I fainted on that fateful night. Besides, we were even distantly related.

March 15, 1950, was a bright day. Vrumek rested at Nachcia's, while I joined the girls at Esther's apartment. She looked beautiful in the rented white gown, her eyes shining brightly, her hair flowing under the veil.

Vrumek arrived with Moshe and Nachcia, walking with self-assurance, his slim body swaying slightly. His face was young looking despite his bald

Vrumek and Esther's wedding,
March 15, 1950.

head, hidden under a light straw hat. Dressed in a suit, the first he was able to afford, he looked handsome and distinguished. His face gleaming with pleasure when his army buddies picked him and Esther up on the chairs to dance and rejoice. They danced the *Mitzvah tanc,* Esther's flushed face and lowered gaze accentuating her bashful personality. Vrumek lifted her face to his, and she smiled happily.

Vrumek and Esther settled in a ground-floor, one-bedroom apartment, sharing the kitchen and facilities with another couple. This was the norm in those trying days of the infancy of the state of Israel.

Energetically, Vrumek began the life of a married man. He not only lived in new quarters but also started his own business. He bought a tricycle on which he constructed a box. On this vehicle he delivered fresh rolls and breads early in the morning to restaurants. Vrumek was satisfied to be his own boss, even though the work was hard and demanding. He was content to be able to provide for his good-natured, easily pleased Esther.

The young country of Israel had buried its heroes, and just as with individuals, with the dulling of the pain came the urgent need to turn toward its new immigrants and their needs. With *olim* arriving constantly and *maabaroth* (shanty towns) popping up everywhere, the need for staff to handle the problems of these newcomers became acute.

I finally found a better position, and I left the restaurant job at Bikowski's. A short substitute job in the department of agriculture and another experience in the department of health prepared me for my final endeavor. I was hired by the AJDC, the American Joint Distribution Committee, which was rapidly expanding its function in the new state of Israel. It's name in Israel was *Malben,* which stood for Mosad Letipul Beolim Nechshalim (Institute for treatment of disabled immigrants).

Tel Litvinski was an enormous military complex located some fifteen miles northeast of Tel Aviv. Having served as a military camp for British soldiers during the Mandate years, it comprised barracks-like low structures serving as living quarters for the soldiers, assembly fields, training structures, kitchens, dining halls, etc. Located inside the camp was a huge hospital of a thousand beds.

The American Joint Distribution Committee, established during World War I by Jewish philanthropists for the purpose of helping Jews in distress, was functioning in Israel. Jews all over the world had been depending on the help of the Joint, ever since its establishment. Even during the Nazi era, when the representatives of the Joint had to do their work clandestinely, Jews were helped.

With the tremendous influx of *olim chadashim,* into the newly established country of Israel, the need of Joint's help was paramount. A small office was established in Tel Aviv on Allenby Street. Just as the country was overwhelmed by the inpouring of shiploads full of immigrants, so was the Joint inundated by throngs of elderly sick people who were in need of special care, which only the Joint could provide. With the waves of people came the need for institutions and professional help. Clerical people were being hired, and hospital beds were being sought.

By the time I was introduced to the Joint, it was renamed Malben, and had offices in a large, six-story building in Tel Aviv. In Tel Litvinski, Malben had acquired the use of five hundred out of the thousand existing beds in the hospital, and these beds needed to be administered.

On the first day of my new job, I presented myself at the hospital in one building's long, empty hall. In the middle of this white-washed, gigantic room stood a desk that looked like an abandoned toy table in a cleared-out toy store. A man in his fifties with graying, bushy hair glanced from behind his spectacles toward the door when I entered. Absentmindedly, he asked me to sit, even though there was no chair available. Introducing himself as Dr. Eisen, he sent me to fetch a chair from the neighboring house. Shuffling the papers around, he seemed to concentrate on his work, while constantly complaining about the lack of organization. He eventually introduced me to his disarray of documents. Not really explaining what it was that he wanted me to do or what would be expected of me, he nevertheless pointed out admittance applications, medical letters of recommendation, and social status history reports.

I sat for hours listening and trying to pay attention to a gibberish of instructions and explanations that made no sense to me at all. The fine Dr. Eisen, a distinguished attorney from Poland, seemed unable to find any logic in what he was doing. He constantly mumbled unintelligibly in a heavily accented Hebrew.

By noon my stomach began grumbling, but I did not dare ask if and when there was a lunch break, concentrating rather on making a good impression. In spite of the uncertainty that possessed me, I hoped to be asked to come back as a hired employee, but nothing was said to me at the end of the day. I came home with a tremendous headache. Nachcia, as always, waited with dinner, wanting to find out how my day had gone. I was quite confused and went to bed early. With trepidation I thought about this new job. Would I be able to perform, or would I end up being embarrassed by having to return to being a waitress?

For many days I sat near Dr. Eisen observing his good-natured helplessness. Slowly I began to get involved. I started organizing his documents. Inching my way through the maze, I learned that the central office of Malben, the medical arm of AJDC, was setting up operation in Tel Hashomer hospital for the benefit of new emigrants. It was Dr. Eisen's job to admit patients referred by the main office, and to administer the number of beds occupied by these patients. It was a tremendous undertaking, with which Dr. Eisen could hardly cope. I was to be administrative secretary. Slowly, day after day, I helped the distraught but kind professor of law master his new field of operation.

Having left behind, in prewar Poland, a flourishing law practice and lecturing position, Dr. Eisen heroically dealt with the trauma of becoming a petty administrative clerk. My respect for the older gentleman gave him much courage, while his fatherly, sympathetic nature gave me the confidence to try do a job for which I was not trained.

Very soon we found out how the war had placed us both in this inept condition. Both of us were trying to establish a new life in the prevailing circumstances. With much patience, understanding, and cooperation, we managed to establish a properly run office. In time, a medical doctor, Dr. Stahler, also of Polish origin, came to Tel Livitski. By the time Tel Litvinski was renamed Tel Hashomer (the hill of the guardian), I was well on my way to being assistant administrator of the five hundred beds being used by Malben.

The AJDC, Malben in Israel, headquartered in Tel Aviv, disseminated instructions and all paperwork throughout the country to all the different institutions: old-age homes, hospitals, and homes for the chronically ill.

Jews from all over Europe, who for centuries had dreamed of the promised land, finally had the opportunity to realize their dreams. The gates of the Holy Land, which had been barred for decades by the British Mandate watchdogs, were flung open to admit its waiting brethren. The infant country harnessed itself to the task, making use of its human resources. Just as the boys from our own contingents had gone from the arrival port to the battlefield, so did the new arrivals work for the absorption of the newcomers.

The needs were many. Housing, jobs, schooling for the young, health services for the old and infirm. The Ministry of Absorption was the busiest arm of the government. All over the country, absorption centers were being built. Haphazardly constructed metal shacks glistened in the hot, sizzling Mediterranean sun, making the occupants broil in the smoldering heat.

Besides Dr. Eisen, Dr. Stahler, and myself, there were also a secretary and four social workers. The work was very interesting, requiring lots of devotion, resolve, and great sensitivity.

Day by day I became more involved in the lives of the patients being admitted through our office. Becoming familiar with all the departments of the hospital, getting well acquainted with the medical staff, I felt the lives of the patients permeating my own life. Through the family members of the admitted patients and via the files of our social workers, I became exposed to the total spectrum of human suffering.

Being surrounded by sick people, however, did not distress me to the point of depression. On the contrary, my own exuberance gave me strength to work hard for the betterment of the patients' fate and destiny. I took personal interest in the individuals who passed through our doors. There were many. Often, when I was perplexed and bewildered, I would cry with frustration, unable to help, but there were also times of enormous happiness derived from the knowledge that I was instrumental in easing someone's pain.

For countless hours I would sit at the bedside of Sophie, an elderly lady from Rumania. I would comb her thick gray hair, prop up the pillow under her head, and listen to the stories of her life, in a small town in Bukovina, where she had been a dressmaker. How she yearned to recompense me for my gestures!

"When you get married," she would say, "I will make you a wedding dress the likes of which you haven't seen in your life."

"By the time I get married, Sophie," I would say, "you will be a famous seamstress and forget about me."

"Oh, no," she would vehemently argue, "I will never forget what you are doing for me and my husband."

But Sophie had breast cancer, from which she never recovered. She left an emptiness in my heart.

When Saada was brought to the hospital for the first time, I turned my head, unable to look at her face. She was a little girl of about eleven, with a perfect figure, rich black curly hair, almond eyes, and velvet-brown skin. But there was nothing else in the face besides the eyes. Where the nose should have been, there was a deep cavity. The deep dark hole extended down to the mouth for there was no upper lip either. The sight was so vile and repulsive, I wanted to get rid of it quickly. Promptly we sent her home to wait for arrangements. My days became a race of inquiry about plastic surgery for Saada. On the first subsequent occasion, we challenged Dr. Appel, a plastic surgeon from South Africa volunteering his time and services, to build a nose for Saada.

Dr. Appel was there to reconstruct the bodies of the many wounded soldiers, work that he did with lots of love and devotion, like many other physicians who had volunteered to help out in these strife-filled days.

And so Dr. Appel undertook the tremendous job of building a nose for Saada. During the next three years Saada became a house guest at Tel Hashomer hospital, and my pet child. She underwent eighteen operations. With his magic fingers, Dr. Appel built for Saada a nose and upper lip—creating a new person in the process. Saada became a confident young lady with aspirations, a pleasure to be with and to look at. Having accompanied her to many of her operations, I became her confidante and close friend. With each additional layer of skin on her face, my attachment to Saada grew, and when she finally left, imbued with self-confidence and satisfaction, I felt like a trainer whose contestant had won a race.

Our task at Tel Hashomer was to administer five hundred beds. The other five hundred beds served the military and other civilian population, not the Malben immigrants. That section had its own administration office, with whom we worked very closely, coordinating the placement of patients. The administrative executive of the hospital, a young, pleasant-mannered, serious man from Haifa, called me one day to say that he was leaving, transferring to Haifa.

"Do you know who will replace you?" I asked curiously.

"Yes, his name is Amos Ben Yaakov. He's coming here from central command."

"Ya a la, really," I exclaimed. "Amos Ben Yaakov! I know him, I know him well."

"Good for you. I thought that you would be sad to see me go."

"Oh, yes, I am really sorry to see you go, but since it did not depend on my opinion anyway, I am glad the replacement is a decent one."

Three weeks later I walked into the hospital administration office on a brilliant sunny day.

"Ayala, what are you doing here?" Amos rose from behind his desk and extended his hand in greeting.

"What I am doing here, you ask. The same thing you are doing here."

"Cannot be," he shook his head. "I thought you came to seek admission for someone into the hospital."

"Right now let's not talk about that," I said with a wink of understanding. "Right now I am admitting people to the hospital, just like you. I have my Malben patients and you have your patients. Believe me, you will be seeing a lot of me from now on, so brace yourself."

"If I had known that, I would have refused the post," he said jokingly. "Come on, let's order some coffee to celebrate."

"Unfortunately, I can't now, duty is calling, I have a few things to take care of, but I'll see you at lunch."

"What time do you go to lunch?" he asked.

"I will give you a ring."

"I can't believe it," Amos said fervently. "In only five years, look at yourself, you have really come a long way. From the little girl I saw in Trofayach, to an executive in a large hospital. How have you done this in such a short time? Even then I knew you had a lot of energy, but it takes more than energy. You have done it, girl, and I am proud of you. You will have to tell me all about it in the most minute detail."

"Oh, Amos, don't make such a big deal out of it. Besides, I can always use some help. It will be good working with you."

I loved my work at Tel Hashomer. The beautiful environment, pretty green lawns, and colorful flower beds in constant bloom could cheer up even the grandest pessimist, like good old Dr. Eisen, who had become so steady in his ineffectiveness. His quiet, good-natured grumbling, mostly owing to the arrogance of Dr. Stahler, who boasted his medical degree but whose stupidity and lack of common sense were detrimental to the smooth operation of our office, could be overlooked.

The international makeup of our staff of social workers only added to the confusion. We had workers speaking as many languages as there were demanding patients. One social worker was from Austria, one from Greece, one from Bulgaria, and one from Rumania. Luckily two spoke English and two spoke French.

Having taken both languages at the Berlitz School of Languages, I was able to put them into practice. The social workers would make their reports in either French or English, and I would then translate them into Hebrew and hand them over to the typist. This aspect of my work introduced me to the patients and their intimate problems and got me even more involved in their lives. Many times my involvement caused me to stay late at the office waiting for a patient, or an evaluation of a patient with the chief of one or another medical department. Becoming a liaison between a patient, the patient's family, and a physician was as routine as squabbling with Amos to extricate another bed in the orthopedic department for my patient. Over a hasty lunch we would haggle for priority for a sick child in the children's ward, and in an office full of people, I would burst in demanding the operating room for my patient.

But there were rare moments when after a tiring day's work we would stay on the premises to have dinner at the dining room and go for a swim in the spacious pool. Relaxed, we would sit for hours talking. I would open my heart to Amos telling him about Yigael while he talked about his girlfriend, Ruchama, whom he left in Degania.

"I was called in to fill this post," he would explain. "I do not have to explain to you how important this work is. They need someone they can depend on. We are building this country, only now it has to be done here at the hospital just as well as on the soil of Degania. Ruchama did not want to understand this. She is a farmer, and nothing will recompense her for leaving the soil, the cultivation of the land. Only in life on the farm of Degania does she find satisfaction to her ideal. My calling brought me here, and I do not regret it."

"Don't you love her?" I asked him in surprise. "Doesn't that count for anything?"

"I am sure I will find someone to love again, and so will she, he said, laughing. I was surprised at the ease with which he spoke about love while I was constantly choked by tears when I spoke about Yigael.

On one cloudy rainy autumn day, it was almost noon when I finally arrived back in the office after attending a conference at Malben Tel Aviv. I was cold, wet, and disheveled. At my desk a young fellow sat waiting.

"He's been here since this morning," Bat-Sheva, my coworker, whispered to me. "I could not send him away."

Patiently the boy sat, his hands in his lap, his smooth black hair neatly combed, and even though his face had some pock marks, it seemed handsome.

"My name is Rachamim Naim," he answered to my question. *Rachamim* means mercy and *naim* means pleasant. "Which is your first name?" I asked, puzzled.

"Rachamim," he answered.

"So Naim is your family name," I intoned thinking, how appropriate, since he seemed to be very pleasant and relaxed in spite of all the hours of waiting, something very uncommon. Patients usually were very agitated, edgy, impatient, and complaining. "Rachamim," I thought, "may God have mercy upon you."

He was dressed very properly in a dressy shirt and long pants, with a tailored jacket, but his feet were bare.

"How did you get here?" I asked, with the pain clutching at my heart and surely very pronounced on my face.

"By bus," he answered, calmly, naturally. All I could see was Rachamim dragging himself up the long road that winds uphill from the gate to our office, on the wet, cold asphalt with his bare feet. Rachamim's feet could not be clad in shoes. Rachamim had been born with his feet upside down. His feet were bent backwards, with soles and heels on the inside. In Yemen, where he had been born, there was no help for him and he grew up a cripple, walking on his top side of his feet, if he could walk at all.

We placed Rachamim in the care of our best orthopedic surgeon. He was hospitalized many times. Each operation he underwent was to break his bones and turn his feet gradually until they were facing the proper way, like everybody else's.

When Amos picked me up late that afternoon, to give me a ride home in his car, I could not stop talking about Rachamim.

"I am getting jealous," Amos said, "for the amazingly moving sympathy and sensitivity you possess. Did anyone ever tell you that you have a heart of gold?"

"Unfortunately, no one," I answered sadly. "You see, even Yigael did not want this heart of gold; he preferred a sack of gold."

"He did not deserve you, I assure you," Amos said, carefully looking at me, his soft caressing eyes so comforting. I felt my anguish being soothed in the cozy confines of the warm car. The pounding rain rattling on the windows outside was like the hostile world populated with suffering people who crowded my mind. Saada with her missing nose, Rachamim and his crippled feet, little Shulamit with her bandaged eyes in the children's post-operative ward. I ached for them, I felt their pain, I bewailed their harsh fate.

I remembered my own sister Goldzia, who had been paralyzed by polio and had lived her life as a cripple. All the joy she missed! My heart was full of pain and full of love. The need I felt to share this overflowing sensation of goodness and joy of life filled me with gladness and sadness. Here in the presence of strong, steadfast Amos I felt comfortable, consoled. At that moment it did not matter that we were so different.

Amos was born and raised on a kibbutz, nurtured with the socialist ideology of the *biluyim* (pioneers), the doctrine of social equality, but only for members in the movement. There was no individuality, no conformation to rules and orders. Nationalism was based only on the land, opposing any inclusion of religion or religious observance. Tradition and history were minimized. The only aim was building a new race of Jew who is strong, free and bold.

I was a religious young girl, steeped in tradition, yearning for observance, warmth, and intimacy, striving to build a life full of love, friendship,
emotional values, and our ancient culture.

Amos felt my mood and asked, "would you like to ride around a bit
more, or would you rather go home?"

I was grateful for his understanding and invited him to Nachcia's for
some hot tea. For a long time we all lingered in conversation, in which we exhibited those differences, but it did not put a rift between us. My sweet sister
served us, smiling, happy to see me content.

Passover was a traditional time not only to celebrate our freedom from
bondage, but also to travel, to vacation, to see the wonders of our country.
It was 1950, the first time I was able to take a trip, a vacation in our normal-
izing life. Once our traditional seder was over, I joined my friends at the
Mizrachi organization for a trip. Since we could not afford much, many of
the boys and girls having to support themselves, we traveled by the cheapest
means. Onto a big truck we climbed, about thirty of us, dressed in comfortable khaki shirts, the boys in pants and girls in skirts, as befits traditional religious girls. Rumbling down the southern exit of the city, the truck rolled
through populated towns south of Tel Aviv. Soon we were crossing Rishon
Lezion and Rechovoth, the region where Ayanot was located.
I would have loved to stop in for a visit but would not dare disrupt the group
plan. Once we were out of the perimeter of densely populated towns, the
scenery changed completely. We were driving through arid land with hardly
a bedouin camp visible on the horizon. The open truck exposed us to the
merciless Mediterranean sun, from which we protected ourselves with elaborate headgear. Some wore hats, others the checkered black and white *kafiya*
usually worn by Arabs. There was no roof or covering of any sort over the
truck, only some ropes crisscrossed overhead, actually holding the sides of
the truck together.

Our mood was jubilant. We were all young and free and trying to be as
carefree as possible. On this, my first vacation, in the land of Israel, the company was terrific, and I loved it. Our joy was expressed in constant singing,
laughing, and joke telling. Soon we were in Beer Sheva, the ancient abode of
Abraham, our patriarch, described so richly in the Bible. After millennia we

The trip to the Negev Desert.

Jewish youth had come back to set foot on this desert settlement, which boasted some small, boxlike, white-washed houses. As in the days of our patriarch, there was a marketplace where the bedouin Arabs would come to barter their goats, sheep, and camel. Sprawled on the dusty ground next to their animals, the turban-clad men in their flowing robes smoked their *nargila*s (long, winding smoking pipes).

We, too, sat on the ground for our repast, producing from our backpacks matza sandwiches, hard-boiled eggs, fruits, and vegetables. Ascending the truck again, we traveled down a narrow desert road with clouds of dust rising all around us. The truck's shaking made us tumble from side to side, causing shrieks of laughter among the squealing girls. We came to a point where the road climbed steeply up a mountain, the engine huffing and puffing heavily. Changing gears, the driver pushed the shaking truck, while we prayed not to have to get out and push the truck up the mountain. Having made it up the hill we were overcome by the breathtaking scenery of the Hamachtesh Hakatan, a natural canyon distinctly showing the layers of the sunken earth. A vast wilderness of barren parched desert as far as the eye could see would maybe fill other people with a sense of helplessness and forsakeness. There we were, looking at this desolate, lonely wind-ravaged land ecstatically, eager to make this land, which was now ours, bloom. We did not know how. We had no immediate plans but we knew that just as only a short time ago making this land our country was a dream, so too would this land miraculously come back to life. We did not know when, but we knew the day would come when this too would be a flourishing garden.

We rolled downhill on the dirt path speeding toward Eilat, the southernmost tip of our new country. Dust-filled, wind-swept, tired, with badly aching bodies from the constant bumping on the wooden planked benches, we finally rumbled into Eilat, a flat desert clearing with a gravel sand beach. Seeking out the softer, sandy part of the beach, we established a camp, spreading our blankets. A wonderful refreshing dip in the cool waters of the Red Sea relaxed us, and the flapping waves lulled us to sleep.

In the morning we visited the only structure found in Eilat, a stone one-story house called the House of Williams, named for a English researcher who spent many years in solitary study of the area. After exploration of the sea with its marvelous coral reefs, exotic fish, and peaceful waters, we embarked on the trek back to civilization.

When the blazing sun hid behind the mountains, when long, dark shadows cooled the dry, choking air, the group leader began contemplating a stop for the night. Far in the distance a silhouette of a camp appeared in the gray dusk—two tents and a few clumped desert bushes. We were greeted by several young men wearing khaki overalls and *kova tembel* (khaki hats) shading their stubbly faces.

With a friendly "shalom," we were invited to spend the night. These were workers building the new road from the north toward Eilat, our dream being fulfilled. We built a fire, and out came our blankets and foodstuffs, while the boys went toward the clump of bushes to fetch some water from a nearby well. Referring to the bushes and the lonely, small palm tree that grew there as the oasis, they compared it to the descriptions in the Bible. This was the desert in which our forefathers wandered. Being a group of religious people, a lively discussion on the Bible, referring to different chapters and quoting commentaries, developed. Before long, everyone got into the customary hand-clapping that signaled the desire to make merry. Of course I was the one urged to sing and entertain. Around the fire we sat, on the dusty hard ground, a *finjan* (long-handled coffee pot) simmering on the crackling branches. Imitating a drunkard, holding a bottle in my hand I stood up and sang my popular "Drai Baal Agules" (The three coachmen), a funny Yiddish song. The laughter and enjoyment were a boost to the already high spirits of the trip. Lively clapping accompanied me in other songs, late into the star-studded night, until exhausted, we separated into small groups to set up sleeping quarters. The more adventurous people built tents from their blankets, others just bundled themselves in the blankets and their *kafiya*s to shield them from the desert dust and chill.

With the first rays of the rising sun, all began to stir. It was time to reload the truck and to part from the local fellows with hefty back slaps and sturdy hand shakes.

Soon we were rolling again on the desert road, leaving behind the scanty oasis and the majestic beauty of the desert. With quiet awe we discussed the grandeur and loftiness of this part of our country, which we had been privileged to visit. Truly we were pioneers of sorts, having been among the first visitors to this yet undeveloped part of the land.

Still dreaming about the wonderful vacation spent, I observed the stark difference between the desert and the rich foliage of the rows of cypress trees shading the road leading to Tel Hashomer. The fragrance of the scenery filled me with exuberance and a fresh interest and eagerness to work.

My first day at the office, however, was immediately overshadowed by problems. A young man born in Rumania, who had dark pomaded hair combed back Rudolf Valentino style and fiery, dark, smiling eyes, was waiting to be admitted to the tuberculosis quarantined ward. Willy was a singer by profession. Plagued by constant coughing, he sang only a monotonous chain of complaints, eager to get started with a healing process for his dreadful disease.

Busily arranging his admittance I was interrupted by a skinny small-framed Yemenite man with thin ear-locks and a scanty goatee. He sat in a corner of the office wringing his bony hands, his lips constantly moving in prayer. Every so often he would get up, shuffle over to my desk, and in his throaty, singsong Hebrew implore me for help.

His twelve-year-old son, Nachum, had died in the hospital the night before. He had to bury his son that day. Being religious, he was distressed at having to sit wasting time while his son's body lay there in the pathology department. The fear of having an autopsy performed on his son's body was causing him agonizing pain. He lived way up north near Afula and wanted to bury his son there so that he and his family could visit the grave often. Until then, all his pleas had been unanswered. The rules of the hospital stated that his son must be buried in Petach Tikvah, the closest cemetery to the hospital, to which the hospital belonged. His tears and sighs were ripping open my wounds.

Having lost my parents, three of my brothers, two of my sisters, my brother-in-law, and my two-year-old nephew in the Holocaust, I, too, was unable to visit the tomb of a dear one. I did not have a grave at all where I could lie down to unite with my departed, to cry my aching heart out. My sympathy was with the father, who had a legitimate claim.

I chose to fight the bureaucracy. I became invincible in my desire to help this fragile, miserable, unfortunate man to gain his small victory over the bureaucracy and attain his goal of burying his son where he wanted.

Amos, whose cooperation I sought, was adamant at my insistence. My disregard over procedure, rule, and policy amazed him. I got angry, I screamed, I implored, I begged, all to no avail.

At wit's end with frustration, I ordered a car from our car pool and presented myself in front of pathology. Dr. Livni, who knew me well, trusting that I was claiming the body for regular procedure, innocently handed me the death certificate. The wrapped body was then handed to me. I did not permit the father to take hold of the body for a specific reason: they would not have let us out of the gate. My heart pounding hard in my chest, I sat in the car, the father next to me, the stiff bundle in my lap. An eerie feeling possessed me, holding this stiff, dead child. I could not think of the consequence of my action, only of the relieved father, whose eyes expressed fear, whose lips kept moving in constant prayer. There was gratitude in his gaze, and I knew that I had acted rightfully.

With an artificially cheerful smile, I greeted the guard at the gate, engaging him in some small talk to distract him from the heap resting in my lap. Once out the gate, we sped at top speed north toward Afula to a *maabara* inhabited mostly by newcomers from Yemen. The grateful mourning father asked me if I could stay for the funeral service. I had to decline, explaining to him that there were other needy people whose problems were mine, too, who were waiting for my help. Far into the distance the wailing of the women rang in my ears, but my heart felt relieved.

I avoided Amos for several days, afraid the Nachum case would surface in our conversation. There were unfortunately enough problems overshadowing the case of the corpse.

I hitched a ride after work one day with Amos.

"I am going home to Degania this Saturday," he said. "Will you come?"

His question caught me by surprise for two reasons. First, why would he want me to come along when he was visiting his home, where his girl-friend was waiting for him? The other was that he knew I would not travel on Saturday.

"I am sorry, but I cannot," I said somewhat apologetically.

"Why?" he said curtly. "I've wanted you to visit Degania for a long time, and you always promised you would."

Not to introduce any romantic reason or suggest suspicion of jealousy, I avoided mention of Ruchama.

"I do not travel on the Sabbath," I said instead.

"Really," he exclaimed. "I cannot believe it. A progressive, intelligent girl like you confined to an ancient restrictive, choking lifestyle. Of all peo-ple, you, who suffered so much because of your religion, have not shed yet the burden of your old European rigor."

I was appalled with his insensitivity. "Maybe I should invite you to my house to show you the joy of observance of real Jewish life," I said with dis-may. "What do you know anyway about being a Jew?"

Amos was insulted. "How can we build a country and live as free people, when our people cannot detach themselves from the medieval tragic image? We have people in Mea Shearim (One hundred gates) in Jerusalem who do not travel on the Sabbath like you, and they also do not serve in the army. Is this the Jewish life that you envision? The always-suffering, always-persecuted Jew? The pale youngsters sitting in a suffocating room learning Torah? Who will till the land? Who will watch it? It wasn't served to us on a silver platter, you know."

"The Jews tried assimilation and the gentile world tried to let them as-similate. It did not work, it will not work," I said. "The crusaders by fire and blood wanted to convert us, Muhammad used his sword to convince us he was the righteous God. In Spain they burned us at the stake, while the czars and the cossacks made pogroms against the Jews. Still the Jews stuck to their belief. This is what kept us together as a people. In Germany the Jews assim-ilated, they believed they outwitted the Gentiles. They wanted us to assimi-late, fine, we assimilated. They exhibited more patriotism to the German fatherland than the Germans themselves just to gain equality. That scared Hitler and the Germans. They did not want Jewish Germans. They wanted

German Germans and Jewish Jews. The tragedy for the assimilated Jews was the worst you can imagine. They were the broken ones, the humiliated ones. We the Jewish Jews were the proud ones; we suffered for our Jewishness. Our religion is our backbone; with the religion we existed as a people for two thousand years without a land. Without religion, even with our land we will not endure. This has nothing to do with building a country. I am helping build the country; my brother, who is religious, sat at an outpost near Latrun with his whole *pluga* (platoon) who are all religious, just like all the others. Don't give me the excuse of the ultrareligious ones, they sit and study; so what, we need them too. They will preserve our heritage, our roots. Someone must do that, too; they are our continuation. Some sit and study medicine, some study aeronautics, or tactics, or politics, or strategies. We need all of them, that is how a country is built."

"You are beautiful when you become so passionate," he finally said. "I will not go home this Saturday. We will go whenever you will be ready."

"I do not want you to change your plan, just like you will not change your mind. I do not blame you, that is how you were brought up. Degania must be beautiful, I am sure I will visit there some day. I do have only praise for the work that was done there, but there are religious kibbutzim who have done the same."

The long road, shaded on both sides by beautiful, full-grown eucalyptus trees, never failed to put me in a relaxed mood. The special small bus just entered the cool stretch of shaded road, soothing my excitement.

"I cannot wait to see that girl." I said to Bat-Sheva my coworker who traveled on the bus with me every day to work.

"I can understand how you feel," she said, raising her eyes from the book she had been reading. "I know how I would feel knowing that there is someone there you are yearning to meet."

"Oh, Bat-Sheva, if you only knew what it is like. I keep thinking maybe it is someone very close to me, a new family member who will fill this tremendous void I have been living with."

The bus passed through the entrance gate, where we descended. With lively strides we walked toward our office.

"I hope she is not waiting for us outside the office, like that time when

Saada was," I said. "I would like to have some respite, some time to get myself together, to be ready. Time to look through the mail and sort things out before she appears."

"Do not forget, that time when Saada came you were at a staff meeting in Tel Aviv, therefore she waited. Today it is still early in the morning. No patient comes so early."

Bat-Sheva knew me well; she could feel my tension. All morning I kept glancing at the door to see if she had come. She did not come, so reluctantly I went to lunch.

"Why are you so nervous?" Amos asked. "You have hardly touched your food. Does this have to do with Yigael? Or is there someone new and exciting on the horizon?"

"Oh, stop it, Amos, your jealousy is driving you nuts. No, unfortunately, not Yigael and not anyone else. You are still my favorite. This is something very exciting, though, and very disappointing. This Monday in my mail, I had an admittance ticket for a new patient. Came from Central Office."

"What is so unusual about that? You always get the admittance tickets in advance for the patients you are to admit. Isn't that what you do here, find beds for the patients who will be arriving? What is the matter with this patient that he deserves so much of your attention?"

"It is very unusual. How would you feel if you had just received an admitting ticket for Amos Ben-Yaakov and you had to find him a bed?"

"You mean they made an error at Central and put your name on the admitting ticket?"

"No, Amos, there is no error. There is a patient by the name Helena Stapler, who is being sent for treatment in our hospital. Her name is identical to mine. I know nothing else about her yet, only that her name is also Helena Stapler. Curiosity eats me up. Who can she be? She must be family, but who? I was expecting her to arrive today. She did not show up."

"Come for a swim after work, it will relax you," Amos said in his relaxing, confident voice. "Worrying will not produce her. In due time you will find out who she is. If she does not show at all, Central Office can always track her down for you."

"You know me better than that, Amos, I cannot wait that long."

But wait I did. A whole week passed before anything happened. A man dressed in a tailored suit and sweating profusely presented himself in our office. He was of husky build. Trailing him was a small woman. She, too, was dressed in a European tailored suit. Her face was flushed with the heat of the day. In her arms she carried a baby. The baby was dressed in a pretty printed dress, her jet black hair hanging in curly locks like Shirley Temple's. Her beautiful dark eyes and small nose gave her the appearance of a doll. Her skin was unusually fair for a dark-haired child. In the corners of her red mouth danced a small smile. They sat down on the bench against the wall. I went over to take their papers. The father sprang up from his seat, his European manners visible. Returning to my desk I read: Helena Stapler, age two, born in Poland. My heart stood still for a second. I sprang back up from my seat and went over to them.

"Let me introduce myself," I said, my voice trembling. "My name is Helena Stapler. Is this your daughter?"

"Oh, my God," the man exclaimed turning to his wife.

"We are finally lucky. You will help us," he said with a positive hopefulness in his voice, turning to me. "Our child is sick. We need help, you will help us, won't you? How lucky, how lucky," he kept repeating.

My heart was breaking. Did these people think that I could make their daughter well, just because my name was also Helena Stapler, and I worked there?

"I will do whatever is in my power," I said, my eyes filling in spite of myself. I cannot let myself go like that, I reprimanded myself. These people were putting all their hope in me. What could I do for them to really help them? I thought hard.

"I will get her admitted, that is sure," I said, trying to calm them.

"That is a very good first step," the mother said with so much hope in her voice. That truly was help, for many patients were turned away and had to wait sometimes for weeks for admittance. The shortage of hospital beds was acute. She was admitted on that day.

A bright sun shone on her small face when I first saw her sitting on the little bench near the entrance door to the pavilion, housing our office.

"Are you waiting for me?" I asked opening the door to let her in.

"I am waiting for Mr. Malben," she said bashfully.

"Yes, this is Malben," I said smiling, used to hearing patients call us Mr. Malben. I never tried to explain that Malben was an organization with a lot of people working, not one person or person's name. They did not care who it was that helped them, as long as they were helped.

She was a shy girl of Yemenite descent, with big black eyes and curly black hair peeking out from beneath a kerchief. She pulled out the papers from her skirt pocket and handed them to me, her eyes cast downward. I saw the diagnosis, and my heart thudded in my chest. I should be used to this, I tried to tell myself, having been working here for so long. But she was so young, only sixteen. She walked silently beside me when I accompanied her to the tuberculosis pavilion. "Do you have any family member who will come to visit you?" I asked, trying to make her feel somewhat more relaxed.

"No," she answered plainly.

"Where did you stay till now?"

"With friends. I am divorced from my husband," she added trying to bury her gaze deeper into the sidewalk.

I was intrigued. I must find time to talk to this girl and find out more about her, I thought, while the head nurse was taking down all the particulars onto her chart.

"I have to leave now," I said turning to Yona, "but I will see you again, Yona Mizrachi."

A sad smile danced at the corners of her thin lips. For a moment she lifted her eyes to meet mine and said "thank you" in a quiet voice.

I was not much older than Yona myself, absorbed in life, friends, and fun. I had my share of hard life and suffering, and I wanted to find someone to love and be happy with. She must have family, this Yona girl. They are most probably still in Yemen. But divorced at the age of sixteen! When did she have time to marry and divorce? How cruel life is for girls. Here I thought what happened to me with Yigael was so terrible, having spent a year and a half dating him and then being on my own anyway. Now I saw it in a different light. Maybe it was for the best; at least I was not divorced.

It was encounters like this one with Yona Mizrachi that made me appreciate my situation, and I was grateful that I had not made any hasty decisions in my personal life. Poor Yona, she eventually poured out her heart to me. What an awful story she had to tell. She was one of six girls in her father's household. They were very poor in Aden Yemen. She did not even blame her father; he'd had no choice, she said, when he sold her to a rich man. She was only thirteen and a half when she was taken to the marriage canopy in her future husband's house.

She was alone in the house, and only a little over fourteen when her pains came. She did not know what to do to stop the pain. Twisting in convulsions on the floor of her kitchen, she cried, but no one heard her. Squeezing her small body into a virtual ball, she choked her child within her. When she was finally found unconscious and brought to the hospital, they did not ask her what happened. She had no power or will to live and made no effort to know what they were doing to her. She only cried and whimpered in pain.

When she returned home, she begged her father to take her back to his house, but he had no money to buy her back, so she had to stay with her husband. He was old and mean to her. She worked hard preparing his meals, but she lived in fear and anxiety. Luckily, she did not become pregnant again. Only when her husband brought her with him to Israel, on the Operation Magic Carpet flight, did she find out that she was damaged for life and would never have children again. In this progressive, enlightened land she learned that she was not obligated to stay with the mean old man who was her husband. She ran away and hid with some people from her home town who had known her family. Eventually her husband agreed to give her a divorce—she was a free woman. Poor sick Yona, she was finally happy. How relative happiness is.

I worked in Tel Hashomer for two years. Patients kept coming and going. I became involved in many of their lives because of my position in the hospital. But when the patients recuperated and left the hospital, our contact usually ended. We all were so busy starting new lives, there was very little room to make time and keep in touch. People scattered throughout the country, and even though our country was small, communication was quite difficult. In the end I stayed in contact only with the personal friends I made. Even from the many girls and boys with whom I arrived, there were few who kept close contact. But we always inquired about each other.

Chapter Seven ✍️

I hadn't seen Aliza, the cook I knew from the rabbi's house, for almost three years. I hardly recognized her when I ran into her at the number 4 bus station on Allenby Street.

"Aliza! How have you been? It's been such a long time." She made me skip the bus ride and dragged me with her. We sat on a bench at Rothschild Boulevard. She was excited and spoke without catching her breath. I sat transfixed, listening and felt two hot drops rolling down my cheeks. I did not dare turn my face away to wipe the tears, afraid to break the spell. She kept talking. She told me all about Niusia.

"It is my private miracle," Aliza said. "Niusia has come to Israel—she now lived here." I could not stop Aliza from repeating Niusia's story word for word.

"When Niusia was in grade school, she hardly had any friends. Her mother took her to school and back, and she would spend the rest of the day at the estate. Her best friends were the farm animals. She spend a lot of time watching the cows and goats being milked. She loved to observe the horses chew their cud and swish away the flies with their long tails. She loved riding to church on Sunday seated next to her mother in the clean, polished coach, her freshly starched dress tickling her legs, the horses smoothly brushed, backsides shining in the sun. She would kneel in church, close to her mother, listening to the whispered prayer echoing her own softly pronounced words.

"Politely she would curtsy and then push her white-gloved hand into her mother's, when the priest would bid them good-bye at the church door and ask the inevitable, 'and how is our little Annusia today?'

" 'Very well, thank you, Father,' her mother would answer and stop to chat for a moment. It was always a nice day, ending when her mother would tuck her in and kiss her good night.

"When she grew up, the coachman would drive her to high school in the city. She was making new friends and began looking at boys through different eyes.

"Somehow, it all changed. She would have liked to spend more time with friends after school, but her mother insisted she come straight home after school. She was allowed sometimes to invite a friend over but never to go to the friend's house. Her mother seemed to be more on edge, getting upset over trivia, raising her voice so often, checking up on her even if she was at the stable or the barn. She became close friends with Kazia, the housekeeper's daughter, which clearly displeased her mother.

" 'We are nobility, you know,' her mother would grumble. 'You cannot befriend just anyone. You must behave according to your class.'

"But Niusia did not care about status, she was lonely and wanted to be able to open up to someone. There were things that began bothering her. 'Why was Mother so nervous when she reached into the cabinet, scooped out an orange, and offered it to Kazia?' she wondered. 'Did it have anything to do with that afternoon when Mother entertained Mrs. Magdalena, and she asked if oranges grow in Poland? Why was Mother so embarrassed? It was a simple question.'

She remembered Kazia's mother, the housekeeper, grumbling something about having to burn the wooden crate from the oranges.

" 'Haven't you burned that case yet?' her mother screamed at Mrs. Genovefa. 'How long does this garbage have to sit around here?' Her mother never behaved that way, Mrs. Genovefa complained.

" 'Is Mommy sick?' Niusia had asked Mrs. Genovefa. Mrs. Genovefa just shook her head and raised her shoulders, leaving Niusia guessing. 'What if Mommy is very sick and does not want me to know?' Niusia wondered, turning and twisting in her bed at night. 'What if she dies?' She wanted to ask her mother but did not dare, Niusia said passionately.

"Eventually she got used to her mother's new attitude. After all, she was a big girl now. She began to see her mother's point. 'We were nobility and that status required that I behave accordingly,' Niusia told me.

"Deep in her heart of hearts, however, she had some doubts. After all, she knew she was not her mother's natural child. She knew her mother loved her and could not conceive living without her. Her mother had spoken to her about her natural parents, how they were killed in a bombardment. Tadeusz, her father, was her mother's brother. Her mother always told her how happy she was to raise her as her own—after all, Niusia was her brother's child.

"And so the years kept passing. Niusia enjoyed school and meeting new people. She knew it bothered her mother when she met Marek at the university.

"Her mother was a devout Catholic, and Niusia, too, was raised to be one. She became fearful when she realized that she was falling in love with Marek. She was excited, yet not sure mother would accept Marek. It bothered her because her mother always scrutinized her friends so severely.

"She told Marek that she was going to talk to her mother. 'I could not go on like that any longer; my grades were falling, and I could not think about anything else but our problem.'

"Marek told her that he loved her and could never love anyone else. He said that in his years at the university of Warsaw, he met many girls, but none was as delicate or had smiling brown eyes like hers. It was his last year in that school. He yearned to finish, to graduate, and then to take her with him. He did not want to lose her, he said, but seeing her distress, he asked if she wanted him to leave the school to solve the problem. He said he loved her and could not see her so distraught.

"She did not want Marek to leave the school. She was a big girl, and had to make up her own mind. 'I loved my mother.' Niusia insisted, but she understood that she couldn't always be near her. She felt her mother would survive without her. She wanted to build her own life with Marek. She loved him with all her heart and knew he loved her, too. They would have to face whatever awaited them together.

" 'It was late morning the day after Christmas,' Niusia told me, and her mother slept late. Christmas dinner was so beautiful, she felt like a little girl again when she was opening the gifts mother handed her from under the tree.

"She had promised Marek she would talk to her mother; she knew she had to do it. Softly she tiptoed to her mother's room, sat down on the edge of the bed. Whatever she had wanted to say suddenly disappeared from her mind. 'Mommy, I am so scared,' she burst in tears. The entire litany she rehearsed so many times just vanished. She curled up in mother's lap and sobbed.

" 'What is it, child, that troubles you so terribly?' her mother asked, stroking her head and lulling her in her embrace.

" 'I love him so, Mother, but I am so scared, I do not want to leave you,' Niusia sobbed.

" 'You don't have to leave me. Why would you have to leave me?' her mother asked, taking her face into her hands, turning it so she could look into her eyes. 'Tell me what is on your mind. Have I been bad to you? Haven't I given you all of the best we could afford? Haven't I treated you kindly and loved you with all my might?'

" 'Oh, Mommy!' Niusia sobbed, 'I know, I know, that is why it is so hard for me. You have been the best mother a girl could have. You always bought me the best and nicest clothes. I never wanted for anything, I was always so happy here. I love you, Mommy, but I love him, too. It breaks my heart, I will not live without him, but Mommy, he wants to take me with him.

" 'So what? You don't have to live here with us all your life. You have to go with your man. You can always come home whenever you wish. You will visit and bring your children when the time comes.'

" 'Oh, Mommy, it all sounds so beautiful, but it cannot be. There is something terrible I never told you about Marek.'

" 'You say you love him, so there cannot be anything terrible about him. He loves you, too, doesn't he?'

" 'Oh, yes, Mommy, we cannot live without each other. We shall both perish if we cannot be together.'

" 'Jesus! Niusia! What is it?' her mother said finally, with annoyance in her voice. 'What has he done? Has he committed a crime?'

" 'No, Mommy, he is gentle and honest and good hearted, and proud and steadfast, but Mommy, he is Jewish, and he wants me to go live with him in his Jewish land. What am I to do? Shall I lose him or shall I lose you?'

"Her mother sat up erect grabbed her shoulders spontaneously pulling her to herself. 'Don't say another word,' she commanded suddenly, 'just listen.'

" 'I was so scared,' Niusia said, 'I buried my face in Mother's shoulder, covered my face with my hands, and held my breath. I thought that something awful is going to happen. Mother's voice was hoarse and unnatural.'

" 'It is the will of God,' her mother said. 'We have lived with a terrible lie. I was very happy when I got you. You know that I adopted you and loved you from the very moment I set eyes on you. But it wasn't meant to be.' She forced Niusia's hands away, she took her face into her own hands and looked straight into her eyes as she spoke. 'You are my child but you are not the child of my late brother. You are a Jewish child given away by your Jewish mother who wanted to save your life. You were meant for Marek from the start. That is why I saved you, when I pulled you from the river. It is finally all falling into place. A tremendous burden is being lifted from my shoulders, a stone removed from my heart. Ever since your aunt wrote to me from Palestine, I lived in fear that God would punish me for my transgression. You are my child, I will always love you but you belong to them. Go, my child, go with your destined one.' "

I had chills running down my back but did not utter a word while Aliza continued telling me about the time when Niusia and Marek came to Israel, about their emotional meeting with Aliza and her son, Eli.

Aliza told me it was another miracle, my meeting her just now, for Niusia and Marek were getting married. She invited me to their wedding.

She spoke about Niusia and Marek hunting for jobs, about the scarcity of resources and money, but most of all she spoke about her happiness. About her dream come true, and about God's will being fulfilled. It felt so good to see her happy and to know that there are sometimes happy endings to sad stories. I, too, was convinced that God's will had been done. Otherwise why would I have had to work three years ago for the *Munkatcher* Rabbi when, after all, my father was a *Belzer Chasid* (follower of the Rabbi of Belz)?

My friend Suzie was getting married to Zvi.

"Who is that fellow who looks so much like your groom? Is he his brother?" I asked Suzie.

"That is Avremale, his cousin. In fact here he comes. Avremale! This is Ayala, I wanted you to meet her."

He was tall and handsome, and I liked his handshake. We danced a little, and later I noticed him glancing over toward me while he was talking to someone else. "Can I see you next Saturday night?" he asked, surprising me, just before we left.

It was intriguing. I was looking forward to the meeting. I dressed carefully and was at the corner of Balfour and Allenby Streets promptly at seven. He was leaning against the lighting pole, and immediately upon seeing me began walking toward me. Well built, handsome, swaying slightly in his gait, he reminded me of someone I knew. Was it Amos, was it Yigael, was it Salek?

His hair was curly, like Yigael's, but his was blond, shining like golden flax. His face was pale like Salek's, but his nose was not hooked, his shoulders broader. His body was large and strong like Amos's but the shade of his eyes was like the clouds on a summer day. He was not as shy as Salek, yet was timid and tactful. He was subtler than Yigael, free in conversation, more animated, mature. He was elegant and sensible with fine manners, something I missed in Amos. In a word, I liked Avremale better than all three of them.

"How did you like the wedding?" he asked as we started walking toward the seashore.

"Oh, it was lovely," I said with enthusiasm. I was in the mood to make a success of this date.

He asked to see me again when we parted in front of Nachcia's place. I consented without hesitation.

On the next date, Avremale waited again at the corner of Balfour Street on Saturday night, as appointed. Poised at the corner, he looked in my direction. His face shone with a smile when he beheld the sight of me. I noticed again how handsomely built he was. He was young and strong and slender, and walked with agility. He stepped next to me sending stolen glances toward me from the corner of his eye. I had the impression that he was assessing me.

"Where would you like to go?" he asked.

"Doesn't matter," I said, "let's just walk down to the seashore. We will find a place to sit in one of the cafés for sure. It is still early."

"See that fellow?" Avremale pointed. "He was in my *pluga.*"

"Why don't you call him over?" I said, "you must have a lot of things to talk about."

"This is neither the time nor the place," he stated firmly.

I had the feeling he didn't want to take a chance of being distracted from our date. How different he is, I thought, from a sabra.

A sabra would not blink an eye to have me stand and wait, while he would go over to the other side of the street to chat with his buddy. The European values in Avremale's behavior were appealing.

The atmosphere in Israel was of doing away with the diaspora Jew. The motto among the sabras was, we are creating a new Jew, whose back is straight and not bent, who is not intimidated. It was attractive to me to be like them, free, proud, boisterous. It was good when I was with sabras, to be what they called *chevremanit* (one of the crowd).

For my own life, however, I wanted someone who would have the same background, who would understand every nuance of the way of life we once had, the gentleness, the politeness, the consideration of the other's feeling. From what I could see, Avremale fit that ticket.

"When you are with a girl, she must be the center of your attention. If she is not, then the date is worthless, and you have no business leading her on," he said, smiling just so slightly.

Not knowing him well yet, I was disconcerted for a moment. Would he be jealous, possessive, domineering? If this were a friend of mine, I would have stopped. Maybe I had something to learn and correct in my behavior. Maybe he was right. He was so proper, treating me like a lady.

By the time we reached the seashore and sat down in a café, I knew that the boy had been with him in artillery, when they fought on the northern front near kibbutz Mishmar Hayarden. "He used to sing so beautifully," Avremale said, "on those long evenings when we were unable to get a pass to go out on the town. We would all gather around him and he would entertain us with Russian and Jewish songs."

I wasn't going to brag right at the beginning by telling Avremale that I, too, liked to entertain by singing. The time for that would come later, I felt.

We spoke about many things. We did not need to beat around the bush. Our needs were the same. We wanted to build a decent home for ourselves. We both had a lot of nothing, but we shared a mutual past, and that was satisfying. When we spoke about our past lives, our joy was contagious, and when the question was our future, we knew what we strove toward without words. A touch of his hand, the look in his eye told me what he felt and what he wanted. I knew he would love me, respect me, and believe in me. He filled my need to love someone with all my heart, to care for and be cared for by, to cherish and adore. I was content at last to have found what I had been searching for, for so long.

We could put all our energies into building a new life for ourselves, intertwined and blended with that of our siblings. Avremale had a brother and sister-in-law. Leon and Fela, like my siblings, struggled in a one-room apartment with shared kitchen facilities. We were equal in so much, with no need for pretending. The little we had we enjoyed equally, without envy, with mutual understanding and sharing. We felt a strong common bond in our past, our tradition.

In the months to come, I found out much about this bashful boy who

Avremale and me at our wedding.

was going to become my husband. His father had died just after he was born. He was a very young boy when his mother, a widow raising four children alone, died. It was his older sister, Tauba, who married very young, who took charge of the family business, a hotel and liquor store. Watched over by his siblings, with no real adult as an influence, he made a life for himself within the large extended family, strictly adhering to family traditions.

The war caught him at the age of nineteen, at a time when friends are more important than siblings. It was the aftermath of the war that brought him back again into the family setting.

With bright faces full of hope and desire, we looked for a real home for the two of us. We were getting married, and we were so happy.

On Rechov Nachmani a quiet side street off Rothschild Boulevard, we found our dream house, a ground floor, one-room apartment with a kitchen and bathroom all our own, no sharing, a real asset. Our joy knew no bounds. Avremale's face shone with pride and contentment. I could feel his proud heart expand in his chest with the satisfaction of a man of means, settling in his own apartment. His subdued smile expressed his happiness. I, the more temperamental, overtly crowed, bragging about my handsome fiancé and our miraculous find of an apartment.

We were so young and naïve, believing that our fate had finally changed. From two orphans would sprout a family, an established home in Israel. We both had saved up some of our hard-earned money for this particular use.

The only problem that arose with our dream house was that it was sold to us under false pretenses. The seller, the previous occupant of the apartment, a man of stature with a broad-shouldered frame and an uncombed long copper-colored beard, the symbol of religious distinction, was a butcher by trade. He possessed large, fleshy hands and a big protruding stomach. With satisfaction, he patted his long beard while we looked at the apartment. He projected himself as a father figure to us, the two poor, orphaned children, when we handed over to him the customary portion of the key money, sealing the deal. With his wife and two sons at his side, he spoke of the wonderful life he had spent in that apartment, which they had outgrown. A smirk danced at the corner of his full red mouth.

Winning our confidence, he quickly arranged with the landlady the signing of the lease. He turned over the landlord's portion of our money to the landlady, and she accepted us as her new tenants, giving the signed lease to us. Everything went smoothly, and we then set the date for our wedding. After the butcher and his family moved out, we rushed to clean the place and set it up for ourselves.

No sooner did the truck with the butcher's belongings leave than we heard banging on the wall. Frightened, we searched for the source of the knocking. The butcher had shown us a shallow closet in the entrance hall where he and his sons hung up their bloodied work clothes. With the clothes removed, the closet was revealed to be just the indentation of a concealed door. The knocking was heard distinctly from behind that door. We ran to the butcher, who explained that a crazy woman lived in the back of the house.

Upon his advice and instruction, we had a brick wall built in the corridor, eliminating the closet space, and the door. It was not, however, the loss of closet space that marred the joy of our first nest. The knocking had become louder and more forceful. Every time I entered the apartment, the banging would stop me in my tracks. Fear would paralyze my movements and instead of cleaning, I would just sit on the floor, hunched, my heart banging to the rhythm of the blows on the wall.

"How can we move in here?" I would ask Avremale, tears filling my eyes. Just days ago, we had been enthusiastically planning our bright future. We had spent all of our hard-earned money, leaving ourselves practically penniless.

Determined to get out before we got in, we postponed the wedding and began our campaign to get our money back. We were angry and sad. Only Avremale's steadfastness and expression of love held up my morale.

The butcher's two sons barred our way when we tried to talk to the father, who was now rude and hostile. Poised in his doorway, his legs spread, his fleshy hands on his hips he coarsely pronounced in his ranting, hoarse voice, "I have nothing to do with you. Go to the landlord." The two younger brutes told us not to bother their father or else they would take care of us.

The landlady, a high-society woman with manicured fingernails and done hair, would send her maid to the door of her Rothschild Boulevard apartment to chase us away. We were disturbing her beauty rest! We were totally distraught. The woman living on the other side of the house turned out to be a lonely older person who had suffered for years the injustice of the landlord and the butcher together. When she originally rented her room she received a lease entitling her to the use of the kitchen and the bathroom, and so did another tenant, who lived in the second room in this two-room apartment. When the butcher bought his one-bedroom, facility-sharing apartment, he immediately closed the door leading from the second room, in which the lady lived. He threatened to slash her throat if she as much as stepped over the threshold of her room into the rest of the apartment. She had lived in fear for years, using a chamber pot for her needs and cooking on a *ptiliya* in her room. In us she saw her golden opportunity to regain access to the kitchen and bathroom. She bought a big hacksaw and was determined to demolish the wall we had built.

Without any scruples, the landlord had issued us a lease for an apartment of room, kitchen, and bathroom, all private. We were devastated. Starting out a relationship, a marriage, under circumstances full of tension was very taxing. Only Avremale's solid attitude pulled us through this trying period in our new life.

We lost much of the money but did eventually get out before we got in. We found another apartment.

When finally our wedding took place, it was a lively affair humbly performed in the rabbi's study hall. We could not afford more than that, but it did not detract from our happiness at finally being able to get married.

Nachcia, Fela (my future sister-in-law), and many of our friends cooked and baked, preparing delicious dishes for the occasion. Male friends schlepped tables and chairs. Everybody enjoyed the party, dancing and eating and participating in mood, in joy, and in happiness at seeing this wonderful union of two lovers, who would build another home in Israel.

In our fourth-floor, one-bedroom apartment, in the heart of Tel Aviv near Dizengoff Square, we set up our residence. With some furniture gifts from Avremale's brother Leon and my sister and brother, a refrigerator purchased with a small down payment and monthly payments, some easy chairs, gifts from our coworkers, and a couple of cheap dishes, we set up house.

On Saturdays, we would join all of Avremale's cousins at his Uncle Meir and Aunt Rifka's house for the customary *cholent* tasting and family gathering. On the long summer evenings we would sit on our open porch, on top of the world on the fourth floor, relaxing after a day's work and getting more acquainted.

Avremale would talk about himself freely now. There were no more dates to go on and no more empty strolls down toward the beach to see and be seen on Allenby Street. We could see all the neon lights from our porch while we were comfortably sprawled on easy chairs. I would sit and listen to him talk and never have enough of it.

I continued working throughout my pregnancy, feeling fine and performing all my normal activities. My growing stomach did not discourage or deter me from any enjoyment. Dancing a lively hora or foxtrot must have shaken my fetus up badly but did not bother me in the least. "The kid will have a braid by the time it is born," my friends would caution me with their old wives tales that heartburn is an indication that the child's hair is growing, when I would complain about attacks of heartburn and nausea.

What did bother me was an attack of nausea on October 24, 1954, some time after midnight. This time it was different. Maybe it was time to wake my husband, I thought. The pains were coming every twenty minutes. When their frequency speeded up to eighteen minutes apart, I shook Avremale and asked him to summon a doctor.

"Don't be silly," he said, "you know it is not your time yet." I was in the seventh month of my pregnancy. He began snoring again, unable to keep awake, while I kept tossing and turning in bed, unable to fall asleep.

I lay in bed thinking, "Maybe he is right. I think about it too much. It cannot be, I am not due till 1955, next year. A sharp pain in my stomach disturbed my calculations. Jolted out of my reverie, I realized that it had been only thirteen minutes since my last contraction. "I am going to try and be a little more patient," I thought, after the pain passed.

I stared at the ceiling in the darkened room, and many visions passed through my mind. "What if this is really it? If I am going to have a baby and it is not the time yet. What will happen to me?" Fear crept into my mind when the next pain came. I thought about Yona, the patient I knew in Tel Hashomer, the Yemenite girl who strangled her baby inside her and was damaged for life and could never have children anymore. "I am not living in Yemen," I scolded myself. "I live in a progressive country. I have a loving husband right here next to me. There is no reason to take chances."

I shook Avremale more forcefully. He saw the panic in my eyes. He jumped out of bed the way he must have jumped out of his bunker in an attack. He grabbed his trousers the way he would have grabbed his gun and in seconds was at the door. Grabbing his bicycle, he pedaled hastily, excitedly, to the Magen David Adom station (named for the Red Star of David, the equivalent of Red Cross), on Balfour Street. It was about ten blocks away.

Meanwhile, I kept up my trips to the bathroom. My patience wore thin. I watched the clock very attentively, noticing that the pains were eight minutes apart.

Totally out of breath, Avremale stormed into the apartment with a doctor in tow. Seeing me hunched on all fours on the floor, cleaning up my most recent vomiting, the physician became unnerved. He sternly ordered me to lie down, severely instructing me not to get out of bed until the ambulance arrived.

"He must be kidding," I thought, glad to see him leave. "I cannot leave the apartment in this shape, in this mess. Who is going to clean up after me? There is nothing wrong with me, anyway. Why can't I get out of bed?" So while Avremale sped again on his bike back to Magen David station, equipped with a doctor's prescribed order for an ambulance, I finished cleaning up.

"Oh, you are back" the attendant said to Avremale. "So, you did find the Doctor on duty, like I told you, by the name displayed on the on duty sign, in the drugstore, right? Now you need an ambulance, right? Okay, go home, I will dispatch the ambulance as soon as he comes in from his previous run. Avremale shook with anger when he repeated the conversation word for word.

"I am not moving from here until I see an ambulance going with me to take my wife to the hospital," he declared stubbornly.

Meanwhile, in my isolated fourth-floor apartment, where no one would hear me even if I screamed, I finished packing my overnight bag, disregarding the doctor's instructions.

At last my husband appeared in the doorway, dragging the ambulance driver behind him.

"We will bring the stretcher up," the man declared after one look at me.

"You are not going to do anything of the sort," I said, insulted and extremely embarrassed.

"Can you make it down all these steps?" he asked.

Gingerly, I picked up my overnight bag, heading for the door ahead of the driver and Avremale.

"Careful," he managed to warn me.

Once inside the ambulance, I succumbed and lay down.

My pains were three minutes apart. I had surely underestimated the gravity of my situation, concerned more with the impression I would make on that stranger.

The time was past two in the morning, the road pretty empty. The driver, obviously more experienced than the two of us, only kept asking, "Are you all right? Do you think you can hold out just a little more? I really do not want to prove my skill and deliver your baby right here. We will be in the hospital in another five minutes."

Indeed he was not driving, he was flying on the empty road. The distance from our house in the heart of Tel Aviv to Petach Tikvah, where the Beilinson Hospital was located, could hardly be covered in half an hour during the day.

I had just had my third bout of pain at three-minutes intervals when we reached the emergency room. The driver stormed into the admittance office, reappearing back in seconds, a wheelchair in tow. I did not resist anymore when he brought the wheelchair close to the door of the vehicle.

Everything began spinning from that point on. I was prodded by a nurse to undress immediately. There was no time for the routine preparations, shaving, etc. When the excruciating pain stopped, I heard the nurse say to someone, "Give him vitamin K." I remembered a book I had read in which premature delivery was discussed and vitamin K mentioned. I could not remember exactly what the consequences were, but I knew that something was wrong.

I tore a pillow with my teeth while a student doctor practiced his sewing on my flesh, and afterwards I lay in bed exhausted, in pain, and crying. With no member of my family present, my thoughts became maudlin. In self-pity I thought, "No one needs me anymore, no one is interested enough to come and see me." I was worried about what would happen at the office, where no one knew what had happened to me and just not showing up for work would be interpreted as lack of responsibility.

Avremale, cognizant that there was no place for him to stay at the hospital in the middle of the night, was grateful that the driver, who was returning to Tel Aviv, offered to take him home. Even if he waited just a little bit, he pondered, there would be no possibility for him to get home.

In bed at home, he could not sleep and could not wait for the nearing dawn. When the first ray of sun hit the window, he ran down Dizengoff Street to find a public telephone. He called the hospital. No information was given so early in the morning.

His plan, so clear the night before, had become totally distorted. What were his options? He could not go to work. There was no use just sitting home. They would not let him into the hospital, at this early hour. He was flabbergasted. He could not decide what he should do next.

Following his instinct, he went to Aunt Rifka's house. There was always a warm welcome there for him. Having just learned what happened, Aunt Rifka prepared some breakfast and send him out to try to call again. Losing his *asimon* (telephone coin) twice, having the operator misdirect his call three times, he finally got through to information.

"Sendyk . . . yes, it's a boy. Visiting hours are from two to three in the afternoon."

Excited, he announced to Aunt Rifka, his heart beating fast, "Mazal

Tov, I have a boy! Chick chack, I took her to the hospital last night, and here I am a father of a boy."

"Mazal Tov, Mazal Tov," Aunt Rifka wiped a tear of joy from her eye.

Uncle Meir came back from services at the synagogue. With a gentle, forceful hug, he wished him "Mazal Tov."

The clatter of rolling carts brought me back to the reality of the hospital room. They were bringing the babies, a murmur floated through the hall. All the young mothers sat up in their beds, undoing the ties of their robes in preparation. A tense anticipation wafted through the room. The patient next to me set her feet down hastily, got up, and walked toward the door. There was anger in her gait.

"Where are you going? They are bringing the babies in," a young woman asked her. "I can't wait to see my baby. Aren't you anxious to see yours?"

"You came last night, didn't you?" my neighbor asked accusingly, and continued out the door. Another woman got into the conversation.

"Never ask such questions," she reprimanded the young mother. "That woman gave birth two nights ago to a premature baby. The baby had no chance. It weighed only a little more than a kilogram."

"Oh, how terrible it must be for her," the young mother said with sorrow. "How stupid of me to ask. It is just that I am so excited about my baby that I cannot keep it to myself. I really can't wait to see him. Here he comes!" she yelled out, seeing the nurse wheel the cart toward her bed.

"Oh, look at him isn't he perfect, isn't he beautiful? Look at his hands, these long fingers." She bubbled over with words of praise while the baby began to scream for his food.

She did not even notice me lying there turned toward the wall. I did not want to see her baby. I did not want to look at his beautiful hands and fingers. I wanted my own baby, but no one brought my baby in. No one bothered to say anything to me; all I had was my pain.

I wanted to get out of that bed and walk out, just like my neighbor had. It was the fear of the pain that prevented me from carrying out my rebelliousness. In the dark, with my head stuck under my pillow, I had time to think.

My thoughts were so sad and morose. "Oh, Mama," I cried, "where are you when I need you so much?" I remembered how Mama made me open all the drawers and doors of the kitchen cabinets, to make my oldest sister Blimcia's passage of the baby open, when she gave birth to her baby. It was on March 17, 1940. I will never forget that date, that event. Mama must have believed in these superstitions, but her presence was such a comfort in those trying times, when we all lived at my sister's house, when the Germans were upon us, when we did not know if the baby my sister bore had a chance for a good life, any life.

Now I had given birth to a baby in our free country, in the holy land of Israel, and I wanted my mother so much. "You would be so proud of me, Mama, your youngest child, your baby. Oh how I long for you, Mama, for your kind word, your soft caress."

"Nurse, nurse," I called out, turning defiantly toward the room. "Why aren't you bringing me my baby? Where is the head nurse, what is taking so long?"

"Do you think you are the only patient here? The head nurse has no time to come to you; she is busy at the front desk."

"I also work in a hospital," I said adamantly. "All I want to know is what is wrong with my baby."

"When the doctor makes his rounds, he will explain everything to you."

I began to worry. What was he going to explain to me?

"Your baby was born prematurely as you know," said the doctor when he came to make the rounds. There were two other white-coated men and the head nurse with him. The nurse, a short plump woman in her early forties, her stiff white cap sitting on her head somewhat askance, was writing in her note pad without even a glance at me.

"Your baby is in an incubator to keep him warm. He is being fed through a tube," the doctor continued. "Tomorrow you may get out of bed, and you will be able to see your baby."

Before I had a chance to comprehend fully what had been said, to react, the whole party was at the next bed.

"What is the name of the doctor?" I asked my neighbor, after they moved on.

"Dr. Baruch. He is the head of the department."

"I did not know. I came in the middle of the night."

"I thought you said you work in a hospital."

"Yes, but I do not work in *this* hospital."

"Then you have no problem. You probably know many doctors. You will find a way to contact Dr. Baruch. Me, I cannot wait to get out of here. They do not even look at me—I only waste a bed."

"Why?" I asked curiously, "what do you mean."

"My baby died; it only lived twenty-four hours. It was born prematurely, it had no chance. I think they did not care enough to save it. After all, I am only an *olah chadasha,* she said, beginning to cry. "You work in a hospital, you said. Do not wait, use your *protekcia* (influence), and they will save your baby. You are so young, you do not understand, but it is not always when you want them that you can have them."

She was a stranger, but I felt so close to her at that moment. I could open up my heart and tell her everything. I was so scared, so frustrated. In this critical moment I had no one to turn to.

"I do know a lot of doctors," I said, crying, "but I have to be out of here to be able to reach them. How will I ever get out of here, when I cannot even get out of bed, and even my husband does not show up?"

"This is your first baby," she looked at me with pity in her eyes.

"Yes, it is, and I was not ready for its coming. I did not expect it for another two months. My office did not expect me to just disappear either. I have so much work to do there."

"Never mind your office, they will find out soon enough, and as for your husband, he is probably downstairs waiting, but they do not let anybody up here before two o'clock, you should know that."

In my distress I had totally blocked out hospital rules, which indeed I knew so well. I wanted to tell her how worried I was for my baby, but it was not fair to complain to her. Her baby was dead. It was clear to me that my baby, too, was in danger. She saw my distress. She sat down at the edge of my bed. I could see her discomfort.

"Don't worry," she said in a motherly tone. I could see that she was not young. This was probably not her first child, I thought, but did not dare make any comments.

"The twenty-four hours will be over soon," I heard her saying, "and your baby will be out of danger. It is the first twenty-four hours that are critical. How much does he weigh anyway?"

"I don't know," I said desperately, and I began to cry again.

Avremale came at two, on the dot. He brought a beautiful bouquet of flowers. He was very excited.

"Do you know how terrible these nurses are? They would not let me in a second before two o'clock. And all the tokens I spent today trying to get through to you! I knew how worried you would be." He embraced me, and I clung to him. My body shook with sobs.

"Why are you crying like this? Aren't you happy to have a baby, a son? When I could not get to you this morning, I ran around telling everybody, Nachcia, Vrumek, Aunt Rifka. They all send you congratulations and will be here to see you soon."

This enthusiastic outpouring of happiness brought the reverse reaction in me. I cried even harder. Here I was, in pain and very worried about our baby, not sure that he would last another day.

"I don't know if it was such a good idea to tell everybody," I said through my tears.

"Why not?" he asked, stunned.

"Because we do not know yet if the baby will make it," I stuttered, more tears welling up in my eyes.

He turned white.

"Don't you want Nachcia to know? Don't you want her to come?"

"Oh yes" I choked out between sobs, "I certainly do want Nachcia, I wish she were here already."

"You are just very upset now," he tried to calm me. "Everything will be all right, you will see."

He did not know what to do next. He hated to see me upset and crying but did not know what to do to make me stop. He just sat there looking at me sadly.

"Please go find out what the baby's condition is," I implored.

"Where do you want me to go? Whom can I ask?"

He was uncomfortable moving around among all these women shuffling through the corridors, their robes open, exposing different parts of their body. Yet he could not ignore my state of mind. "I will ask to see the baby," he said a little hoarsely, and left the room.

It was only when Nachcia showed up that things began looking a bit less disastrous.

"Come, I will help you out of bed," she said, "and we will go see the baby."

Tenderly she took my arm. Every step of mine seemed to affect her; she was a mirror of my pain. With a tense face, she watched me shuffle through the corridor. We saw a small crowd at the window. "Look how he kicks his little feet," a woman was saying to her young companion. The baby, a dark crop of hair and dark, wrinkled skin, looked like a little old man struggling, kicking. We looked at the little bassinets lined up against the wall, craning our necks, trying to read the name tags. My heart pounded with fear. There was none that carried the name I was looking for. I felt weak, faint. I had no desire to wait there any longer for the nurse. My sister supported me, but it was not so much my legs that needed the support, it was my soul.

I thought about my neighbor who had lost her baby. I pitied her and felt sorry for myself. So many thoughts swam through my head. How would it be to come home empty-handed after this ordeal? How would all my friends greet me, expressing their regrets, talking softly, embarrassed?

"I want to go back to my bed," I said.

"Avremale," Nachcia commanded, "go ask where the baby is, and have them bring it to the window." There was no trace of doubt in her voice. My husband was already reaching for my arm. "Come, I will show you where the baby is," he said with satisfaction, leading me away from the window.

A smile broke through my tear-filled eyes. How lucky I was. My baby was alive, my husband at my side, my sister so happy. As if with a magic wand, all the worries were wiped away, like a dark cloud that passes and is gone, revealing a sunny sky that warms every part of the body, refreshing and replenishing. On the arms of my sister and husband, I approached the other window, through which we could see a tiny skull resting in a bassinet that looked much too big. There were slim little hands and even slimmer legs. The body was covered by a tube emanating a bluish light. The baby did not move at all, but we could see the little chest rising and falling with every heavy breath. I watched intently, but all I could see was his breath, like a short puff. Hypnotized, I stood there and searched, sometimes getting panicky when I could not see the chest rising. What if that was his last breath?

Nachcia could see my tension in the way I stood there transfixed, never taking off my eyes off that tiny figure in the incubator.

"He is going to be okay," Avremale said, trying to be cheerful, but I detected the uncertainty in his voice. The nurse began urging everyone to leave, and I returned to my bed. "Do not tell the news to the whole world yet," I said cautiously, when they were leaving.

"I am sorry," he said apologetically. "How could I have known?"

Wanting to cheer me up, Avremale told me what had happened when he went to Aunt Rifka's. When he told them the wonderful news, his cousin Aryeh, trying to compliment him, said, "Avremale, what a fantastic *baal melacha* (tradesman) you are. You know how to execute a job." Then, turning to his brother Zvika, whose wife, Suzi, had just given birth one month earlier to a little girl, he said, "Not like you—a girl, half the job."

"Half the job, but twice the pleasure. That is why you, my brother, have two girls," Zvika retorted.

Then Zvika turned to Avremale and asked, "What are you going to name the child?"

"Of course, Zvika knew that I would like to name the baby after my father," Avremale said. "It was my turn now to retaliate to Zvika's sharp tongue for all the stinging remarks I had to take from him while I lived in their house. 'Would you have any doubt?' I said to him with a pleasurable smile. " 'Certainly I am going to name him Zvika, after you. [Naming a child after a live person was not an option among Eastern European Orthodox Jews.] After all, I owe you one for having introduced me to my lovely wife, and you know I have no money of any consequence to pay you, so this is my reciprocation, my extension of honor to you. You will from now on always be, in my house, the revered and honored one.' "

Avremale did make me smile.

He hugged me tight, and I could see his predicament. He wanted to shout to the whole world, "Look at me, I have a son, a kaddish, an heir, a bearer of my name!"

After they left, the conversation turned to a young mother by the name of Zivia. She had just given birth to a healthy, sturdy boy. That did not mean Zivia had no problem. Zivia's father had passed away just two months earlier, and she was devastated. She wanted to name the baby after her father. She was anxious for the baby to carry that name, but how could she name him Zalman, her father's name? The kids in school would not stop pestering him by singing "Zalman yesh lo michnasayim arukot ad habirkayim" (Zalman has pants going down all the way to his knees), a shameful, insinuating song. They would call him names. Zalman was not a Hebrew name; it was a Jewish name, smacking of diaspora. "How can I do this to my son?" she pleaded. "He would never forgive me." It was a battle between her loyalty to her father and an obligation to her son. It was the past against the future. Zalman—the name reeked with the stench of *galut* (diaspora), of Jews bent and broken in body and spirit, of Jews covered in dark clothes and dark clouds of oppression, wearing the badge of shame, being pushed around, trampled. Her son was going to be a sabra, a young Israeli born free, in a free country. He was going to be proud, walk tall and erect. He was going to be bright and brave, and happy. He was going to be independent, he was going to be a leader. How could she ruin his life by naming him Zalman?

I was glad at least not to have that problem. We were going to name the baby Zvika. My husband wanted to name him after his father. I was glad to please him, to see him happy, and besides, my brother's name was Zvi also, so it would do for both of us.

I was sent home after four days, but the baby remained in the hospital. My distress was boundless. There was no telephone nearby. To use a public phone, I had to go down three flights of steps, walk three blocks, and find a unoccupied working one. I would have to stand in line at the post office to purchase telephone tokens. That accomplished, I had to be lucky. Most of the time either the nurse was too busy to talk to me, the operator would let me hang on till the token dropped in and then disconnected the phone, or there would be no one available to tell me anything.

"Why should you be a nervous wreck?" Avremale agreed that it would be best for me to return to work. At the office I had a telephone at my fingertips, a great convenience.

They were thrilled to have me back at the office. Ziporach, my replacement was ecstatic.

"Can you imagine what it would have been like to take over this job, which we planned to work together on, for two months, on such short notice, without you?"

But I could not concentrate on my work. The milk in my breasts was stinging in painful pressure. The soreness and stitches made sitting impossible. My biggest distress, however, was a gnawing bewilderment over the fate of my baby. I was not permitted to take in the extracted breast milk, even though everybody agreed it would be beneficial to the baby. My having to extract and destroy was tormenting. The baby was not gaining weight. To my horror he began losing weight, eventually coming down to 1.70 dekagrams, having lost one-eighth of his body weight.

I could not visit much, and when I eventually got in, what I saw frightened me. He was attached to a tube in his leg, to be fed intravenously since he could not absorb any food. The cautioning words of my hospital-bed neighbor kept gnawing at my insides with painful realism. "You said you worked in a hospital, you know many doctors."

I dreaded bothering Dr. Langer, with whom I worked. I remembered well how distasteful it was to ask for *protekcia* and be turned down; I had seen it happen in Tel-Hashomer. Just like all my colleagues, I had felt at the time that no one should get preferential treatment just because of friendship with a certain official or doctor. But this was the life of my baby, and I was not going to consider etiquette. What had to be done must be done.

Dr. Rappaport's brother was chief of internal medicine at Hadassah hospital in Jerusalem. Dr. Rappaport liked me very much. I called him. Would he ask his brother to find out the status of my baby?

Suddenly I was permitted to visit every day. The nurse even took the time to explain to me that the baby had an intestinal infection and therefore was fed intravenously. Everything possible was being done. It was such a final-sounding verdict. Everything possible was being done, but what did she mean to say? "If he lives he lives, and if not . . ."? He was her patient, but he was my baby, and I wanted him to live. Even if Dr. Langer did not want to get involved, even if he rejected me, I had to try. I had to make every effort, try every lead.

Dr. Langer seemed to sense my troubled mind. It was not my usual disposition. My head bent with sadness, my voice filled with choking tears and humility, I came to him asking for help.

"Ayala, why haven't you said anything all these days that you have been back? I am not going to call Dr. Baruch or anybody; we are going there right now. Come."

His hand lifted my chin. "Everything is going to be okay. I am going to attend to this baby now."

"But Dr. Langer," I protested, "we can not go there now. It is still before ten in the morning. They won't even let us in at this early hour."

"Come, come, come, and stop worrying so much." We marched straight to his car. It was still much before noon when we reached Beilinson Hospital.

I could not believe my eyes. Dr. Langer whispered something to the guard at the entrance, and we marched right through. Like a trooper I marched right behind him, stepping on tiptoe, fearful of disturbing the hospital routine, afraid someone might at any moment stop me and ask the usual: Where do you think you are going? No one barred my way.

The ordinary hospital routine seemed absolutely undisturbed. We went straight to pediatrics and faced the nurse at the front desk.

"Dr. Langer to see Dr. Baruch," Dr. Langer introduced himself.

"Second door on your right." How plain it was, how easy, how simple.

"Herr College" (colleague), Dr. Langer exclaimed, extending his hand in greeting.

"With whom do I have the pleasure of speaking?"

"Dr. Langer, and this is my secretary, Mrs. Ayala Sendyk."

My hand was cordially shaken too.

"It upsets me to see that my secretary is unable to perform her duties as usual in her very efficient manner, being very distressed with the condition of her baby, who is your patient. Can you update me on the state of this case."

"Sendyk . . . Sendyk . . . oh, yes, didn't Dr. Rappaport just call me from Jerusalem on this case? Mrs. Sendyk must be a very important asset in your organization."

"Yes, indeed, she is," Dr. Langer smiled amicably. "I would greatly appreciate your personal involvement."

"Oh, absolutely, Herr College." It was the turn of Dr. Baruch to be congenial. "The baby had some—" and he named some medical terminology and diagnosis. He gave me the impression he did not want me to understand. Inconspicuously, I moved toward the door, letting them discuss it openly. I was sure Dr. Langer would explain to me clearly.

I would have liked to slip quietly through the corridor to the baby ward, unnoticed, but did not dare. I was thinking about asking Dr. Baruch if we could see the baby, when I saw Dr. Langer shaking hands with his colleague. Dr. Baruch again extended his hand to me. We said our polite good-byes, and I followed Dr. Langer down the long corridor. He seemed tight-lipped, and I did not know how to approach him. Only when we were already in his car did he begin talking. Staring out the window, with not even the slightest glimpse toward me, he blurted out angrily, "Remind me to call him every day."

I was puzzled. Should I be happy now that Dr. Langer had taken such a vivid interest in my baby, or should I be alarmed with the seriousness of my baby's fate? I just sat there absorbed in my thoughts.

"Those idiots!" he blurted out again.

I became really intrigued. "What happened? Please tell me the truth."

"They will not let you bring in your mothers' milk, yet some incompetent night nurse fed this tiny baby some unrefrigerated, spoiled milk. This delinquent gave him stomach poisoning."

I could not overcome my ambiguity. It was shocking to find out that I could have lost my baby, and not because he was born prematurely, but owing to some negligent, careless, incompetent nurse. On the other hand, how lucky I was not to have adhered to proper etiquette, acceptable conduct. I was so glad to have followed my heart, to have asked Dr. Langer for his intervention. Dr. Rappaport's call had also made a difference.

I went back to work. I waited impatiently every day for Dr. Langer's discussion with Dr. Baruch and for the progress report. With nerve-wracking acuteness I followed the delicate balance of the baby's weight. I prayed for the baby to gain back his lost dekagrams, since only when he had regained his birth weight would they consider sending him home. But his weight kept going up and down like a yo-yo, and our nerves were being stretched to the point of snapping. Three times we were told he had reached the acceptable weight required for his release; Each time by the time we came to pick him up he lost a few dekagrams, and we would be sent home empty-handed.

The tension, the apprehension, the excitement, were very taxing. The soaring and dropping spirits took a toll on both of us. On the fourth trip, with hope at the lowest ebb, with shoulders slumped and hearts downcast, we sat and waited for the nurse to come out with the verdict.

The door opened and through it came the nurse, baby in hand. My heart skipped a beat. Finally, we were taking our baby home. I squeezed Avremale's hand. The nurse put the baby on a table, unwrapped his diaper, and undid his shirt. There in front of us was a tiny creature not even close to meeting the expectations of new parents. Babies were sweet and cuddly, plump and soft; this baby was a tiny skeleton. His hands were like twigs, his legs like matches. His body from below his chin to his ankles was red, like a raw piece of meat, with open wounds around his thighs, crotch, and stomach. I looked at my husband and back at the nurse. My fear of touching this tiny soul was alarming. The dread of hurting him by my touch was devastating. I wanted to run away, leave this little bundle of pain, and flee.

"Take him, here he is", the nurse was saying.

"How am I to care for him? What am I to do?" I asked, totally distraught.

"Take him to your pediatrician," she said with calm indifference.

Not expecting much in this fourth try, I had not even brought a shirt with me. Delicately, I put the baby onto the blanket, loosely covering him, afraid to hurt him. We did not take the bus home. We brought our baby home in a taxi.

A new world opened to me. Gone was the world of office, of girl talk with my coworkers, of schedules and appointments, of patients, forms, and paperwork. Gone was the freedom of going out every Tuesday with friends to sit and talk, play games and sip cool drinks. Gone was the world of freedom and time on your hands, of going and coming as you please, whenever or wherever your legs took you. There was a new routine, a new order to our lives, dominated by this tiny creature in the crib. There were hours of mixing formulas, blending the *Eledon* powder with the water until it would meld into a fine, smooth liquid. There was washing and boiling bottles and diapers. There were trips to the drugstore, searches for *protekcia* to acquire an extra bottle. Bottles were rationed and very hard to come by. With a baby that needed to eat every two hours and bottles at a premium, life was not easy. There was never any more than one hour of sleep for me. There were salves and ointments to be applied, baths to be given more than the usual. There were full cotton wraps to keep the tiny body warm in the chilly winter air in the unheated apartment. There was fatigue and exhaustion and weariness of body and spirit. But there was also satisfaction and relief when the red, rough, painful, sore skin would show signs of healing, when it became pink and sweet smelling. There was comfort and succor when he drank the bottle to the end, and when he splashed his tiny fists in the bath. There was praise from neighbors and family and even the pediatrician. That experienced, well-established doctor said to me once, "I have been practicing pediatrics for thirty-five years but I've never seen a baby like this before. You have done a miraculous job saving this child."

Indeed, when I had brought my child home he was a neglected, diseased child. Now there was a new life filled with happiness, blissfulness, and fascination. The bond between my husband and me was cemented with the product of our love. There was no need for nights out with friends. Avremale would rush home to behold the smile of his offspring, to cuddle his son in his arms. Enjoyment was a walk on Saturday afternoon to the park to have the

My son, Zvika, and me.

baby breathe the fresh pure air and absorb the weak afternoon sun rays struggling through the treetops into his shaded baby carriage. There was the thrill of watching him raise his head and turn over, and all the other miraculous things a baby does, like sitting up, smiling, playing. At the age of three months his *Brith Mila* (circumcision) was performed and he was named Zvi in Israel.

Chapter Eight ⌒⌒⌒

I met Gutka in the Mizrachi organization. She pushed up close to me when I sang, applauded with vigor, and shouted loudly for more. She clung to me when I seemed receptive. She lived in *tzafon* Tel Aviv (the northern part of town) and we would walk home together after a meeting.

I liked her from the beginning, and our friendship developed over time into the same relationship I had with the other girls of our group, deep caring and understanding. Gutka was a warm, cleaving girl. She had no one in the whole wide world, and was happy to get close to someone she could trust. Gutka had survived Auschwitz. We seldom spoke about Auschwitz; among survivors there was no need for words to know the feeling. When Gutka's sparkling blue eyes would fill with tears, I would know what she was thinking about. Gutka had told me about her little sister, Rifkale.

"They tore her little hand out of mine, at the selection in Auschwitz," she would say, tears choking her, unable to say any more. But I could feel the wrenching of her heart, when her pretty, milky-white face would get red with the blood rushing to her head. I could see the fear of the cruel Nazi still gripping her, the enormous ache, each time she sighed and mentioned Rifkale. Sometimes she would talk about the terrible guilt that tortured her.

"Why couldn't I hold on tighter to her hand? Why did I let them tear her away? I should have struggled. I should have gone with her. I should not have let her go. She was so young, so small, so forlorn. She looked at me with a question in her eyes. 'How can you let me go without you?' She was so scared."

Gutka would still clench her hands when talking about it. She was like someone holding onto the hand of a dear one who is hanging over a cliff, making an inhuman effort, straining muscles to their utmost capacity, feeling that hand slip slowly, inch by inch. Suddenly that hand slips out, and she is gone. With that hand goes the person she loves so, her little sister, Rifkale. She plunges into the abyss, and Gutka remains standing above, her hand still clenched. Always will that moment come back to her, with her regret: "If only I had a tiny bit more strength; if I just clenched my hand harder over hers."

This was the scar on Gutka's heart, her little sister, Rifkale. Even though she had lost all her family—her mother, her father, her brother Moishele, and her kid brother, Avremale—it was Rifkale she could not get out of her mind.

The scar on her own forehead, a deep ugly cut received from the German whip, which she covered with a lock of her pretty blond hair, seemed nullified and unperturbed in the shadow of her emotional scar.

Gutka lived as a boarder in Mrs. P's apartment. An older widow reluctant to become a burden to her own children, Mrs. P was happy to have Gutka there. She was happy to have someone to keep her company, especially on those long sleepless winter nights when she would walk around her apartment. It was so comforting and soothing to have someone there. Gutka was an immaculate girl, a wonderful companion. She was an accomplished cook and housekeeper, using the skills she had learned in those wretched times in the Lodz Ghetto, after her mother died, leaving her, at age twelve, in charge of her father and his household.

Mrs. P was extremely happy with Gutka, but Gutka was lonely for company of her own. Like all of us *olim chadashim,* she was ambitious. She, too, wanted to set up her own household, find a man to love, and rebuild her shattered life. This determination, this desire for normal family life, was the thread running through the circle of survivors. Each one of us, as lonely as we were, would seek out the company of the others for the understanding and strength we drew from one another.

Gutka was in her early twenties, just like myself, a pretty, sincere, bright girl. In spite of having lost all of her family, she adhered ardently to the Jewish faith, following her family tradition, walking in the footsteps of her mother and father. Our mutual feeling that our parents deserved to be proud of our behavior, and that this behavior was conditional on religious observance, was what made us such close friends.

I became very attached to Gutka, and when I met Avremale and married, I felt Gutka's apprehension. She wondered if I would remain the trustworthy, close friend I had been, or if I, like other girls, would become so absorbed in my marriage that there would be no room for my friendship with her. Somehow I felt more comfortable with Gutka than with any other friend, and I was not ready to give her up for anyone. There was room enough in my heart and my schedule for her. Even when our son was born, our contact did not diminish. And even with my busy schedule, I still made time for us to sit and talk.

We would talk about the fellows she went out with, about the future she was dreaming about. I would hear her talk about her mother's demise in the Lodz ghetto. From her I learned all about Lodz ghetto, about the *Shpere* (the curfew the Germans imposed for a whole week of deportations), when they had to hide out at the cemetery, subsisting on crumbs. I got to know her brother Moishele, the *iluyi* (genius) in the study of Judaism at the age of seventeen. I knew her baby brother, Avremale, whom she hid under the bed in a raid, and who was dragged out from underneath it by the cruel Germans. "I could not save him," Gutka cried.

Gutka was not envious of my having a brother and sister, and yet she was keen to stick with us, to experience family life, which she so eagerly searched for and missed.

When Gutka finally met Maurice, also a survivor, who had come from America with the intention of finding a girl to marry, she knew he was the one. Maurice was handsome, warm, and affectionate. His blond hair and fair complexion, his straight, tall posture, reminded her of her brother Moishele. Gutka fell deeply in love. She shone like a star. One could mistakenly believe that her scars were healing by the magic touch of Maurice. She brought Maurice to our house as soon as she felt comfortable enough to introduce him to our family. We liked Maurice right from the start. He was personable, pleasant, smart, and thrilled with his find.

I was pleased that my friend had found happiness. What I was not happy about was that Gutka had to follow her destined one and leave for America. I knew I would miss her awfully, but I was not jealous, either; on the contrary, her happiness was my joy. I was fervently hoping that she would build a happy life for herself and was convinced that her happiness would reflect back to me. I knew that we would be friends forever.

Maurice left Gutka in our custody while her papers were being processed. She was extremely scared of beginning life again in a strange land where she knew no one. It was not the language barrier that occupied her mind. Gutka had been taken to England upon her liberation from the concentration camp. She had lived there for a while and managed to learn the language well. She was just thoroughly apprehensive about what awaited her in the new country.

We spent a lot of time together after Maurice left, and she kept worrying. How would she be able to cope there all by herself, without me, her only true friend, who always listened to her, who accepted her unconditionally?

All my prodding and colorful descriptions of the glamorous life in the most adventurous, exciting, rich, and interesting country in the world did not bring her much comfort. Only my promise to come to America would help soothe her. She took my fantasy seriously and procured an application from the American consulate for us to fill out. Once the application was in our hands, she did not relinquish her pressure until we filled it out. All she wanted was to take it back to the consulate herself, to be sure that we were not making empty promises.

More at ease after she filed our application, she talked about our living close to each other again, how we would always be friends, how we would raise our children to be friends, too. Inspired by her cheer and enthusiasm, I became excited about an easy life of luxuries and splendor in the fantastic land of America. We shared a happy time, a delightful indulgence, when we went shopping together for her dowry. Sparse as it was, consisting only of two decent dresses and a couple of other items, every article acquired was a valuable possession.

Our precious time spent together was somewhat overshadowed by the slowly creeping in consciousness of our impending separation. As she was not going out on dates anymore, she had all the time in the world to spend with us. Even after Avremale, tired after a day's work, would say good night and retire to the bedroom, we would sit at the small table in our small foyer/dining room, talking late into the night. Like two school girls, we would plan what it would be like when we met again in America.

"You have not even left yet," I would say. "Why are you getting all worked up?"

"Because I know how I will miss you."

That day in February 1956 was an otherwise uneventful day. Avremale was home from work having dinner and Zvika was playing on the floor next to his father's feet when Gutka came to say good-bye. We cried, we hugged, we kissed, we embraced, we promised. We looked long and deep into each other's eyes, mutely swearing to keep that fierce bond between us alive. That

Gutka and Maurice.

closeness, that fire would not become extinguished, we knew, by the distance between us. We were very determined to keep that contact alive. We knew there would be long letters, but we were determined to meet again.

There was a sudden emptiness when the door closed behind her. For many a day I stood at the window looking at the falling rain, thinking of Gutka. The evenings became longer, and I sat on the couch in the living room, my hands mechanically knitting little sweaters for Zvika. He had just started walking, cruising in front of the sofa, while I sat bundled up, a blanket on my knees to shield me from the cold that penetrated the unheated apartment.

I wish a letter would come, already. She must be busy setting up an apartment. I hoped they have a nice heated one. It was the end of summer 1956, and the political situation in Israel was not very encouraging.

It was rather late. We had just come home from our usual Tuesday evening out with our friends. Hanale, the baby sitter, had gone home. We were just about falling asleep when the knock on the door came. Avremale went to open the door.

"We were expecting this call," he said to the caller. "We were just talking about it this evening. Menachem, one of our friends, was called just yesterday. We were aware that it would come to us, too; we just did not know when."

In a way it was a relief; the waiting was nerve-wracking. The *fedayeen* had been active, tearing our southern communities to pieces, attacking and destroying our property, killing or maiming our people. It was time to react, to teach them a lesson. Jewish blood had been spilled for too long. It could not go on like that; the Arabs understood only one language, the language of force. An eye for an eye, a tooth for a tooth, blood for blood. They must be hit tenfold or there would be no peace.

Leaving me with a little baby and going off to fight was not glamorous, enticing, or rewarding but we both knew it had to be done. Avremale needed to protect his most precious property, his wife and child, so it was my determination to be brave in the face of danger. We had become so used to danger, we had learned to control our feelings, to keep in check, not let it overcome us. This land was our home whether we lived in the city or at the southern border, which now needed action, protection. There was no doubt in our minds that military retaliation must be carried out to the best of our ability. We were positive about its success. Our confidence in the ability of our forces to defend our people was unquestioning.

Avremale dressed quickly. He was silent, subdued. After all, he knew where he was going. He embraced me and held me tight for a short while. We both knew he had to go. It was a hug filled with stress and pain. I tried not to think about it as I looked into his eyes, trying to retain the picture of his face. "Be careful," I said. There was a faint smile at the corners of his mouth when he gave me a quick kiss and left. I stood rooted to the spot. I did not know where he was going or when he would be coming back. I was a young woman with a baby in my arms alone, with my husband just gone to fight the enemy, an enemy coveting our destruction, craving our land, this part of the earth that had opened its arms to accept us when we were searching for a place to live upon our liberation. This strip of soil was bequeathed to us by our ancestors, promised to us by God himself. It was the foothold to which every human being is entitled.

So why was I afraid, left here alone on the fourth floor walk up with my baby? All the years of suffering would suddenly come back to haunt me in such times of crisis. I had to be brave, I would reprimand myself. My husband was brave, all the citizens of this country were brave, and so must I be.

From previous battles he fought in, I knew that he would walk up quiet, almost deserted King George Street toward the Mugrabi Theater, where the waiting trucks would take him and his buddies to the former British army camp in Sarafand. "Here comes *jinji*" (red head), his friend Zigi would announce, saying, "did you think we would leave you behind? Is that why you came late?"

Swerving like a maniac on the empty roads, the driver would push hard on the gas pedal, and they would make it to Sarafand in twenty minutes. There they would line up to receive their personal equipment, take possession of the cannon, and move right out.

Half the night they would spend digging, setting up their cannon in a field behind a slope. The lieutenant was a typical Israeli commander, shoveling the hard, dusty earth, setting an example, always first, always hardest working, always encouraging.

There were no commands being shouted, no salutes, no standing at attention, no shoe polishing, in Zva Haganah Leisrael (Israel Defense Forces). The commander was a buddy, a friend, a man caring for his men, a man carrying the responsibility with awe and respect, with dedication and devotion.

When they finished digging in, they would sit around waiting for the order to come—the kibbutzniks, the refugees who hardly spoke Hebrew, the trained soldiers who had served in the British army, the experienced partisans who fought in the deep forests against the Germans, and the decorated commanders who fought in the Russian army reaching all the way to Berlin.

Avremale would tell me stories about some of the soldiers in his unit, boys who cried with fear when the cannon blasted and courageous men eager to silence the enemy who was attacking their homes, killing their wives and children.

Then the commander would search the horizon and spot the scout who would bring the order, and they would synchronize their watches. At the precise hour, they would begin loading the shells, covering their ears to soften the blast and counting, one for mother, two for father, three for Shmulik, four for Rivka, five for Shula, six for Moti, seven for Eli, pouring out their

Avremale (*left*) with his army buddies during the war, 1948.

anger like little children wanting to punch the bully in the nose. Their mission completed they would rush home to their families.

Avremale came back tired and dirty. I lingered in his embrace squeezing Zvika between us. "We mopped up," he said, "but who knows for how long the quiet will last?" He had new stories to tell about this battle.

Saturday afternoon, as usual, we walked down Dizengoff Street, pushing the baby carriage. The sidewalk cafés were full again, and strollers held hands and licked ice cream. At Dizengoff Square, fathers followed their toddlers around the benches or carried them piggyback. The little ones squirmed with excitement, their mothers sitting on the benches gossiping.

"Your husband is not back yet?" a young woman asked her neighbor. "How good it is to have him home," I thought. "Thank you, God of Abraham, Yitzchak, and Yakov, for saving my Avremale."

In our old home in Poland, in my own family, my sister Nachcia was the most religious one. In a household where tradition and religious observance was strictly adhered to, Nachcia was what we in Yiddish would call *poypstlecher vie der poipst* (popier than the pope). The sleeves on her dress always reached past the elbow, exposing not even the flesh of her arms, so modest was she in her appearance. At Passover, on the last two days, when even Papa would allow it, Nachcia would not eat *gebrocked,* meaning, she would not soak her matza or eat *kneidlach* (matzo balls). In the very strict observance of the laws of *kashruth* (keeping kosher), it made the matzo leavened bread. A fellow who would be a prospective suitor for Nachchia would have to wear a beard and side curls and be very learned in *Torah.*

Having lived through the Holocaust changed many lifestyles, but not so my family, not at all my sister Nachcia. I, too, continued living in the old traditional lifestyle I knew so well. In my behavior and conduct, I always lived up to Papa's and Mama's standards. They were always present in my mind, and I would never do anything improper, indecent. My brother Vrumek conducted his life the same way, adhering to our family tradition in observance of religion.

Nachcia was still the righteous person she had always been. She lived to do good, to help, to care. The means she had at her disposal were minimal. With a husband who was an invalid of the War of Independence, and a very meager income, she worked very hard to make a nice home for her family. Her family did not, however, take precedence when someone in need asked for help. She was kind and generous, and her house was always a haven for guests. My friends, her friends, Vrumek's friends, all found an open door, a warm welcome, a cool drink, a shower.

When the time came when her one-room apartment became absolutely too small for her family of four, they moved to Bnei Braque. There she felt very much at home. Much of her activity was concentrated in the synagogue and the people of her neighborhood.

The relationship we had enjoyed as sisters began to suffer, not emotionally but physically. Not a day had passed until then that we had not seen each other. With no phones for either of us, and only the sporadic public transportation at our disposal, the contact began to diminish. Nachcia had two children and I, too, had a child, making my time not my own.

Sometimes when Avremale was home at night and all the chores done, I would summon the last of my energy to travel on three buses to visit Nachcia and her family in Bnei Braque.

Until late we would sit and talk, watching the clock, being careful not to let my stay extend past the last bus. It would be quiet in the dark streets of Bnei Braque when Nachcia walked me to the bus stop. Rabbi Akiva Street, the main street of the town, with its quaint little stores of children's wear, groceries, and vegetable stands, full of shoppers during the day, was quiet, dark, and abandoned. It was past the hour when mothers would sent young children to purchase that extra ingredient needed to finish supper, long past the morning hour when women in house dresses ran out for milk and bread to feed hungry babies. The residents of the town were asleep, the streets deserted and empty. Only here and there could some lone footsteps be heard. A rabbi, a scholar, a student hurrying from his yeshiva in his long black coat and wide-rimmed black hat reminded us so much of our home town of Chrzanow, where similar *chasidim* (devotees) engaged in the same manner of Torah study and walked the same path of late-night study hours, where women did not wait up for their student husbands, but fell asleep exhausted from the day's chores and burdens.

Where were they all, the pious husbands, the modest, pure wives? The Holocaust has swallowed them, despite their chaste, decent, holy natures and lifestyles. There had been no allowance made for their purity. Together with the assimilated, the atheists, the indecent, the simple, they died as Jews.

There in Bnei Braque, Nachcia felt at home among the new generation of extremely orthodox people who cleaved to our Torah and its teachings, to our rich and precious tradition, to our tragic history. There in the cradle of our birth, our homeland, where no one would disturb them in the trend of their thought, that silver thread wound through generations. There I saw my sister thrive, living the life of a matronly, pious, righteous woman, happy to do charity work. A sick woman in need of medication, a new mother just home from the hospital with her newborn baby, a young scholar away from home—they all were on her mind. Just like Mama used to prepare her little pots of food for her needy, so did Nachcia continue the tradition of helping the less fortunate.

Hard were our partings at the bus stop, for I longed to be near her; I missed her warm, soft, motherly touch, her wise advice, her constant caring. Yet I had my own life to live, my own husband, my own son to return to. I would kiss her good night, board the bus, and head home to my own nest.

Just as the country struggled through hard times so did we as individuals attempt to maneuver the loads upon our shoulders, scrupulously adhering to our traditional lifestyle, never desecrating the Sabbath. Unable to share the Sabbath with Nachcia, we spent it mostly with Vrumek. Saturday afternoon, rested and refreshed, we would stroll down the lively Dizengoff Street of Tel Aviv with its fancy shop windows, and multitude of cafés, to Keren

Kayemeth Boulevard, where Vrumek lived with his lovely wife, Esther and his little Tovale, on the ground floor in a one-bedroom apartment, sharing the kitchen and facilities with another family. Very centrally located, his house became the center and meeting place for our friends.

Full of energy, good humor, and sociability, Vrumek loved to entertain guests. He would put up extra folding chairs on his little porch and serve cold drinks and sweets. When it became very crowded, people standing with no place to sit, Vrumek would jokingly say: "Wait a minute, I am just going to run across the street to my neighbor Duvid'l to borrow some chairs." The neighbor he meant was no other than the most famous Duvid'l, David Ben Gurion, the prime minister. There on the tiny terrace at Vrumek's, we would discuss former battles and future plans, politics and party adherence, border incursions and El Fatah (a terrorist band) infiltrations, tactics and military strategies and crises.

"Well," Vrumek would say, "we are influenced by our neighbors. Paula and Duvid'l discuss politics with their friends in their kitchen across the street, so we may discuss the same here on our porch."

"I bet you if they knew what was going on here, they would join us," someone remarked.

Vrumek never tired of socializing. He could outdo Esther in preparing, serving, and entertaining. He was a hard worker, getting up daily long before the sun made its appearance to run his tricycle down the empty city streets before the hustle and bustle began. Of his own making and construction, the three-wheeler, with a big wooden crate attached to it, served as his business location on wheels. Severely independent, ambitious, and enterprising, he did not want to work for anyone else. Always striving to fulfill his potential as a businessman, a trait he inherited from our father, he began by selling bagels to the stores. It was his own idea to build this delivery tricycle, contact a bakery where he could purchase some bagels, and start a business of distribution. With no money for investment, it was an ideal way to start, and he was always aiming for bigger and better things.

In the cool early morning, before anybody was out in the streets, he pedaled his bike to the bakery to pick up his merchandise and then sped to the downtown business district on Herzel Street to reach all the coffee shops and breakfast restaurants. A fresh supply of hot bagels ready for the quick breakfasts of the working public was the goal that helped him push those pedals with strength and vigor.

Vrumek had served in the Central Command infantry during the war of independence, and he remembered it well. Many of his tales and stories centered on the battles he had been in. Vrumek talked about the battles fought near Abu Gosh, where he had seen some of his friends gunned down when they were climbing the hill in broad daylight, while the Jordanian Legionaries were sitting up at the top. One could recognize the trauma, tension, and fear by the quiver in his voice. "We knew the Arabs were up on the mountain, but orders were orders. We had no ammunition left. We were praying hard."

Vrumek was not the giving-up type. Vrumek's survival during the Holocaust was not purely a miracle. He saved himself with ingenious, dexterous inventions born in his own head. They were acts of bravery, risks taken, decisions made relying upon instinct, and his extraordinary sense of survival that came with danger.

Vrumek was still called to action every time there was tension on the borders, but the situation was different. Vrumek was a married man, a father, a breadwinner, with a business from which no one could release him. His bicycle would stand in front of his house idle while its owner fought the enemy. Like all the soldiers of Zahal (Israel Defense Force), he felt his life being disrupted. The tension, the inability to plan anything, to live his life with his family, was like having an uninvited, unwanted intruder present. The duty to have that intruder eliminated was the force, the compulsion the energy used in the actions. The nights spent again in bunkers, on hilltops, with fierce fighting were culminations of stress periods, intervals in a life of constant pressure. There were dreams of ending the constant fighting and the life of instability, dreams of enjoying our precious new-old land, like a man enjoying his new bride whom he has not seen in a long while.

Vrumek loved life. His dream was to take his family and go traveling, to show his wife, his lovely bride, the country, the places he loved so well. Since he had come to this land, he had worked and toiled and fought and protected, never having had the time or opportunity to see this strip of land for which he fought, to open his lungs to the cool breezes on green fields, to pick a fresh orange in the vast orange groves. He wanted to show Esther the places where he would have liked to take her on her honeymoon, where instead he had trekked with a rifle slung across his shoulder.

Esther was a quiet girl, not pretentious, not demanding, satisfied with her small, one-bedroom, half-the-use-of-the-kitchen-and-bathroom home, happy with her husband, on whom she depended unquestionably. That made Vrumek even more eager to guide and care for Esther and his baby Tovale.

Vrumek also carried upon his shoulders the responsibility of being the head of a family, caring and watching over his three girls, his sisters, Nachcia and me, and our cousin Hania, who had lost her husband, Yaki, and was left alone with two babies. Yaki's family was considerate, kind, and moderately generous, but emotionally Hania was totally alone. Having barely regained her confidence, balance, and will to live, she then lost her husband and was left with two babies under the age of two.

Our cousin Hania was like a third sister. Having survived the camps together, the bond between us grew stronger with every tragedy. Unable to visit Hania much and see for himself how she was faring put additional strain on Vrumek. It was also my reduced capacity to visit Hania that curtailed our contact.

Before I was married, I would spend time with Hania whenever an occasion came to take a ride there. Being unattached made it possible for me to stay with Hania and her children, giving her a breather. The children loved having me around to play games, read books, tell stories, and take them to the beach to build castles in the sand. With me they could do exciting things that mothers of little ones seldom have the time to do.

Now I was a mother myself, with an unusually demanding baby absorbing all of my time and effort. Effort was a main ingredient in our lives. In spite of it all, we always made that effort to stay in touch and be together for the holidays. By hook or by crook, with husbands on active duty, with babies ill, we somehow always managed to be together for the holidays, to continue being a family. With Vrumek in charge, with Nachcia cooking, preparing, doing most of the hard work, with Hania dragging her two babies on buses to come to Tel Aviv, we still managed to make the holidays a special time of family reunion.

Chapter Nine ✑

The tension at the southern border between Israel and Egypt was ever increasing, with the incursions of *fedayeen* hordes. There were constant murders of civilian population, and damage to Jewish property. The burden of the summer heat was intensified by the skirmishes in the Negev.

We were still going to the beach for leisurely strolls and splashes but listened more attentively to the radio broadcasts. Daily incidents became commonplace, and more and more onerous.

On May 22, 1956, we learned that the ruler of Egypt, Gamal Abdul Nasser, closed the Strait of Tiran, to Israeli navigation. The strait was the only waterway available to Israeli ships traveling from the Red Sea through the Gulf of Aquaba to the southern Israeli port of Eilat.

In July another news communiqué announced Nasser's intention of nationalizing the Suez Canal. It was a shock to the population of Israel. With breathtaking unease Israel was watching the reaction of the Americans, whose relations with the Egyptian ruler became strained over the Aswan Dam, and the British and French governments, whose interests in the Suez Canal were notable. Obviously the commanders of the Israel Defense Forces could not afford the luxury of watching and waiting for the reactions of the other governments. Decisions and action had to be taken.

Israeli citizens could only wait until the call to arms came. It was Zvika's second birthday, October 25, 1956, when the call came. As often happened, it was unexpected, undesirable, but acceptable.

Avremale dressed quietly and quickly. For a longer moment than usual, we held each other. I could sense his consternation. He was leaving his wife and child behind, going into battle. Like his forefathers before him, he was going to do battle, to defend this holy piece of land, which was our home after having been regained in bloody battles.

After two thousand years of exile, it was our generation that was going to secure this land for our children, throwing all we had into its defense. We were young and desirous of life, and yet we were sure that our path of action was the only and just one.

I remained standing at the door, contemplating my own course of action. The baby was peacefully sleeping in his crib. The night was still young but sleep did not come any more to my tired eyes. The eerie quiet of the night, which always brought demure thoughts, was prolifically working. The discomfort of my second pregnancy added to the dread. There was no one to stand beside me, to take my hand, to lead me to safety, to comfort me in my dismay. Bits of conversations from previous days floated like dark clouds through my mind.

They were going to bombard us. Tel Aviv certainly would be a major target. We had to observe total blackout. I needed to hang some blankets against my windows. Maybe I would wait till morning, buy some black paper to paste on the glass—it would be less stifling, I thought. How would I run around with the baby on my hands? There surely would be lines in the stores.

I got off the bed and began organizing some blankets. "How am I going to climb up to the top of the window?" I was wondering. "How am I to hang them? On what?" It was always Avremale's job; he was so handy around the house, he would find an easy way. But he wasn't there and I had to do it myself. Tears were running slowly down my face. What if he did not come back at all? This was how Hania was left with two little babies. How many wars must we endure? Thoughts like that slowly crept through my mind.

I remembered sitting in my old home, in our kitchen. There were blankets hanging from the windows. The air was thick and suffocating. My helpless, paralyzed sister Goldzia was bound to her bed. Mama was wringing her hands. "What if a bomb falls? We will be buried here in our kitchen." Oh, Mama, you were always so worried for Goldzia. Wouldn't it have been better to have died then? How asphyxiating was it when they choked you to death, Mama? How many wars can we survive, how many battles can we fight, how many people must we sacrifice?

I climbed on a chair, I climbed on a table, I hung the blankets on the open windows. The hot air in the room became heavy. An indecisive dawn was rising on the distant horizon. The baby woke up. It was necessary to dress him and feed him. Mechanically, my hands attended to these familiar chores. What next? I really should not stay there all by myself with my child, on the top floor of a four-story building. "Maybe I should go to Vrumek's," I thought. "Even if Vrumek is not home anymore at least his apartment is on the ground floor. I could stay with Esther. We would be together. There is some moral support in being together, stress is easier tolerated."

Hastily I began gathering some clothes for Zvika, packing a bag. Some diapers, some toys, extra shirts and shorts. "Oh, what about food? He needs to eat. How will I carry all this, shall I take the carriage? It will take so long to get there by carriage. Maybe I can catch a bus. I can not take a carriage on the bus." Tears were choking my throat. The baby looked sadly at me, sensing my predicament. I had cramps in my stomach. Hot, sticky sweat was crawling down my back like rows of marching ants.

I stood in the little foyer, bag in hand, when the knock came. "Who could that be, at a time like this? Probably one of my neighbors, maybe to invite me to come down one floor." I opened the door with an intense tug. A deep sigh escaped my throat.

"Vrumek!" I could not believe my eyes. "Vrumek, why are you here?"

Vrumek did not sit down. Standing in the doorway, rapidly speaking he explained. "I was called late. I am on my way to my unit right now. I just managed to send Esther away with Tovale, putting them in a taxi. They went to Sala, Esther's sister. Then I remembered that you are alone, and just could not leave before stopping here and making sure." He looked at the bag in my hand.

"I am glad you have something packed. There is no time, we must hurry. Come!"

He took the baby. I locked the door and followed him.

"Where am I going?" I asked as we were striding down the street.

"You will go to Sala and be there with Esther. You cannot stay here all by yourself."

"How will I get to Sala?"

"We will see."

I could see Vrumek searching for a way as we were going down the street. Unsure himself what to do next, he never wavered in his decision to have me get out of town. I understood how serious our situation was. Obviously Vrumek, being a soldier and a father, realized better than I the danger we were in. I followed him silently, taking big strides to keep up with his haste. We went out to Dizengoff Street. Buses were still running. They were crowded, filled to capacity, but the people of Israel, sensing the urgency, were making allowances. They squeezed and pushed and made room for more passengers, trying not to leave anyone behind. The driver, like a broken record, would usually announce: "No ascending anymore, there is a next bus right behind me"; but now he sat grimly behind the wheel, patiently waiting and urging the passengers. "A little more, there is still some room inside."

"I have to be near the central station anyway," Vrumek said. "I will try to get you onto a bus going to Rishon Lezion."

We ran to the pier from which the bus to Rishon usually left. We didn't bother to go first to the cashier to buy tickets. The commotion at the central bus station was overwhelming. The station was flooded with people running in all directions; no one knew which bus was going where. There was no one giving directions. Some buses were standing idle on the platform, with no drivers to drive them.

I saw Vrumek's impatience. He could not stay with me; his obligation to report to his unit was burning under his feet. But he didn't want to leave me there all by myself with the baby on my hands, with hardly a chance to get to Rishon.

"Let's try for a taxi," he suggested anxiously.

Back we went to where the taxis used to take people to Rishon. There were hardly any taxis, and when one would come, people would assail it, almost fighting for every seat. Seeing a taxi approach, Vrumek jumped in and sat down, frantically motioning to me to follow him. Before I could reach the door, all the places were taken, but I understood his strategy—Vrumek got up and let me slide in onto his seat. We waved a quick good-bye and were off.

As soon as we were out of the city, we heard the sirens wailing. I thought the driver might stop so we could take cover, but he kept going. Soon he began letting people off. He did not turn off the road for anyone; he just let them exit the taxi and continued on. As it happened I was the last one out. The taxi sped on, and immediately disappeared on the horizon.

There I was in the middle of nowhere, on the road, with nobody around to ask for directions. I knew Sala's address but had never been there before. Normally there must have been a bus running this remote route. Maybe not very often, but it would bring me close.

I did not know how far I was from the main bus station or even in which direction the station was. Certainly I did not know in which direction to turn to reach Sala's house. But I could not stand there on the road. Zvika held on tightly to my hand, sensing my tension. There were fields on both sides of the road. Some trees grew in the distance, forming a small oasis. There was a path leading into the field. I turned and took the path. My back was aching because I had been squeezed in the taxi with the baby in my lap and the big bag on top of me. I remembered that we had not eaten for a long time. I looked at my watch, which read 4 P.M. The bag was weighing heavy in my hand, and Zvika refused to walk. I had to carry him the rest of the way.

I plodded through the field, trying to encourage myself to continue in spite of a growing fear building in my subconsciousness. Where was I going? To Sala, of course, I would be there soon. Somehow I had to be able to find it. There must be someone passing by sometime. I walked, at first briskly, wanting to reach my destination as soon as possible, but the weight of the bag and the baby on my arm slowed me down. I was getting tired very fast and lost all sense of direction. When I reached a clump of trees I had seen before, I realized that I was going in circles. The gray sky was getting a tinge darker. The thought of continuing my walk into darkness panicked me. Again I heard sirens wailing in the distance and did not know what to do. Shall I fall down to the ground? There was no shelter whatsoever in the empty field. I could not make Zvika even more anxious, so I continued walking. Darkness descended very suddenly.

Through the darkness I could see in the far distance a small light. Someone had forgotten to adhere to the blackout. What luck! I walked directly toward that light, in a somewhat more optimistic mood. When I finally reached the house in question, all the lights were extinguished. The people must have realized their mistake. Totally blinded, I could only follow some faint sounds. I knocked, and a woman came to the door. She did not know Sala but directed me toward the address. By then it was pitch black. I could not even see that there were houses where I was.

With the child tired and myself exhausted, I finally reached Sala's house. Sala came to the door when she heard my knock. She and Esther were astonished to see me and could not figure out how I had made it there. It was wonderful to see them. Sala was marvelous; she grabbed Zvika from my arms and put him down to sleep. I wanted to break down and cry and cry, but there I was one of three wives with husbands on the front, with babies in our arms.

The house consisted of one room and a kitchen. I could not fathom how we would manage, yet Sala began immediately pulling out blankets, spreading them on the floor to create makeshift beds.

The scene reminded me of another time. We had reached the city of Krakow, in Poland, having walked all night. There were so many people in the house, all sleeping on makeshift beds, that there seemed not to be room for another person. Blankets and pillows were spread on the floor, and we all slept. Esther and Sala were there, too; it was their aunt's house we were in. Many members of my own family were there—Blimcia, Nachcia, Vrumek, Heshek, Papa. We had been fleeing from the advancing German army.

It was Papa who saw the futility of our situation and did not want to stay. There was only one thought on his mind, to get back home. As long as we had a home, that was the place to be, war or no war. Once you lose your home, you yourself are lost.

How right Papa was! I could see that, in the crammed quarters of Sala's apartment. Sala was wonderful, so similar to her aunt in Krakow. But I was away from home. All these thoughts churned in my head as I lay on the blanketed floor cuddling my son close to my body, feeling his rhythmic breathing.

Sala's aunt, Krakow, Poland, Sala, Rishon Lezion, Israel, another generation, another war. How many wars were we to endure, how many wars can one live through and survive? I was bearing another child; how many wars would this child have to experience? Would we finally become free and able to live in peace?

The news that came in the morning from our radio transistors was not good. Our forces were battling the Egyptian army in heavy artillery battles. There were constant announcements of casualties. All our ears heard was so many dead or so many wounded. "Where is my Avremale?" I kept thinking when they spoke of artillery battles, and then, "where is my brother Vrumek?" Vrumek was in the infantry; Sala's husband David was in the air force.

With the morning sun came some improvement in our living conditions. The children could stay outside in the small yard that served as living and dining room. Sala put up a little folding table and served breakfast to the children. The goat in the neighbors stall was the best entertainment for the three of them. They fed it, gave it water to drink, pulled the straw apart, and then gathered it again. They pulled on the goat's beard, on its tail, they were busy—it was a blessing.

By evening we were back in the hot, close room, where the blackout made it still more suffocating. We curled up, each with her child, a bag of clothes for the child and emergency articles at our side. When the sirens began wailing, we grabbed our children and bags and ran outside. The children continued to sleep in our arms, while we waited, listening. We heard the roar of airplanes, unable to determine whose airplanes we heard, the enemy or our pilots. We stayed outside, three frightened women with three sleeping children, worried for three fighting husbands.

How different this war was from the War of Independence. We were a regular country with an elected government and a unified citizenship. There were no more separate battles being fought by Haganah, Irgun, Lehi; there was now a central command that conducted the war. In the war of independence, however, we had been young girls with no responsibilities. What a difference that made—a boyfriend is not a husband.

And so another day passed as we idled in Sala's backyard, listening to the radio reports of more wounded and more casualties that rattled our nerves. We had no word from anyone of ours. After six days we heard from a neighbor who had received a message from her husband; he had been able to call and confirm that he was okay.

As days passed, I became very upset with myself for being there, away from home, and the message from the neighbor was the straw that broke the camel's back. "What am I doing here?" I thought. "What if Avremale is able to call to send a message to me? How will he know where to find me? How will I know if he is searching for me? This is absolutely absurd, to sit here stashed away in a peaceful corner, out of touch. I have to go home," I decided. Esther and Sala thought me totally crazy and did not even want to hear of it. They didn't want to let me leave. There were no buses running and any other transportation was questionable at best. "How do you think you can get to Tel Aviv, and what do you propose to do there all by yourself even if you do reach it? Where will you run at night from your fourth floor apartment if there is a raid?"

My mind however was made up, and no one could budge me from it. Papa's words kept coming back to haunt me. I had to try. Another passing day would wear my patience thin; my physical discomfort and emotional stress were taking their toll. I became impatient, irritable, petulant, and that was not fair to Sala because she was so good to me.

In the morning I gathered my stuff and went out to the road. Neither Esther or Sala wanted to accompany me to the road, hoping I would get discouraged and turn back. I stood a long time on the road, until a taxi passed that had a seat available. Somehow I made it all the way home, dragging Zvika beside me. At the entrance to the house, my neighbor Shoshana greeted me, exclaiming loudly, "Oh, my God! Where have you been? Why didn't you tell me where you were going? Who does such a thing?"

I did not mind her yelling at me. It felt good to be home. "There was no time to stop in to tell you when I was leaving," I said apologetically. "My brother was on his way to his unit. He was in a terrible rush and took me along to central station. I was with my sister-in-law in Rishon."

But she was not listening to my explanations, keeping up the complaint. "How does one go away without leaving word where to be found? What is a husband to do when he comes home and finds the house empty, and does not know where his wife and child are? Do you know what this does to his morale?"

I could not understand at first what she was talking about.

"Your husband, Avremale, he was here. He came home, he asked me where you were, and I did not know," she said accusingly.

I became frantic. "When? How? Where? What do you mean he was here?"

"He said he managed to get a pass to go to Tel Aviv, so he made a quick stop at home, but you were not here."

"Where did he say he had to go back to?" I wanted to know, "Where did he come from?"

She had no answers to all my questions, just stood there, hands on hips. "These are not things a soldier discusses with his neighbors. You should know that." Seeing how upset I was, she changed her tune. "Don't worry so much. Thank God he was here, which means he is okay."

I walked slowly up the three flights of stairs, blaming myself. I had missed a chance. Why hadn't I come home right away? I had wanted to, I had this feeling that was pushing me to go home, but I had come too late. Finally I broke down and had my cry.

Two more weeks passed before I saw my husband again. We flew into each other's arms and could not separate for a long, long time.

The mood of the country was ecstatic. We had won another war. Our enemies lay defeated, shamed, frustrated. Our men had captured territories they had hardly dreamed about. We hoped that would be our last war.

Egypt's seizure of the Suez Canal in fall of 1956 triggered another war in the Middle East. The French and English, having participated and accomplished their goal, went home, leaving Israel triumphantly in possession of the Sinai Peninsula. This fact would not sit well with Egypt's president, Gamal Abdul Nasser, or the world powers, whose interests in the Middle East were paramount. The best friend and ally of Israel, the United States of America, pressured Israel to withdraw its forces from the conquered territory, to protect its own dominance in the region and appease its Moslem clients. Israel's savoring of her victory was short lived.

It was the end of 1956. We were just over another war. The men were back from the front, applying their renewed energy to their jobs and daily endeavors. As in the previous war, we had buried the dead but not finished mourning when the Americans speeded up the pressure to relinquish the territories conquered. Having captured the Suez Canal, in the three-power cooperation between England, France, and Israel, the soldiers of Zahal were sitting on the other bank of the Suez Canal, on the African continent.

The people of Israel were bitter with disappointment. The U.S. government, always our friend, was pressing Israel against the wall. Obviously their own interests took priority, in view of the political climate and strategy favorable to the Americans. Politics is a dirty business, not dominated by justice or sentiment, but guided by power struggles and favorable gains.

It had been years since I had seen Aliza, the woman cook whom I had met in the rabbi's house, at the time of my arrival in Tel Aviv. When I ran into her in the *kupat cholim* (health station), Aliza's hair was disheveled, her face dark with the expression of pain. For a moment her eyes lit up when she saw me and deduced that the child in the carriage was mine. She was happy to see me and to learn of my happy marriage and baby son.

I sensed the burden of grief in her voice even before I asked the questions. I kept talking about myself and my family, fearful of hearing what she had to relate. Was it Marek, the husband of her niece Niusia-Chanale, who had come to live in the Jewish land, taking his bride with him out of Poland? Would Chanale, who was raised as a Catholic, but was really a Jewish girl, have to mourn together with her people the loss of her husband? Was it Aliza's son, her only child, the essence of her life, to whom she devoted all she possessed? I could not stall any longer.

"How is your family, Aliza?" I asked carefully.

The question triggered an avalanche of emotion. She burst into a lament, unable to control herself. The hurt was so fresh, the scar so open. Through her sobs I heard her bitter tragedy emerge—her son, her only boy her hope, her love, her future, her interest in life.

"You know how hard I worked, how I never minded doing it. It was all for him. He was so brilliant, he was so good, he studied hard, did not demand much. He was not like the usual boys. He knew my limitations, being a widow supporting him and myself. He always promised to make it up to me when he grew up, when he would be on his own. I knew he would have taken care of me when the time came. His young life he gave for our land, for our existence, for our freedom. What am I to do with this freedom without him?"

I sat there unable to find the words to console this mourning mother who just buried her only son, her sacrifice for our homeland.

It carried me back all those years to the rabbi's house, where Aliza, the happy widow, would console me for having lost my family in the Holocaust. Aliza, who always found a good bite to fatten me up. Aliza, who craved with all her heart to find her little niece, Chanale, and bring her under her roof. I remembered her joy and happiness when Chanale was finally reunited with her and her son, and the pride with which she always spoke about her son, her Eli. There she sat in front of me, a tormented, broken woman. What a price we were paying for our dream, our free country—the bodies of our fallen sons hardly cold yet, and the cold world already standing at our doorstep demanding to relinquish and abandon what we had conquered with so much blood and grief. How were our mothers to endure this? They would not have any more sons to give.

Was my son going to have to do the same? Would President Eisenhower's promise be good two decades later? The buried soldiers would never know, and the living would slowly thrust the memory of battle into their subconsciousness, making room for life to go on.

We stayed together a long time, and I found out that Chanale was a nurse working in a hospital in the rising desert town of Eilat, where she and Marek had settled. They were pioneers, building the arid land of our fathers into a paradise for our children, if only our enemies would leave us in peace.

There was a period of calm after the storm. The country received an economic shot in the arm: the German government in Bonn was paying up for the crimes committed by the Nazis against the Jewish population of Europe. Sadly, the Jewish state was benefitting from the loss of six million Jews. Money and material were streaming into the country. The beneficiaries, however, were hardly the survivors. They were required to submit claims, produce witnesses, bring documents, prove their medical necessity, while the kibbutzim built bigger plants with modern machinery of German production.

Avremale was home savoring the calm, the freedom, the joy of indulgence with his son. With vigor he immersed himself in his work, happily pursuing his ambition. He had always aspired to become independent in business, to establish a factory of his own. He came from the city of Alexandrow in Poland, where the majority of the population engaged in the manufacture of socks, a trade he had learned as a youngster. He wanted to do the same on his own. In a long process of paperwork, he applied to purchase machinery. Months kept passing while we waited and hoped. When the answer finally came from the bureau of commerce and industry, it was shocking to us. It stated, "Since you have not supplied any proof of being an exporter of this type of merchandise, your application for machinery must be denied. Priority is being given to exporters."

"How can I ever become an exporter if I am not being given a chance to manufacture?" Avremale asked of all the clerks and officials in whose offices he spent days pursuing his goal.

The argument that the agreement with Germany was made in the name of the survivors, which we both were, fell on deaf ears. The fact that he was a *chayal meshuchrar* (war veteran) and that Moshe, Nachcia's husband, his partner-to-be, was a *neche milchama* (disabled veteran) meant nothing to the government officials.

"There is this man, Shladow," Avremale would complain, "who is single. He has no family to support, he did not serve in the army, he did not suffer in Europe, he had no factory before, but he has a party membership booklet. His application was approved. He has a factory now. His party friends decide who should benefit from the German reparations, money the Germans pay for the blood of our parents, for our slavery."

Avremale with our daughter,
Sharona.

No complains had any validity. Avremale was not a party member. Our idealism was being worn away.

The birth of our second child was approaching and certainly making us apprehensive. I woke on Thursday morning, February 21, 1957, earlier than Avremale. I felt an urge to talk to Avremale. I shook him awake.

"What happened?" he asked anxiously. "Is it time?"

"No. But I must tell you the dream I had. You know that I have not seen my parents, even in a dream, throughout all these years. And you know how I always wanted to see them again, even if it would be only in a dream.

"Well, I was lying on a bed and was in labor. I really felt the pain. On both sides of the bed at my head, stood my parents, my mother on my right and my father on my left. They each held one of my hands in theirs, and with their other hands were patting my head. They were so comforting, tranquil, and calm. They said to me, 'Do not worry my dear child, everything will be fine. There's nothing to worry about, we are here with you.' When they disappeared I knew what I would name our daughter. My mother's name was Sarah, my father was Symche, which also is Ron, both meaning joy. We are going to have a daughter, and we will name her Sharona."

Avremale looked at me in amazement. He had never seen me with such an expression on my face. My face was radiant with such confidence that he did not dare dispute or contradict me. He did not even dare ask, "how can you be so sure we are going to have a daughter? After all, it was only a dream."

He let me talk and just sat there in bed next to me, listening.

"I saw them so clearly. They looked so alive; it was so real. I know now that they are watching over me and will not let anything happen to me, their baby, their youngest daughter. They want to be with me forever. In my daughter they will live, this dream will be fulfilled."

The next day, Friday afternoon, I gave birth to a beautiful baby girl, whom we named Sharona.

Epilogue

My very dear sister, Nachcia, passed away in Bnei Braque, Israel, in 1971. I sat next to her in her hospital bed, seeing her fade away. For me her demise was a tragedy akin to the death of our parents. Her daughter, Sarah, has five children and six grandchildren, all living in Israel. Her son, Symche, has six children and four grandchildren. Nachcia lived to see only one grandchild. I keep in touch with Sarah, Symche, and their families and we have established close ties.

My dear brother, Vrumek, passed away in 1980, in the United States. I was with him to the very end. The pain of his loss still lingers.

His wife, Esther, passed away in 2001. Their daughter, Tova, has three children, and his son, David, has one child. We maintain a close family relationship. Vrumek, like Nachcia, only lived to see one grandchild.

My dear cousin Hania lives close to her two girls, in Kfar Saba, Israel, where she started out. She also has a son, Pinchas, from her second marriage. She has seven grandchildren and six great grandchildren. We do keep in close touch.

My good friend Gutka lives in the United States with her husband, Maurice. They have two daughters and three grandchildren. We are in contact as close as if we were family.

Most of my friends have married and have children who are respectable, prominent members of society, contributing to the welfare of humanity in different fields of endeavor. I am very proud of all of them and know that they will carry on the tradition of their families, and their people.

My son, Zvika, is married to Lea and has two children; our daughter, Sharon, is married to Alan and has five children. We are extremely proud of their accomplishments.

On the Shore by the Sea

On the shore by the sea
On a dark cloudy night
On the shore by the sea
We dream to see the light.

For we know that past the sea
Lies the land we must make free.
It is the land of *Zvi El*
Our ancient *Eretz Israel.*

Eretz even the ocean cannot keep us away
Eretz we will come we will be there one day.
Even on all four, we will reach your shore
On ocean liners or in little boats.
Even on all four, we will reach your shore
On ocean liners or in little boats.

April 1946

Nachcia

The orchard fruit will shine with gold
The river Jordan lively stream
The vast wheat field will grow bold
Her child's smile sweetly beam.

Near the open peaceful grave
Reposed on the moist earth
Forsaken, abandoned, alone
Bitter weeping, moaning, heard.

Lonely, pale, stands the boy
Tears are rolling down his face

Murmured prayer utter lips
Oh, have pity, mercy, grace.

You have triumphed death, so fast
Spreading mourning and despair
May your triumph be the last
Pain and sorrow fill the air.

She won't see fruit shine with gold
She won't hear her baby's call
She won't feel wafting spring breeze
Sorrowful the Jordan rolls.

February 1971

Vrumek

Was it destined from the start
That at sixty we should part
From Vrumek my only brother
He the last one and no other?

Our childhood spent together
Like a dream a fairy tale
His love so richly given
Never stopped never failed.

Is it true that here lies buried
My whole family's last shred?
Will I never see the smile
Of his kind and sweet bright face?

Are we sitting here in mourning
For the one that we so loved?
Is the sun to go on shining
Even though he is not with us?

Are we going to keep on living?
Are flowers to be in bloom?
Is the world to keep on turning
When we *shivah* sit for him?

Is it possible tomorrow
There will even be a smile
Ring of laughter from a baby
To be cherished for a while?

Is it true that we have lost
Our crown, our precious jewel?
In this coffin we have buried
Our hearts with his soul.

July 30, 1980

Avremale and me.

Glossary

aliyah: Immigration.
aliyah beth: Illegal immigration.
Am Israel Chai: The people of Israel live.
asimon: Token.
ayala: Young doe.
baruch haba: You're welcome.
Betar: Revisionist Zionists.
bevakasha bou: Please come.
biluyim: Pioneers.
boker tov: Good morning.
Brith Mila: Circumcision.
capos: Jewish foremen in concentration camps.
chasid: Jew following the tenet of a specific rabbi.
chayal meshuchrar: War veteran.
chayal Ivri: Hebrew soldier.
chayelet: Female soldier.
cheruth Israel: Freedom from bondage.
chevre: Guys.
chevremanit: One of the crowd.
Chrabina: Countess.
chuppa: Bridal canopy.
degel: Flag.
fedayeen: Terrorist groups.
finjan: Long-handled coffee pot.
Folksdeutsche: Naturalized German.
galut: Diaspora.
Greczynki: Greek.
Hagadah: The book about the exodus from Egypt.
Haganah: Jewish military underground.
Hashomer Hatzair: Socialist Zionists.
iluyi: Genius.
jinji Redhead.

Judenrat: Jewish leadership in the ghetto.
Judenrein: Cleansed of Jews.
kafiya: Checkered black-and-white headgear usually worn by Arabs.
Kiddush: The blessing over the wine.
kipot: Head coverings.
kneidlach: Matzo balls.
kova tembel: Khaki hat.
landsleit: People from one's home town.
maabarot: Shanty towns.
madrich: Leader.
Magen David Adom: Red Star of David.
matzevah: Monument.
mishlat: Military outpost.
moshav: Agricultural settlement.
nargila: Long, winding smoking pipe.
neche milchama: Disabled veteran.
noter: Local policeman.
ocer: Curfew.
ola chadasha: New immigrant.
olim: Immigrants.
pluga: Platoon.
poypstlecher vie der poipst: Popier than the pope.
protekcia: Influence.
ptiliya: One-burner cooking device.
sabra: Native-born Israeli.
shikun: Government-built subsidized housing.
shpere: The curfew the Germans imposed for a whole week of deportations.
shuk: Marketplace.
tefilin: Phylacteries.
Yehi Shem Hashem Mevorach: Blessed be Your Name.
Yehudi galuti: Diaspora Jew.
yeke: Person of German descent.
yishuv: Jewish population of Palestine.
yishuv: Settlement.
zemiros: Sabbath songs.
Zionim Klaliim: General Zionists.
zdrastwicie: Welcome.
Zva Haganah Leisrael: Israel Defense Forces.